D0874030

FOR SCIENCE IN THE SOCIAL SCIENCES

FOR SCIENCE IN THE SOCIAL SCIENCES

David Papineau

St. Martin's Press   New York

793343

© David Papineau 1978

All rights reserved. For information, write:
St. Martin's Press, Inc., 175 Fifth Avenue, New York, N.Y. 10010

Printed in Great Britain

First published in the United States of America in 1979

Library of Congress Cataloging in Publication Data

Papineau, David, 1947–
    For science in the social sciences.

    Includes index.
    1. Social sciences—Methodology.   I.   Title.
H61.P28   1978   300′.1′8   78–14193
ISBN 0–312–29812–9

To my Mother

Contents

Preface

Much of this book has grown out of my lectures in the Department of Sociology at the University of Reading in 1973–77. Versions of Chapter 3 were read to the Sociology Staff seminar at Reading and to the Philosophy Society at Birkbeck College, of Chapter 4 to the Philosophy Club at Reading, and of Chapter 6 to Philosophy seminars at Bradford University and at Macquarie University. I am grateful to all those who responded to what I said on those occasions.

I would also like to thank Valerie Cook, Barbara Young and Jennifer Moore for typing my manuscripts at various stages, and Ken Robertson, John Cottingham, Geoff Harrison, Jim Tiles, Mary Tiles, Malcolm Hamilton, Tank Waddington, Terry Stokes, Graham Nerlich and Liz Jacka for reading and commenting on drafts of various sections.

Sydney   DCP
December 1977

Introduction

This book covers a number of problems in the philosophy of social science. Each chapter deals with a relatively self-sufficient topic. But there is an underlying theme running through the book—a defence of the view that the social sciences can and ought to conform to the standards set by the natural sciences.

This is not a popular view nowadays. The 'positivist' tradition in the social sciences is currently held in extremely low repute. It is not really my intention to buck this trend. I agree that much social scientific work aimed at emulating the natural sciences has been both unproductive and fundamentally misguided. But I would not attribute these failures to the intended aim as such. That is, I think there is nothing wrong in itself with the idea that the social sciences ought to emulate their natural counterparts. The real trouble has been that those social scientists who have aimed at being 'scientific' have characteristically suffered from one misconception or another about exactly what is involved in being scientific. And it is this, rather than wanting to be 'scientific' as such, that has hampered the 'positivist' tradition in the social sciences. Critics of the tradition have in general shared these misconceptions, and so have objected to the scientific method as such, when a more appropriate target for their often justified criticisms would have been particular assumptions about what that method requires.

One example of this tendency is the notion that the application of scientific methods to the study of society somehow requires that we suppose there is a level of distinctive 'social facts' existing external to the reality comprised by human individuals. In Chapter 1 I show that there is no basis for this Durkheimian conception of external social facts. But I do not of course intend this to discredit the possibility of a scientific study of society. On the contrary, my aim in starting with this topic is to clear science's name, from the outset, of its unfortunate associations with the Durkheimian conception.

On a more general level, the term 'positivism' itself illustrates the kind of misconception I am complaining of. Amongst social scientists this is widely taken to refer simply to the thesis that there is a methodological

1

unity between the natural and social sciences. On the other hand philosophers of natural science use 'positivism' (and the more specific 'logical positivism') to refer to one specific view of how the natural sciences work: for them 'positivism' is the extreme empiricist view that scientific reality is exhausted by what can be established by direct observation. This interdisciplinary semantic difference is a perfectly understandable consequence of the divergent interests social theorists and philosophers have taken in the work of Auguste Comte, the original 'positivist'.[1] And it is easy enough to avoid any confusion it might engender—I myself shall do so by simply avoiding the term 'positivism' altogether. But, still, the semantic awkwardness is symptomatic of the unfortunate fact that those concerned about the foundations of the social sciences standardly take it for granted that adherence to the methods of the natural sciences means careful and exclusive attention to the observable appearances.

It is not as if the 'positivism' of the philosophers of the natural sciences were an uncontroversial view. Perhaps it has been at certain times in certain circles. But in recent years there has been a general realisation, in the Anglo-American world at least, that there is far more dreamt of in natural scientific theorising than is allowed by positivist philosophy of natural science. In Chapter 2 I shall examine various arguments against the idea that observation plays a dominant role in the practice of the natural sciences, and show that science is in important aspects an open-ended and intellectually creative process. The view of science I develop will accommodate the insights of such writers as Hanson, Kuhn, Feyerabend and Lakatos.

At the same time I shall resist the more extreme suggestions of some of these writers, by showing how science is still an objective process in which observation plays some part in directing scientific theorising towards ever-improving representations of reality. But notwithstanding this objectivism the view I eventually reach will be far indeed from 'positivism' (in the sense of an excessively strict empiricism). And so I hope that those who find it difficult even to countenance 'positivism' (in the sense of a continuity between the natural and social sciences) will grasp that I am by no means recommending the avid concentration on purely observable matters generally favoured by those social thinkers who have tried to ape the natural scientific method.

In Chapter 3 I consider the possibility of the social scientist being able to find out about causes, given that any generalisations he comes up with will almost invariably be statistical in form. In this chapter the thrust of my argument is slightly different. For here I do think that those scientifically-oriented social thinkers who have been concerned with this problem have adopted the right approach. In recent years there have been developed a number of techniques for inferring causes from statistical data. The difficulty here is that, while these techniques have a certain obvious intuitive appeal, there has been no detailed explanation, so far as I know, of their logical foundation. In particular, there has been no account which relates these statistical techniques to the standard philosophical analyses of causation as a deterministic relationship. So there remains a suspicion in many people's minds about whether the social sciences can really hope to discover causes. I shall try to allay this suspicion by presenting, in broad outline, an explanation of exactly how and when it is possible to move from statistical premises to conclusions about the ability of one event to determine another.

In Chapter 4 I look at the explanation of human action. Perhaps one motivation for the Durkheimian idea that a scientific approach to society requires supra-individual social facts is the fear that human actions cannot possibly be explained scientifically on an individual level. This worry is defused in Chapter 4. I show how individual human actions can perfectly well be explained scientifically by their causal antecedents. But I do *not* assume that this requires us to ignore people's reasons, to forget about the beliefs and desires behind people's actions. The behaviourist prejudice that there is something unscientific about people's mental states is something else that has done much to give 'science' a bad name. What I show in Chapter 4 is that, given a proper appreciation of scientific methods, there is no barrier to scientific theorising about the connection between people's thoughts and their actions, and indeed that we already possess a reasonably adequate scientific theory of this connection. I also show in some detail how this scientific theory is adequate—indeed required—to yield an understanding of the way that social rules and meanings are invariably important for the explanation of actions.

Chapters 5, 6 and 7 are less directly addressed to my main theme. Each is oriented in the first instance to a particular conceptual problem faced by the social scientist. Nevertheless, they can be considered to lend support to the underlying thesis. For it turns out that the general points developed in the first four chapters about the nature of natural scientific methods and the application of such methods in the social sciences are in each case crucial to our satisfactorily resolving the problem at issue.

In Chapter 5 I consider the question of how individual humans relate to large-scale social developments, or at least such aspects of this question as remain after we dismiss the Durkheimian conception of distinctively external 'social facts'. I distinguish three such residual issues. Firstly, is there an admissible level of inquiry which examines social developments purely in the large, without seeking to reduce its analyses to the individual level in any way? Secondly, in what way, if any, is history as a whole a determined process? And, thirdly, in what way is a sociological perspective on society consistent with the idea that people can often change their social situation by the exercise of their free will?

I then turn, in Chapter 6, to the problem of understanding an alien culture, and in particular the problem of interpreting the belief systems found in traditional societies. I point out some difficulties inherent in the different standard analyses of such belief systems and suggest a line of approach which promises to avoid these difficulties. In so doing I broach a question which often presents itself to those who entertain the possibility of a 'sociology of knowledge'—if we explain a 'scientific' theory sociologically, do we thereby discredit it as proper objective knowledge? This issue is taken up again in Chapter 7, in the course of a general discussion of the relationship between facts and values and the possibility of a value-free social science. I there show exactly when and why 'external influences' undermine a putatively scientific theory's claim to objectivity. I conclude by considering the view that the whole idea of studying society scientifically itself conceals illegitimate evaluative commitments.

Throughout the book I have tried not to assume any specialised training, either in philosophy or in the social sciences, on the part of the reader. But I am only too conscious that I may not always have succeeded in this; that on occasion the argument may move too fast for the reader unfamiliar with the ground. I fear that this will be especially true of the latter half of Chapter 3, parts of which are inevitably on a level which might be difficult for the reader without any experience in the standard social scientific statistical techniques. Fortunately the precise details of the arguments involved here are not presupposed by the rest of the book (except for a part of Section 3 of Chapter 5) and so those who want to avoid them can do so easily enough.

My first concern in this book is always with the problems I discuss as such, and only secondarily with what other authors or schools of thought might have said about them. The problems are knotty and frustrating enough as it is, without the extra burden of having constantly to trace connections and differences through the literature. As a general rule I discuss other authors only when it is a positive aid to exposition to do so, or when a position under discussion is unquestionably the intellectual property of a particular individual or group. This does mean that I have omitted to detail exactly how the views I defend here differ, contradict, or concur with those adopted by various important schools of current thought. I can only hope that I specify my own views clearly enough for it to be obvious to those interested how I would stand on related positions.

A different kind of omission is that I ignore two of the traditional topics in the philosophy of the social science, namely, the logic of functional explanation and the use of ideal types. I have discussed ideal types elsewhere.[2] And there are a number of writers who in recent years have shown satisfactorily that 'functional explanations', when valid, are nothing more than special and disguised cases of causal explanations.[3] While there is no doubt more to be said on these topics, and in particular on the way practising social scientists have misused the methodological tools in question, it would not have furthered the general argument of this book to do so here.

One last introductory word. I nowhere give an explicit definition of what I count as the 'social sciences'. This is in a way deliberate. I certainly intend the notion to cover what is standardly done in academic departments of sociology, anthropology, economics, and political science. But the usual academic attempts to demarcate between these disciplines, and between them and others, are difficult to take seriously. It will be quite good enough for my purposes if the reader starts with some rough and ready idea of what the social sciences are, and allows the arguments of this book to suggest more about what they should be.

1 Social Facts

1. DURKHEIM AND INDIVIDUALISM

What are the social sciences supposed to be about? Since Durkheim's *Rules of Sociological Method* at the end of the last century it has been an article of faith amongst most sociologists that there is a distinct order of *social facts* which in any society exist over and above the totality of facts about its individual members[1]. Durkheim characterised these 'social facts' as *external* to the individuals in any given society, but as nevertheless exerting a *constraint* on those individuals. Examples of such social facts for Durkheim were laws, norms, roles, institutions, currents of opinion, regular patterns in such statistics as crime rates or suicide rates, and features of natural environment. These social facts were not to be seen as consequences of any inherent psychological characteristics the individual members of society might have, but rather as things which imposed themselves on those individuals from without. Insofar as individuals displayed psychological attitudes and forms of behaviour consonant with the social facts external to them, these 'individual manifestations' were the results of independently existing social facts, not the basis of the way society was.

The uninitiated often find something counter-intuitive in the idea of social facts independent of and surplus to facts about individuals. Everybody, it is true, will allow that there are facts about societies which are not facts about particular individuals. For example, that the average age in Britain is 30·12 years is obviously not a fact about any particular person in Britain. But at the same time everybody will also be able to see that such facts about society do not really involve anything over and above facts about the individuals in that society. To say that the average age in Britain is 30·12 years is just to say that 30·12 years is the answer we get if we add up the age of everybody in Britain and divide by the total number of people. In speaking of average ages we are not referring to any aspect of reality other than that comprised by facts about some number of individual people. What many people do find suspect is the idea of social facts whose essential feature is that they are not so reducible to individual facts. Consider a society like Britain, they will say. There is the geographical location and the natural environment, there are some buildings and cows and so on, and then there are the people doing various things and with various ideas in their heads. Where in addition to all this, they will ask, can we find some separate level of reality containing these supposedly distinctive social facts?

This natural scepticism about the Durkheimian view I shall call *individualism* for the purposes of this chapter. According to individualism, all so-called 'social facts' are really like average ages. That is, all characteristics of societies ultimately consist of nothing more than certain aspects of the characteristics variously or jointly displayed by their individual members. They are not something 'emerging' at a new autonomous level of reality when societies are formed.

The existence of a norm, for example, is not for the individualist some mysterious psychic aura or force influencing the individuals in that society. It is simply a matter of the members of the society in question all holding that certain actions ought not to be done and tending to behave accordingly. Similarly, the individualist will hold that for a certain role to be established is for there to be some cluster of norms specifying what certain people should do, which then again cashes out as there being some cluster of attitudes and related activities common to the members of the social group in question. Correspondingly the individualist will reduce institutions to sets of roles and norms, and hence to facts about collections of individuals.

The more reflective individualist will allow that there is often more involved in a putative social fact than might appear at first sight. When we talk of two people getting *married*, for instance, he will admit that we are implicitly referring not only to the attitudes of the couple in question and the others present at the ceremony, but also to the ideas those in the larger society have about what is appropriate for or allowed to couples who have been through such a ceremony. And, insofar as marriage involves specifically legal rights and obligations, the individualist will also see us as implicitly referring to the institutions of government and justice, and hence to all the attitudes and behaviours involved in the roles and norms constituting those institutions. But, notwithstanding this complexity, the individualist will still wish to insist that we are in the end referring to nothing more than collections of facts about the individual members of society.

Eventually I shall conclude that the individualist's scepticism is the right response to the Durkheimian view of social facts. But before this can be established, a tangle of related issues needs to be analysed and unravelled. There *are* a number of plausible arguments which seem to show that the individualist picture is crucially incomplete as a representation of social reality, and which seem to support the Durkheimian line. I shall begin by considering in some detail three such arguments, and showing that although they point to important considerations they fail to prove the Durkheimian case.

The first argument goes as follows: 'Social facts such as norms, roles, institutions, etc. continue to exist and exert an influence on particular individuals whatever those individuals themselves think and do. So the existence of such social facts must involve something more than what individuals think and do'.

The second argument will be: 'People do not think and behave in the same way when in social groups as they would as isolated individuals. So the properties of social situations cannot derive solely from the thoughts and actions of aggregates of single individuals'.

And then, thirdly: 'People in different societies have the different characteristic thoughts and behaviour patterns they do because of the different norms, roles, etc. which are accepted in those societies. But, if this is the right approach to explaining "individual manifestations" of social difference, we cannot *identify* social facts with the sum of their individual manifestations—for it is no explanation of something to say that it results from itself'.

For Durkheim, and for many since, it is precisely the distinctive nature of social facts that makes an independent science of society possible. Roughly the idea is that it is only insofar as men are made by independent social facts, rather than the other way round, that the sociologist can study an objective subject matter in a scientific manner free from considerations of individual psychology. In arguing against the Durkheimian view of social facts I do not want to suggest that the social sciences cannot be proper sciences on the model of the natural sciences. For I do not go along with the general Durkheimian idea that the existence of supra-individual facts is somehow a necessary condition of any scientific approach to society. Indeed part of my motivation for criticising the Durkheimian view of social facts is to make it clear from the outset that when I argue for a scientific approach to society I will not be trying to give an implicit defence of supra-individual social facts.

Before proceeding it will be helpful to clarify a couple of terminological points. Firstly, as will have been clear, I am using 'Durkheimian' to refer to the specific notion that social facts involve some level of reality other than that comprised by collections of facts about individual people. In adopting this terminology I do not especially wish to suggest that this notion was either central to Durkheim's overall intellectual position or that it exhausts what was important or original in his thought. Indeed my argument can in a sense be read as showing that Durkheim's important theoretical innovations can be accepted without adopting the 'Durkheimian' view of social facts. And I shall suggest in passing later that it was only because of a certain conceptual disarray in his period that he was led to adopt the 'Durkheimian' view at all. Still, there is no doubt that Durkheim has been widely associated with the 'Durkheimian' view of social facts, and the familiarity of this link makes his name the natural and obvious way of designating this view.

Secondly, I shall from now on use the term 'social fact' in a sense which is neutral between the Durkheimian and individualist positions. That is, I shall assume that there is agreement that the discussion, roughly speaking, is about large-scale features of society, called 'social facts', and that the dispute is then about the nature of such social facts—do they have a reality over and above that comprised by individuals? This will be much more convenient than using 'social fact' to refer to the distinctively Durkheimian notion, with the dispute then coming out as to whether social facts exist or not—for we would then be without any natural term for specifying what it is that the individualist is denying to have any supra-individual reality.

2. 'INDIVIDUAL CHANGES DO NOT AMOUNT TO SOCIAL CHANGES'

To illustrate the first argument Durkheim considers such a socially defined role as that of a husband or brother. He points out that any particular individual who refuses to acknowledge or fulfil the obligations involved will nevertheless feel the force of the social fact all right, in the form of pressure for him to conform. So, Durkheim argues, the social fact is external to the individual and not merely a matter of his internal consciousness and behaviour. Moreover, argues Durkheim, this is true of each and every individual in that society—if he is a husband he will be pressured to conform whatever he himself thinks about the allotted role. The conclusion drawn is that the role in question must exist over and above any facts about the attitudes and actions of all the individuals in the society.[2]

The individualist will reply that Durkheim's argument involves an obvious fallacy. It is true that any one person being of a different mind does not make a difference to the presence of a social fact; but it does not follow from this that if *everybody* were simultaneously to become of a different mind that the social fact would still be the same. One may as well say to a room full of people, 'If any one of you were to leave there would still be more than ten people here—so if all of you were to leave there would still be more than ten people here'.

The individualist takes the existence of a certain rule to be nothing more than most of the individuals in the society in question holding that certain forms of behaviour are appropriate for people in certain categories. The 'external pressure' the nonconformist experiences is nothing but other people's consequent negative reactions to his deviance. Durkheim's point is then the truism that where large numbers of people are involved the subtraction of one makes no effective difference. By contrast, and consistently with the individualist theory, the subtraction of all would make all the difference.

At this point, some might be tempted to accuse the individualist of making the naive humanist assumption that social changes can always be effected by autonomous changes of heart on the part of the general population. Now, it is indeed true that the individualist holds that social changes *are* in large part changes in the psychological states of society's members. But this does not commit him directly to any particular view on what such changes are *due* to. We need, so to speak, to distinguish the *what* from the *why* of social facts. In this chapter it is the former we are concerned with—we want to know what social facts are made of, what their constitution and nature is. The *why* of social facts will be discussed in Chapter 5. As we shall see there, the question of how changes in social facts are to be explained raises a number of interrelated problems about historical accidents, free will, and alternative levels of explanation. We cannot solve all these problems immediately. But, without going into the matter too deeply, we can point out here that there is no obvious reason why someone who is an individualist on the 'what' of social facts should be committed to the idea that social facts can be changed by free human decisions. Even if he takes social facts to consist, roughly, of the actions and states of mind of numbers of people, he can still hold that such actions and states of mind are always determined by prior factors outside the control of those people, such as, for instance, by their natural or historical environment. Indeed, it is not even clear on the other side that a Durkheimian has to *deny* that social facts can be results of autonomous human decisions. It is true that Durkheim himself did deny this, for he held that social facts were the only things that could affect other social facts,[3] and this, together with his view that social facts are entirely on some supra-individual level of reality, obviously implies that human decisions cannot explain changes in social facts. But the idea that only social facts can affect other social facts is an additional claim, independent of the Durkheimian position on what social facts are made of. Suppose social facts did 'emerge' at a separate level of reality whenever individuals were grouped together in certain ways, and that such facts were thenceforth able to exert an influence on those people. Why should this *in itself* rule out the possibility that on occasion certain people might decide freely to bring about those groupings of individuals which would lead to the emergence of such social facts? Radio waves appear as new and independent phenomena, able to produce effects, including effects on people, whenever certain kinds of equipment are operated. But this does show that people cannot choose to bring about those waves, by operating that equipment.[4]

So views about the constitution of social facts have no direct consequences about the possibility of their being changed by some kind of autonomous human resolution. If there is something wrong with individualism, it is not that it is guilty of some kind of naive humanism.

3. 'INDIVIDUALS ARE ALWAYS AFFECTED BY THEIR SOCIAL SITUATION'

The second pro-Durkheimian argument was premised on the idea that people think and behave differently in social groups from when they are on their own. One popular example of this phenomenon is the way in which hysteria can develop in a crowd of people, each of whom would behave perfectly normally by himself. For the Durkheimian this will simply be an extreme example of the characteristic way that people are affected by their social surroundings.

The initial individualist response to this line of argument will probably be that there is nothing in it he wants to deny. He will say it is a truism that people react to the social circumstances they are in. New surroundings can provoke new desires, fears and anxieties in people. And, even more obviously, people will choose different ways of achieving their aims in different situations—a man who always likes to be admired will know that what impresses his acquaintances in the bar will not necessarily do the same for his boss's wife. But this is no great insight. Why should the fact we are affected by those around us show that there is some supra-individual order of social facts? People might think and behave differently in different social surroundings, but still all we seem to have is people thinking and behaving in various ways, albeit in response to other people. Social facts might not be reducible to what the people involved would be like on their own, but this does not show they cannot be reduced to what the people are like in the situations they actually are in.

Thus the individualist finds no great mystery in phenomena like crowd hysteria—it is for him simply a matter of a collection of individuals behaving hysterically, no doubt because each has a large number of excited people in close proximity. There is of course one further feature of such examples which needs explaining. Being with a large number of other people does not in itself actually disturb most of us—it is being surrounded by numbers of *hysterical* people that we do not like. This makes for a problem about what starts crowd hysteria and similar phenomena in the first place. But this is scarcely a serious difficulty for the individualist. Presumably crowd hysteria erupts when some few individuals start being hysterical on their own, either for quite idiosyncratic reasons, or because, unlike the rest of us, being in any large confined group makes them hysterical whether or not anybody else is. Interesting as these refinements are, they do nothing to show that we cannot understand everything that is going on perfectly adequately in terms of the way the various individuals in the crowd are behaving in response to others' behaviour.

At this point the Durkheimian might try another tack. He can argue that the important question is not whether individuals react in the obvious ways to their social surroundings, but rather whether their underlying psychological dispositions to display those reactions themselves depend on the social background. The individualist picture of things suggests that behind people's varying reactions to changing surroundings there are stable and inherent features of character and personality. Thus, while he admits that immediate social events (the boss's wife, a large crowd) trigger off certain responses, the individualist still presents these responses as manifestations of standing internal dispositions (a desire to impress others, a tendency to get hysterical in certain situations).

The Durkheimian will want to object to any idea that behind people's responses to immediate social stimuli there are inherent psychological dispositions which do not vary from one social context to the next. The historical and comparative evidence makes it clear, he will say, that ultimate ideas about right and wrong, about proper ambitions for men, about how the world works, etc., are not inherent to the nature of individual human beings but rather part of the external social context.

So, he will continue, mental and behavioural differences between societies cannot be accounted for simply in terms of people responding to obvious features of their immediate situation according to their native psychological dispositions. It is this, rather than any superficial examples about crowd hysteria and so on, that the Durkheimian can insist shows that there are external social facts. Insofar as the inherent dispositions of individuals are inadequate to account for the different ways people behave and think in different societies, we have no alternative but to recognise the existence of external pressures acting on them—that is, that there are social facts existing outside individuals.

It will be of some help in sorting out this argument to consider some basic points about the development of individual human characteristics, and in particular to compare our contemporary theories about this with those current in the nineteenth century. In the last couple of paragraphs we have been skirting round a distinction that comes very naturally to us, namely the distinction between genetically innate and environmentally acquired characteristics. Genetically innate characteristics are those ensured by the genes the human individual is endowed with at conception. Environmentally acquired characteristics are those which depend also on the contingencies of what happens to the individual after conception.[5] Our theories of inheritance add a further aspect to this distinction. An individual can pass on to his descendants his genetically innate but not his environmentally acquired characteristics. This follows from the fact that the environmental acquiring of characteristics does not produce corresponding changes in the genes an individual bequeaths to his descendants.

For most of the nineteenth century there was nothing like our theory of inheritance and the resulting distinction between innate and acquired characteristics. It is true that people have always asked if certain traits resulted from 'nature' or 'nurture', whether they were determined from conception or by later circumstances. But until the last quarter of the nineteenth century it was also almost universally assumed that any characteristics 'nurtured' in one individual would in turn be passed on to his descendants as part of their 'nature'. Even Darwin accepted this 'inheritance of acquired characteristics', and indeed his theory of inheritance by 'pangenesis' was explicitly tailored to account for this. Where Darwin and his followers differed from previous evolutionists like Lamarck was not in denying that any nurtured characteristics would be passed on, but in doubting whether new characteristics did actually get nurtured in individual development often enough to account for the evolution of species without bringing in natural selection as well.[6]

The significance of this for us can be brought out by considering the standard nineteenth century view of differences in thinking and behaviour between different human societies. For us these differences must be *either* genetically innate *or* dependent on enviornmental differences. The issue simply did not arise in this form for most nineteenth-century thinkers. They assumed that once social character- istics had been acquired, from whatever source, they would automati- cally form part of the inherent nature of succeeding generations— though at the same time these characteristics could always be 'un- acquired' too, and so cease to be passed on through inheritance. Nineteenth century debates about the possibility of 'improving' an 'inferior' race should thus not be understood as concerned with our question of whether 'inferiorities' derive from different genes or different environments—for them all social characteristics were *both* inheritable *and* susceptible of environmental modification. The question they disputed was rather how many generations it would take for superior characteristics to be nurtured and so become nature for succeeding generations.[7]

In the 1880s August Weismann formulated the theory that the 'germ- plasm' in the cell nucleus was (a) the basis of inheritance and (b) unaffected by the environmental circumstances of the individual carrying it.[8] It is interesting to speculate on whether the development of the germ-plasm theory and related ideas played any part in the emergence of the idea of external social facts. The discovery that all inheritable information is carried in an unchanging cell nucleus would obviously have reduced the plausibility of the previously accepted view that all differences in social mores, patterns of thought, etc., are somehow built into different peoples' inherent natures.

But, if this was an influence on Durkheim's thinking,[9] the way he puts his conclusions suggests that he failed to free himself entirely from traditional thinking about inheritance. For it is one thing to deny that certain characteristics are genetically innate, but quite another to claim that they are not individual characteristics at all, but features of some supra-individual reality. From the modern point of view there is nothing difficult in holding that though certain individual differences are not genetically innate, they are still nothing more than differences *in* individuals. All that has to be recognised is that those differences are produced by factors external to the individuals, rather than by their genes. Still, it is easy enough to see what might have led Durkheim to say what he did. Having rejected the view that social differences could be explained by the inherited characteristics of different races, he could then have slipped back into the old way of thinking according to which *any* internal characteristic common to the individuals in some social group would be part of their inherited nature, and so ended up insisting that social differences must somehow be external to individuals altogether.

We can sympathise with the conceptual struggles Durkheim probably faced in formulating his insights about the nature of social facts. But we need not succumb ourselves. For we are nowadays clear that traits can be 'internal' to individuals in the sense of being part of their real psychological make-up, without being 'internal' in the sense of deriving from their genes. So, contrary to what the Durkheimian argument earlier in this section insinuated, the individualist can reduce what people do in society to the expression of their internal character and dispositions without in any way being committed to the view that those psychological traits are genetically innate. Even if social facts are more than the sum of people's genetic characteristics, this does not show they must be more than collections of socially acquired characteristics.

4. 'SOCIAL FACTS EXPLAIN THEIR INDIVIDUAL MANIFESTATIONS, SO CANNOT BE THEM'

But there are still difficulties for the individualist. The Durkheimian can now appeal to the third argument mentioned earlier, and press the individualist on the question of how we are to explain the 'individual manifestations' of social facts. We are now agreed that the characteristic attitudes and patterns of behaviour displayed by individuals in different societies are not to be explained by genes. The natural alternative seems to be that it will be the presence of some social fact itself that produces its individual manifestations. But then how can social facts *be* collections of their individual manifestations?

To take a simple example, suppose we were to ask why the individual members of some society have a repulsion to and disapproval of eating beef. It seems undeniable that the initial answer will standardly be that they have each had those attitudes instilled in them by the existence in their society of a norm or taboo against consuming beef. There is of course a further question about why the norm got set up in the first place. But this is a further question—given that the norm is there, we can perfectly satisfactorily invoke its presence to explain why each individual has come to have an antipathy to eating beef. But this then seems to show that the norm must be something existing external to those individual antipathies. If it were identical with them, how could it explain them? We cannot explain something by itself.

What the individualist will want to say on this is that each member of society gets trained into the accepted social attitudes and behaviour by his contact with other individuals who themselves uphold the accepted standards. The people in the above example would throughout their life have observed that others shunned beef, and no doubt have been corrected and even punished when they showed any inclination to eat it themselves. The natural outcome of this process would be for the individual to adopt the principle that eating beef is deplorable himself.

There is nothing in this story, the individualist will say, that forces us to recognise any supra-individual forces. All we have discovered is a typical pattern, repeated throughout society, of individuals with certain characteristics socialising others by producing those same characteristics in them. That social characteristics are not transmitted *genetically* from one generation to the next does not show they are not so transmitted at all, that there must be some process outside generational interaction keeping the characteristics there. (Though again we can appreciate how the lack of a clearly articulated conceptual structure for distinguishing genetic from cultural inheritance might attract someone to this notion.)

The individualist will see the kind of cultural transmission outlined as typical of any case involving norms, roles or institutions. A norm is a principle of behaviour which is upheld by the members of some group, in the sense that they approve of or expect conformity to this principle and consequently both conform themselves and tend to constrain others to do the same. Whenever such a general pattern of attitudes and expectations obtains, new individuals will naturally come to adopt them as well. So norms, and, derivatively, roles and institutions, have a tendency to perpetuate themselves. This tendency can of course be disrupted by various factors. But for all that, it is a natural and understandable process that in the absence of countervailing pressures characteristic attitudes should persist over time and generations.

This self-perpetuating property of social facts is what allows the third pro-Durkheimian argument to get under way. There *is* a sense in which the individual manifestations of a social fact are results of the prior existence of that social fact. But it does not follow from this that it is wrong to equate social facts with their individual manifestations. The trouble is that when we say 'the individual manifestations of a social fact

are results of the presence of that social fact' we are in effect
equivocating on 'social fact'. We can use 'social fact' to refer to the set of
attitudes people have at some precise moment of time. Or we can use it to
refer to a continuing process of certain attitudes persisting over some
period of time. In most contexts this distinction between two senses of
'social fact' does not matter, precisely because the kind of social facts we
have in mind are characteristically persisting things, which, once they
are there, tend to stay there. But in the present context this distinction is
crucial. For it shows how the individualist can allow that a 'social fact'
explains 'its' individual manifestations without being committed to the
fallacy of circular explanation. In such cases, he can say, the 'social fact'
that does the explaining will be the *previous* presence of certain attitudes.
What gets explained is the 'social fact' consisting of the *later* existence of
such attitudes. There is a sense in which these are the *same* persisting
'social fact'. But it is not in this sense that the former explains the latter.
It is only when we confuse the two senses of 'social fact' that we are
inclined to think that the individualist is trying to explain something by
itself.

5. SOCIAL FACTS AS THEORETICAL ENTITIES

So far the individualist has resisted a number of arguments *for* the
Durkheimian position. Perhaps this will encourage him to go on the
offensive and offer a definite argument *against* the Durkheimian view.
One such argument was hinted at at the beginning of this chapter. The
individualist can complain about the *unobservability* of any supposed
supra-individual social facts. We can perceive people and houses and so
on all right, he will say, but where can we perceive any additional social
facts? And does this not make it pointless to continue discussing them?
If we cannot detect whether or not a social fact is present in any given
situation, then surely their existence can be no more than arbitrary
speculation.

This argument is not as crushing as it might first appear. For one thing
the Durkheimian can ask, *ad hominem*, about the psychological traits to
which the individualist wants to reduce social facts. Can we observe
people's values and thought-patterns? It is not at all clear why external
social facts should be more suspect than internal mental states.

But, more to the point, the Durkheimian can question the implicit
premise that only observable things exist. The modern physical sciences,
for instance, seem to have discovered all kinds of perfectly real but

unobservable entities, such as magnetic fields, radio waves, and subatomic particles. According to physical theory, such unobservables are responsible for many of the everyday phenomena that we can observe directly, like electric motors, radio music and solid matter. Why should social facts not be conceived of on the same model? Admittedly they cannot be observed directly, but why should they not be like 'theoretical' entities in physics, detectable indirectly by reference to their observable effects? For the Durkheimian supra-individual social facts are responsible for many of the things that individuals do. He can argue that this is in itself a justification for supposing their existence. Just as the theory involving magnetic fields is validated by its success in accounting for certain observable phenomena, so can ideas about supra-individual social facts be justified in terms of their utility in explaining what people do. Indeed, the Durkheimian might say, he never really needed to produce special arguments *for* the existence of social facts in the first place. There is no onus on him to prove that his social facts *must* exist, any more than the physicist needs to *prove* to a persistent sceptic that magnetic fields exist. By the nature of the case, such conclusive demonstrations are impossible and unnecessary. It is justification enough that the theoretical entities one postulates yield a satisfactory explanatory account of the relevant observable phenomena.

The individualist can object to this response that the account of theoretical entities being taken for granted by the Durkheimian is by no means uncontroversial. There is a perfectly respectable school of thought which holds that 'theoretical entities' are only admissible in science insofar as they can be reduced in principle to observable indicators, in just the sense that the individualist wants to reduce social facts to their individual manifestations. And there is another school of thought which allows that it might be handy to think in terms of irreducibly unobservable entities, but which holds that nevertheless we should not suppose such entities to really exist.

The argument is threatening to get out of hand here. A number of deep issues in the philosophy of science are crowding in. So I shall leave the debate between the individualist and the Durkheimian up in the air for the time being, and turn to some general questions about scientific theorising. This will be part of my more general project of assessing the possibility of a scientific understanding of society. But it will also enable us to come back and resolve the debate about social facts at the end of the next chapter.

2 Scientific Theories

1. EMPIRICISM

We were all once taught that scientific conclusions gain their authority from careful observation and experiment. It was this empirical component in scientific method that was held up as making science superior to such superstitions as astrology, alchemy, divination and magic. The idea was that the one thing we could be certain of were the results of experiments and other observable phenomena. Science guaranteed its conclusions by sticking to what could be proved from such data.

This long-conventional view was classically systematised in the philosophical tradition called empiricism. In this chapter I shall point out some deficiencies in empiricism, and discuss some ideas which will promise to remedy these failings. It is a moot point whether the resulting view ought still to be considered a version of 'empiricism'. It will certainly be a long way from the historical origins of the empiricist tradition.

I shall for the moment use 'science' without prejudging whether any or all of the social sciences are 'sciences' in the same sense as the natural sciences. And I shall draw on examples from the social sciences when they are convenient for the development of my theme. But my first priority will be to develop an analysis which deals with the natural sciences. This tailoring of my analysis of 'science' to the natural rather than the social sciences is in the first instance merely a semantic convenience. Eventually I shall argue that this rubric covers the social sciences as well. But this conclusion will have to come at the end of this book.

Classically, empiricism held that any idea we have—be it of a fire, a triangle, or a house—stems originally from sense experiences.[1] We can conjoin these ideas to form judgements. Judgements conjoining ideas in themselves unrelated are *synthetic*. Synthetic judgements are shown true if the ideas conjoined actually go together in experience. For instance, the judgement that metal gets hot in fire is verified if experiences of metal which has been in fire go together in actuality with experiences of heat.

19

Since all ideas are implanted via the senses in the first place, any judgement is in principle so decidable by reference to sensory experience, and should be accepted only if actual sense experience does verify it. Except, that is, for the special case of *analytic* judgements, where the ideas conjoined are intrinsically related to each other. For instance, with the judgement *triangles have three sides* the first idea involved includes the other, and anybody who comprehends those ideas will be able to perceive the truth of the judgement straight off by reflection alone, without recourse to any actual experiences. This ease of deciding analytic judgement reflects the fact that, unlike synthetic claims, analytic judgements do not say anything about reality, but merely report on relationships between ideas. (For all that analytic judgements can be of serious interest. Most empiricists would consider that all mathematics is analytic.)

In the twentieth century logical positivism has transposed empiricism into a linguistic key.[2] Logical positivists treat of sentences and meanings rather than judgements and ideas. But the essential features are unchanged. The 'verification principle', the defining slogan of logical positivism, decrees that if a sentence is meaningful, then its meaning must indicate what observations would show it to be true. Sentences are to be accepted as true only if the verifying observations are actually made. The exceptions, of course, being analytic sentences, whose truth follows directly from the meanings of the words in them. Analytic sentences convey information about the meanings of words, rather than features of the world.

Empiricism has a problem with induction. Proper knowledge— science—is supposed to be guaranteed by the certainties of sense experience. This demand seems to be satisfiable easily enough for singular statements specifying that a particular object at a particular place and time has a certain property. But science is not so much concerned with such singular statements as with *universal generalisations* specifying that *all* things of some kind have some property ('all metals in fires get hot', 'all falling bodies have constant acceleration'). Induction is the process of reasoning from observations to such universal generalisations. The problem is that the premises of such inferences can never guarantee the conclusions. At best, our observations can only cover those instances of a generalisation which have occurred up to *now*, whereas the generalisation itself makes claims about all those cases that will come up in the infinite future. However many positive instances we observe, it is always possible that a counterexample will occur in the future—that the next bit of metal put in fire should remain cool, that the next falling body should have a variable acceleration.

The problem of induction is not just a logical curiosity. Even if it was once viewed in that light, the demise of classical mechanics at the turn of the century has brought home to philosophers of science that the possibility of inaccurate extrapolations from necessarily limited data is a real danger to even the best-confirmed scientific theories.

What then happens to the empiricist principle that proper scientific knowledge must be *guaranteed* by sense experience? Some heroic members of the tradition, notably Hume and Schlick,[3] have concluded that universal generalisations cannot be part of proper knowledge after all. But most have preferred to weaken the requirements for good science. Instead of requiring that accepted scientific judgements be provable and proved, they merely ask that they be testable and that they have stood up to some tests. Universal generalisations are certainly testable, even if not provable, in the sense that it is always possible that the experiments we perform or the observations we make should turn out to falsify them. So the substitution of testability for provability allows universal generalisations to be included in science all right. Indeed Karl Popper has built a whole philosophy of science on the principle that what distinguishes science from non-science is its 'falsifiability'.[4]

This weakening of the empiricist requirements on science does not really *solve* the problem of induction. Even if the requirement of testability succeeds in picking out what people standardly and intuitively count as proper science, it leaves us with a problem of explaining why such proper science is a good thing. We have still been given no account of why success in past tests should be a good basis for accepting generalisations which predict the future.[5] But I shall not pursue this. I doubt there is any good alternative to simply accepting as a first principle that the past is somehow an informative (if fallible) guide to the future. So let us now turn to some further difficulties faced by empiricism.

2. THE PROBLEM OF THEORETICAL TERMS

As was mentioned at the end of the last chapter, many of the entities and properties discussed by scientists do not seem to be accessible to the senses in any obvious way. Magnetic fields, radio waves and subatomic particles were examples offered from physics. And on the face of it there seem to be similar unobservables in the less hard sciences: for example, geologists have continental plates, psychologists have instinctive drives, economists have elasticities of demand, and sociologists have class structures.

The incorporation of such invisible, intangible entities in scientific theories is an embarrassment for empiricists of whatever ilk. For if we cannot in practice detect the presence of certain things, how can we assess judgements about them, either for truth or falsity? It is clear enough what kinds of experiences would be relevant to the truth or falsity of 'all swans are white'. But what about 'the same volume of all gases at a given temperature and pressure always contains the same number of molecules'? However are we supposed to tell, given a sample of a gas, how many molecules it contains? If we cannot see or touch them, how are we to count them?

Recent philosophers in the empiricist tradition have been loath to condemn all talk of unobservable entities as arbitrary nonsense. The most sophisticated approach to 'the problem of theoretical terms' is offered by the *double-language model*.[6] On this model there are two languages in any branch of science. On the one hand is the *observation language*. This conforms to the standard conception—terms in it are supposed to get their meanings by being associated with elements of sensory experience. Then there is the *theoretical language*. Theoretical terms get meanings indirectly, by being related to terms in the observation language. These defining relationships are specified by 'correspondence rules', or 'co-ordinating definitions'. For instance, 'a standardly calibrated mercury thermometer will read x if it is in contact with a body at a temperature of $x°$ C', is a correspondence rule connecting the theoretical term 'temperature of $x°$ C' with the observational expression 'standard thermometer reading of x' ('standardly calibrated' here of course referring to basic physical characteristics of the thermometer specifiable independently of its measuring centigrade temperatures correctly). So the basic idea of the double-language model is that our grasp of theoretical terms derives from generalisations which stipulate their relationship to observation terms. And this grasp then enables us to test statements about unobservables indirectly, but perfectly objectively, by assessing those observation statements to which they are related by correspondence rules.

A question of continuing concern to proponents of the double-language model has been exactly what kind of definition of theoretical terms we get from correspondence rules.[7] The simplest answer is given by what I shall call *translationism*. On this view, for any theoretical term there is always some—possibly quite complicated—observational expression which is precisely equivalent in meaning. This means that theoretical language is in principle quite dispensable, in that anything said in it would always equally well—if not equally conveniently—be said using the observation language only. For the translationist, theoretical talk is just a useful shorthand for making complex observational statements. At bottom, talk of 'temperature' is just talk about thermometer readings, talk of an organism's 'genes' is just talk about the distribution of certain observable characteristics amongst its relations, talk about 'class structure' is just talk about certain patterns of interactional behaviour, etc.

For all its simplicity, translationism is false. Theoretical talk cannot in fact be replaced by observational talk without changing the meaning of what is said. The basic obstacle is that theoretical terms characteristically enter into a *number* of 'correspondence rules'. Temperature, for instance, can be measured not only by mercury thermometers, but also by gas thermometers, alcohol thermometers and any number of other devices. Which of these measuring procedures gives *the* observational meaning of 'temperature'? The problem for translationism is that there seems no non-arbitrary way of selecting one of these procedures over the others.

Why not just take it that 'temperature' is defined simultaneously by all the different ways of measuring it? This makes a kind of sense, but such a 'multiple definition' would be no good for the translationist. Consider what would happen if we came across a case where two of the procedures built into the definition of 'temperature' actually gave different results when applied to the same body. What then would be the 'temperature' of the body in question? At first sight this might seem a silly question—surely it is just a matter of finding out which procedure is unreliable. But remember that we are being supposed to get our grasp of what *temperature* is solely from what we have agreed to be the observational signs of it. So we have no further court of appeal when those signs differ amongst themselves. In such a case although we would be in no doubt about the *observable* facts we would *not* be able to decide what to say about the body's 'temperature'. Our 'multiple definition' would fail to give a precise observational equivalent for statements involving 'temperature'. This is not just an artificially contrived difficulty. In general scientists do take it at any one time that there are a number of alternative ways of detecting their theoretical posits, be they temperatures, electric charges, IQs, or political attitudes. And then they often discover subsequently that what they previously thought to be equivalent ways of measuring the same thing give different results in certain circumstances. If all they have to go on is a 'multiple definition' for their theoretical term the observable facts will leave them at a theoretical loss.[8]

There is a school of thought that holds that the absence of precise observational definitions for theoretical terms is a *flaw* in scientific language. This is *operationalism*. Operationalists accept that translationism is false—in practice scientists do not select some one privileged measuring procedure to give each theoretical term a precise observational meaning. But nevertheless operationalists think scientists *ought* to do this.

Their reasoning is that the existing looseness of theoretical language puts the objectivity of science at risk. They are concerned about the kind of case just discussed, where different procedures for measuring some theoretical quantity give different answers. There is a danger in such cases that the different answers will favour different theoretical positions. Consider, for instance, the debate about whether 'IQs' are genetically or environmentally determined. Suppose that some 'IQ' tests give answers which indicate a low correlation between scores of siblings reared apart, while other 'IQ' tests give answers which make this correlation relatively high. There seems nothing to stop the two sides to the debate each adopting those measurements that favour their view and discarding the others. And then, the operationalist fears, there would ensue a confused, pointless and irresoluble debate, precisely because it had not been laid down and agreed which one measuring procedure amongst the various alternatives actually *defined* 'IQ'.

The possibility about which operationalists are worried is real enough. Indeed operationalism was originally developed by Percy Bridgman largely in response to the confusion engendered when relativistic physics questioned the principles behind certain classical procedures for measuring spatial and temporal intervals.[9] But, even if we admit there is a real danger here, it is doubtful that the operationalist cure is preferable to the disease.

Consider what the operationalist programme would actually involve. We would no longer be entitled to our 'ambiguous' term 'temperature'. We would need to distinguish 'mercury thermometer temperature', 'gas thermometer temperature', and so on, with a different term for each way of measuring temperature. The same goes for all other theoretical terms. And this means we would no longer be able to say, for instance, 'water boils at 100 °C at standard atmospheric pressure'. This would fragment into a multitude of distinct generalisations, one for each combination of ways of detecting 'temperature', 'pressure', and 'water'. Suppose for the sake of argument that these three terms are each associated with ten correspondence rules. Then we would need a thousand generalisations to say what in our present unreconstructed language can be implied by thirty-one (by the thirty correspondence rules plus the original statement of water's boiling point).

This schematic example only hints at the damage operationalism would do. Scientific theories as they presently exist are articulated structures of great expressive power. Imagine a theory as a kind of pyramidal framework made of struts. The observational terms are the points at which the framework is moored to the ground. The theoretical terms are the points at which the struts making up the framework join. The struts then represent the generalisations which link the theoretical terms to observational terms and to each other. Some theoretical terms will be linked directly to a number of observational mooring points. Other more abstract theoretical terms, higher up the structure as it were, will be linked indirectly to observational terms through being linked to numbers of the former theoretical terms. And so placing a strut between theoretical terms up in the air will create a great number of pathways indirectly connecting up various observational points on the ground, the more so the higher up the framework that strut is. Or, to relax the metaphor,[10] formulating an abstract theoretical generalisation will systematically imply a wealth of generalisations relating observational terms. Thus a statement of the boiling point of some substance will imply that *all* the different tests for temperature will each give a certain answer for anything satisfying *any* of the tests for being that substance. The same point will apply, to an infinitely greater degree, to such basic theoretical assumptions as the physicist's $F = ma$, or the neo-classical economist's postulate that competitive prices are fixed by the intersection of supply and demand curves. It is precisely because theoretical terms do not conform to operationalist strictures and are each linked to observation in a multiplicity of ways that they provide such a powerful and economical mode of expression. If each theoretical term had to be tied to just one observational term, they would no longer be able to facilitate science in the way they do.

It has come to be generally accepted by empiricist philosophers of science that a strict adherence to operationalism would make science effectively impossible. Science needs to have theoretical terms which are not precisely definable in the observational language. The content of a theoretical term, what it means, can still be seen as depending on how it is linked to various points on the observational 'ground' by the structure of generalisations it enters into. But it is only because *all* such links together contribute indiscriminately to its meaning that it will have the distinctive utility it does.

But there then remains a question as to how seriously we should take theoretical language. Given that claims about 'electrons', 'genes' and 'elasticities of demand' cannot be considered as definitely equivalent to claims about specific observable facts, are we entitled to suppose that the entities apparently referred to in such claims really exist? According to *instrumentalism* we are not entitled to suppose this. Instrumentalists argue that since our senses cannot verify claims about unobservable entities theories about such things cannot be counted as anything more than 'instruments' for ordering and summarising observational claims. They allow that, as the pyramid metaphor illustrates, theories about unobservables are in practice essential tools for this organising purpose. But they insist that as such they should not be viewed as actually reporting anything about reality—a tool, unlike a statement, does not *say* anything.

Realists defend the rather more natural view that theoretical entities really do exist, in just the same sense as such medium-sized physical objects as tables and chairs. In support of realism it can be argued that postulates about unobservables do more than simply summarise in an economical way generalisations about observables. They also character-istically explain *why* those generalisations are true. Suppose we wanted to know why there is always a rainbow when sun and rain occur simultaneously in a certain relative position. This demand would seem to be satisfied by a demonstration that the observable regularity in question is a logical consequence of the laws describing how light waves are refracted in water. The realist will allow that theories about unobservables like light waves are in a sense useful as a means for systematising regularities about observables like rainbows. But for him this is merely a by-product of their far more fundamental ability to show us what *produces* those regularities. And insofar as those theories do have this ability then of course light waves and so on must exist—if there really were no light waves to be refracted and reflected in raindrops, we could scarcely take rainbows to *result* from the behaviour of such light waves.

The instrumentalist will of course respond that talk about unobserv-ables manages to 'explain' what we observe only in the anaemic sense that it organises the total mass of observable regularities into manage-able groupings. The formation of rainbows is 'explained' by our theories only in the sense that our theories classify them into the same category of phenomena as the 'bending' of sticks in water, the workings of lenses, etc.

Given the frame of reference developed so far, there is a strong argument for preferring instrumentalism to realism. We have now accepted that it is inevitable that theoretical terms should only be imprecisely related to observations, that all the various links between a theoretical term and observable ways of detecting it should be considered on a par in contributing to its import. But, in accepting this, we have left ourselves with no way of allaying the worry which motivated operationalism. There seems to be no reason why scientists should not always be able to hang on to their favoured postulates about unobservables when faced with unexpected experimental results by simply preferentially discarding such assumptions about the relation of their unobservables to observables as threaten their position. And it is this apparent arbitrariness about what theoretical postulates are to be accepted which makes it hard to maintain a realist position about unobservables. If there is nothing to decide who is right when scientists disagree on postulates about unobservables, then how can they be disagreeing about an objective reality?

The difficulty here is not just that a scientist might always be sincerely mistaken in accepting some postulate about unobservables.[11] In general, of course, error can arise from a number of sources—inconclusive evidence, faulty reasoning, etc. But even if we can never be certain we have eliminated such possible sources of error, we still generally have some conception of what would have to obtain for a given statement to be true. Even if we cannot be sure, we generally know at least what we are looking for. With statements about unobservables we seem to lack even this. Our analysis seems to give us no proper hold at all on a notion of correctness or incorrectness for statements about unobservables. When a scientist defends his favoured postulates as consistent with whatever evidence comes along, it is not just that we cannot *prove* him wrong—the trouble is that we seem to have failed to attach any content to his *being* wrong. This gives us serious reason to doubt that theoretical statements refer determinately to independently existing objects and properties. If they did, then in principle at least the correctness of such statements would depend on the facts constituted by those entities.[12]

The point I am making can be related to a philosophically familiar issue. Our problem about theoretical language is a special case of the difficulty which has for some time been recoganised to arise for the distinction between analytic and synthetic statements.[13] If it were a clear matter which generalisations involving theoretical terms were analytic, which were true by virtue of the meanings of those terms, then scientists would be constrained in how they responded to new evidence. When revisions were called for they would be required to hold analytic postulates fixed. And this would direct them objectively and specifically to the revision of synthetic generalisations. But we have recognised that the various generalisations by which theoretical terms are more or less directly linked to observables cannot be seperated into those manifesting the authorised meanings of those terms and those which are merely empirically revisable synthetic hypotheses. It is this which seems to allow that nothing can ever force a scientist to revise any given theoretical postulate, or, for that matter, force him not to revise any given such postulate. In a sense, any theoretical dispute cannot help but be a debate about concepts as much as about facts. Because the meanings of theoretical terms are not determinately tied to observational language the scientist seems free to attach such meanings to his theoretical terms as will allow him to say what he wants to say. If he decides to hold on to certain favoured postulates about unobservables, then he is in effect treating those postulates as analytic and allowing them to dictate what concepts he will attach to his theoretical terms. ('*Forces* are whatever we have when accelerations occur'; '*Intelligence* just is that innate intellectual ability everybody has to an equal degree/derives from their parents'.) An opponent who wants to reject such postulates cannot just appeal to the facts—for as much as anything he is disputing the content to be attached to the relevant terms.

The instrumentalist, unlike the realist, finds nothing uncomfortable in the scientist's apparent freedom to mould his theoretical talk as he wishes. He contrasts this with the way in which observational judgements, determinately tied as they are to elements of sensory experience, are directly and objectively responsive to what the evidence shows. Observational judgements he takes therefore to report on an independently existing reality. The fact that different theoretical judgements can be equally acceptable in the face of the same evidence he finds no more surprising than that different hammers can drive nails into wood.

3. THE THEORY-DEPENDENCE OF OBSERVATION

The instrumentalist presupposes a clear distinction between observational and theoretical languages. Theoretical discourse is suspect, but observational languages are not. However, this distinction is by no means uncontroversial. In the last decade or two a number of writers have questioned the traditional analysis of observational languages, and indeed whether a distinction between observation and theory can be made at all.

On the official view, observational expressions get meaning by association with elements of direct sensory experience. It was because of this that observational judgements were supposed to be directly and straightforwardly answerable to the facts, unlike theoretical claims which seemed to depend as much on the scientist's prior intellectual commitments as on what the evidence showed. But is the information we are given by our senses a direct representation of reality, uncontaminated by our prior theories? An initial difficulty for the traditional conception of an observational language is that many of the perceptions prompted by our sense organs seem to involve quite definite theoretical assumptions. To take an example of N.R. Hanson's, what the trained physicist perceives when presented with an X-ray tube is quite different from what the uninitiated layman will experience. The layman will see a glass and wire thing, like a funny light bulb; but the physicist will see it *as* an X-ray tube, as a distinctive piece of equipment with certain definite uses.[14] Again, what the layman watching a cloud chamber will see as indeterminate squiggles will be directly perceived by the experienced physicist as definite kinds of subatomic phenomena. Further instances offer themselves. The phonetician or sociolinguist will be able to directly discriminate phonemes or accents indistinguishable to the man in the street. Geologists can immediately categorise rock formations and social psychologists unthinkingly code answers to open-ended questionnaires in ways impossible for the untrained. What examples such as these suggest is that even the immediate material of sensory awareness can often incorporate all kinds of assumptions deriving from abstract scientific theories.

Perhaps these examples are less than convincing. The judgement that something is an *X-ray tube* carries implications about its ability to produce X-rays. How then can such a judgement be part of direct sensory perception? Direct observation can show us the shape, the colour, the hardness, etc. of an object—but surely not that it will produce X-rays. Thus it might be argued that the assertion that something is an 'X-ray tube' does not issue directly from pure elements of observational experience, but comes only after we *interpret* those observations in the light of our theoretical assumptions, after we move out of observational language into theoretical discourse.

The difficulty with this defence is that it is dubious whether what we are given in experience is ever pure in the sense that it is free from interpretation in the light of our general assumptions about the kind of entity observed. In general the entities we perceive are more than our senses entitle us to. Perceptual curiosities like duck-rabbits and Necker cubes illustrate the point. Even though we are given a constant input to the sense organs, we nevertheless switch back and forth between seeing the drawing as a rabbit and seeing it as a duck, or between seeing a cube one way up and seeing one the other way up. While our everyday perceptions do not of course switch back and forth in this way, these examples show that what we are immediately aware of in observation has a content which *adds* to what we get by way of sensory input. Our perceptions involve judgements about further properties of the thing perceived, beyond what is guaranteed by the impressions of our sense organs. When we see a cat, say, our perception is of something which exists in three spatial dimensions, which is alive, which is not going to disappear into thin air in the next second, etc.; it is not just a two-dimensional pattern of textures and colours.

At this point, a defender of the observation-theory distinction might try a different tack. He might admit that if we attend to the content of the conscious experiences which accompany assertions we are not going to be able to distinguish some category of expressions which report on a reality which shows itself directly to us. But perhaps we can make the distinction without bringing in conscious perceptions at all, by considering directly the way linguistic behaviour responds to conditions in the external world. Why not count as observational expressions those we are trained to use unthinkingly and immediately in direct response to the reception of certain physiological stimuli at our sense receptors? And then theoretical terms will be those we only apply indirectly, after time and thought, as when we use our accepted theoretical postulates to move inferentially from direct observational judgements about a particular situation to its unobservable characteristics.[15]

What kind of conscious experiences we have when we respond to the prompting of our sensory receptors would on this view be quite irrelevant. What makes a term observational is our being conditioned to use it directly when the external world interacts with us in a certain physical way—that we might at that moment imaginatively conceive of certain abstract entities would be beside the point.

Nevertheless this shift in approach is for our purpose of no significance. The new line is no more successful in distinguishing observational from theoretical languages than the earlier one. We can accept the picture of scientists being trained on the one hand to use expressions directly (observationally) and on the other to use expressions indirectly (inferentially, theoretically). The difficulty is that nearly all scientific terms whatsoever seem to have uses governed by *both* kinds of procedures. Examples like 'X-ray tube' show that even the most apparently theoretical terms are sometimes applied in direct response to sensory prompting. The physicist does not first register its observable features, and then use his theoretical generalisations to infer that it is an 'X-ray tube'. He will assert this straight off. Similarly the quantum theorist does not first register the shape of the squiggles in the cloud chamber, and then laboriously compute that it must be an 'electron – positron pair'—he has learnt to tell what those squiggles are without thinking. Conversely, even the most overtly observational terms like 'red' can on occasion be applied on the basis of inferences from the applicability of other terms instead of directly, as when we judge that something is red, not as a result of looking at it, but from knowing the wavelength of light it emits, or from knowing that it is iron at 1000° C. So a distinction between observational and inferential *procedures* does not distinguish between observational and other *terms*. For many, indeed most, terms seem to be usable both observationally and inferentially.

Instrumentalists had good arguments for thinking that electrons and force-fields do not exist in the same way as tables and chairs do. Since there seemed no objective constraints on what conclusions scientists should adopt about unobservables instrumentalists inferred that theoretical language failed to relate determinately to an independent reality. What happens to instrumentalism now we see there is no good basis for distinguishing 'observational' from 'theoretical' expressions? Does not the instrumentalist now have to allow that electrons are as real as chairs? But it would be too quick to conclude that we all have to be realists now we have abandoned the observation – theory distinction. For perhaps the real upshot is that chairs are as unreal as electrons.

Let us reconsider. We no longer have purely observational or purely theoretical terms. Any scientific term will standardly have both direct observational and indirect inferential uses. But we can still speak of a scientific term being used to make an *observation report* on those particular occasions where it *is* used observationally, where it is applied directly as a result of sensory prompting, or, on the alternative conception, as a result of its association with a certain kind of conscious perception. (We can even for convenience talk loosely of a term being more or less observational in general, according as it is more or less often used observationally—in this sense 'red' would be 'more observational' than 'electrically charged'.)

However, observation reports no longer have the status they had within the double-language model. According to the old model observation reports had a certain authority, in virtue of issuing from a direct and uncontaminated sensory contact with reality. This authority can no longer be presupposed. For consider the situation where some observation report conflicts with an independent inferential judgement about the situation in question—where, say, our direct report that something is 'red' conflicts with what we have inferred from its chemical constitution about the wavelength of the light it must be emitting. One thing we might do is conclude that there must be something wrong with the chemical and electromagnetic theories on which our inferential judgement is based, and revise them accordingly. But on the other hand we could decide that there must be something wrong with our observation report, with our ability to tell that things are red by looking. Now we have realised that term 'red' is not tied purely and solely to a certain observational procedure, there is nothing that rules out the latter step as absolutely inadmissible. If the use of the term 'red' is governed by inferential as well as observational principles, why not stick by the former when there is a conflict? And, indeed, this is precisely what physics has been led to do in certain contexts—it has concluded that our direct observational judgements of colour are unreliable for objects moving at high speeds relative to us.

Effectively the same point can be made in relation to the conception of observation reports as issuing from association with conscious perceptions rather than physiological promptings. The crucial consideration is that such perceptions transcend what sensory input can possibly guarantee. For what this means is that our conscious sensory perceptions must be allowed to be *fallible*. If such a perception involves a judgement about a particular situation which contradicts our general assumptions, together with our other information about that situation, then one alternative open to a defender of those assumptions will always be to reject the perception itself. If part of what it is to perceive something *as* an X-ray tube is to judge that it will behave in certain ways in certain circumstances, then it seems perfectly admissible to reject the perception if we discover inferentially that it does not behave so.[16] Of course it will always be possible to retreat in such cases to talk of how things *look*. ('Even if it's not an X-ray tube, it sure *looks* like one'; 'Even if that star's not actually red, it does *look* red'.) But apart from any general philosophical problems about such talk, this ploy will have the precise effect of cutting sensory judgements off from what, on the double-language model, they were supposed to ensure—guaranteed access to external reality.

As with his judgements about unobservables, the scientist's apparent freedom to play fast and loose with observation reports also derives from a certain looseness in the meanings of scientific terms. If it were definitely part of the meaning of 'red' that it applied to anything normally trained English observers judged to satisfy it, then it could be argued that it was simply illegitimate semantic juggling for scientists to deny that things were red just because it did not fit into their general assumptions to admit they were not. But our rejection of the observation – theory distinction leaves us no grounds for always according such observational uses of scientific terms authority over inferential uses.[17] And so the scientist seems quite properly free to mould even the meanings of relatively observational terms into accord with his favoured postulates.

This was why I suggested earlier that the demise of the observation – theory distinction did as much to make talk of chairs suspect as to make talk of electrons respectable. The instrumentalist arguments now seem to be applicable to observation reports as much as to judgements about unobservables. On this level too there seem to be no objective constraints, even in principle, preventing a scientist always defending certain judgements by adjusting the meanings of his terms in the way dictated by his favoured postulates. But if this is so, and there is no content to the idea of a scientist being *wrong* in accepting or rejecting a given observational judgement, then in what sense can even observational expressions be held to relate determinately to an independent reality?

4. THE NEW RELATIVISM

It might seem absurd to maintain that even scientific decisions on observational matters are at bottom arbitrary. If science is not objective, what is? Nevertheless there are philosophers of science who in recent years have given accounts of science which come close to embodying this surprising view. Perhaps the most prominent amongst these are Paul Feyerabend and T. S. Kuhn.

There are differences between these two, of which more shortly, but they concur in their scepticism about objective theory choice in science. (From now on the term 'theory' will refer to any set of interconnected generalisations—our earlier identification of 'theoretical' with 'unobservable' has become pointless now we have rejected the idea of separate languages for observables and unobservables.) Both Kuhn and Feyerabend agree that the empirical evidence can never force the scientist to abandon a commitment to some favoured set of general postulates. Even when those postulates are framed in terms that can be applied in direct response to observation, the scientist can always deal with apparent counter-evidence by reinterpreting it to fit his chosen postulates. Kuhn and Feyerabend independently adopted the term *incommensurability* to indicate the impossibility of objective choices between alternative theories in a given domain.[18] Competing theories are characteristically 'incommensurable' in the sense that there is no common set of data against which they can be tested to see which is superior. Since the content of *all* scientific concepts is inseparable from the structure of the surrounding theory, two competing theories will necessarily be framed in different languages, even at the level of direct observation. The 'facts' relevant to one theory will thus be distinct from the 'facts' relevant to its competitor. In a sense the adherents of different theories will work in different worlds—each will study the 'reality' created by the theory he has accepted.

Kuhn and Feyerabend draw rather different morals from the incommensurability of theories. Feyerabend urges the proliferation of competing theories.[19] He is concerned lest received scientific views become self-supporting dogmas which continue to hold sway simply because they have a monopoly on the formulation of facts. To combat this danger he recommends that scientists should continually strive to develop new alternatives to accepted theories, and in particular to aim at precisely those alternatives which conflict with the reality presented by received orthodoxy. For Feyerabend, appeals to 'established facts' can only restrict scientific practice. Instead he recommends epistemological anarchism—'Anything goes!'[20] And he is able to support this radical prescription by reference to a number of convincing historical case-studies, in particular from Galileo's work, which suggest that certain important scientific advances were in conflict with any number of established and obvious 'facts' when first introduced.[21]

Kuhn presents science as a far more conservative enterprise.[22] Kuhn takes it that scientists working in a given field at any time all share a *paradigm*. There are a number of strands in this notion. Central is the idea of a community of scientists sharing a lasting commitment to certain fundamental postulates. In addition, Kuhn is referring to scientists' recognition of certain classic problem – solutions as exemplary examples of how to do science—he argues that these examples give scientists a tacit and intuitive understanding of how to deal with new problems. Various other ideas are on occasion involved. But in any case, Kuhn takes it that the scientist's commitment to a paradigm will so condition what he makes of the evidence that there will be no possibility of that paradigm being empirically disproved.

Kuhn argues that most of the time, during what he calls 'normal science', scientists do not question their paradigm in any way, but seek merely to solve puzzles within it, to extend the range of problems to which the paradigm yields standard solutions. If an individual scientist fails to solve some puzzle, that failure reflects on the scientist and not the paradigm. It is taken for granted that the paradigm will prove adequate to the problem once the matter is competently and properly investigated.[23]

Periodically the tranquillity of normal science is shattered by a 'scientific revolution'. These are intense, traumatic episodes in which one paradigm is replaced by another. Remember, there is no question of the empirical evidence *forcing* such developments. If anything it will be the personal motivations of scientists that account for the change. After a paradigm has reigned for a long time, soluble problems will become harder to find. Certain puzzles will resist solution and create an atmosphere of intellectual unease. And so younger scientists entering some field will cast around for some radically new approach which offers a new set of problems for them to make their names with. The older scientists who established their reputations within the confines of the old paradigm will characteristically be resistant to the new ideas, but after a while they will all retire or die off, and the new paradigm will settle down to another period of normal science.[24]

Though primarily concerned to describe science as a historical phenomenon, Kuhn is also judging how science *should* proceed.[25] Unlike Feyerabend, he does not see progress as best ensured by constant contention amongst competing ideas. On the contrary, he argues that it is only when the unquestioning acceptance of a paradigm ensures a general and longstanding agreement on fundamentals that there is any possibility of the strengths and weaknesses of a given approach being properly explored. For Kuhn, perpetual proliferation would simply stultify science, by stopping anybody ever getting down to proper research. In support of this view, Kuhn points to the kind of advances that the history of science shows to have resulted from sustained commitment to such lasting traditions as Newtonian mechanics.

To many philosophers the dispute between Kuhn's conservatism and Feyerabend's anarchism will be of little significance beside their basic agreement that scientific conclusions are at bottom relative to the scientist's theoretical preferences rather than the empirical evidence. Indeed they will query whether, given this, it makes any sense for Kuhn and Feyerabend to debate whether conservative or liberal strategies are best for science. Best for what? If all theories are equally capable of dealing with the empirical data, if they are all equally adequate pictures of incommensurable realities, then what does it matter how science proceeds?

5. THE METHODOLOGY OF SCIENTIFIC RESEARCH PROGRAMMES

However the discomfort that many have felt in swallowing the relativism of Kuhn and Feyerabend has been matched by a difficulty in formulating a position that deals satisfactorily with the issues they raise. Perhaps the most sophisticated response to the relativist challenge is to be found in the writings of Imre Lakatos.[26] Lakatos's central notion of a *research programme* is not dissimilar to Kuhn's paradigm. A research programme is characterised by a 'negative heuristic', a commitment by the programme's adherents not to question the more fundamental postulates, or *hard core*, of their current theory. The 'hard core' is related to the empirical data and gives rise to definite predictions only with the help of *auxiliary hypotheses*. These will include assumptions about how specific kinds of experimental situations relate to the entities discussed in the hard core, about how interfering factors will affect the simple relationships the hard core postulates between those entities, about instruments for detecting and measuring those entities, etc. Thus the Newtonian research programme could be considered to have as a hard core the three laws of motion and the law of universal gravitation. Then auxiliary hypotheses would specify such things as the specific kinds of forces that would be found in various experimental situations, the way air resistance, say, affects the gravitational fall of bodies through the atmosphere, the instruments that can be used for detecting stars, for measuring masses, distances, or times, etc.

Work within a research programme proceeds as follows. A particular set of auxiliary hypotheses can be said to define a particular variant, or *version*, of the research programme. A particular version will give rise to predictions which can be experimentally tested. If the experimental results are not as expected we have an *anomaly*, and scientists will seek to defend their hard core by revising their auxiliary hypotheses so as to formulate a new version of the research programme which avoids the anomaly in question.[27]

Lakatos is inclined to side with Feyerabend against Kuhn on the value of competition—he thinks it desirable that different research programmes should be pursued simultaneously in any given field of science. But, more significantly, he differs from both of them on the possibility of objective decisions between competing approaches. He allows, it is true, that there is no question of a simple experimental disproof of a given programme. The hard core of the programme so constitutes the content of the scientist's concepts as to make him always look in the first instance for a way of reinterpreting anomalies as consistent with his basic assumptions. But nevertheless Lakatos maintains that contending programmes *can* be objectively compared by reference to their relative *progressiveness*.

A research programme is constantly faced with anomalies which call for revisions of the programme's auxiliary hypotheses. One kind of solution would be to abandon one or more of the auxiliary hypotheses responsible for the anomaly. Thus we might simply reject certain thermometers, attitude questionnaires, or IQ tests as not measuring what they were supposed to measure, when investigations using these measures came up with theoretically unanticipated results. But such a step would be *ad hoc*, or *degenerate*, in that it deals with the anomaly by decreasing the content of the research programme by simply eliminating the possibility of the confuted predictions. Lakatos says that scientists are required to suggest *progressive* modifications of their programmes. By this he means that they should always *replace* their auxiliary hypotheses by substitutes which lead to new predictions. Thus we might suggest that certain correction factors should be applied to the results of our measuring procedures in certain circumstances, or device new kinds of thermometers or questionnaires, etc. Lakatos suggests that scientists are only justified in sticking to a research programme as long as it continues to be revised progressively, and provided that, in addition, the new predictions those progressive revisions give rise to are on occasion borne out.

Lakatos's requirements for a research programme are fairly moderate. It is not necessary that all its new predictions should be borne out, just that the programme should sometimes be successful in extending its explanatory range to new facts. Moreover Lakatos urges that we should even be tolerant of temporary *ad hocness*, provided progressive suggestions are made in time. Lakatos himself has a number of interesting historical case-studies showing how programmes which at one time were failing later recovered and achieved important advances. But, notwith-standing this moderation, Lakatos maintains that he has identified standards that, in the long run at least, will allow objective decisions between competing scientific positions.

What of the theory-dependence of observation? It was this, and the consequent problem of total incommensurability, that earlier gave the final blow to the idea of objective choices in science. It might seem quite unclear how Lakatos's approach can circumvent this difficulty. Indeed, Lakatos seems simply to take it for granted that observations of failed predictions can unproblematically refute a given version of a research programme, and to ignore the possibility that the defenders of that version might instead reject the observation reports themselves. He thus seems to be open to our earlier arguments which showed that the procedures giving rise to observation reports do not automatically have the semantic authority to override any general postulates they might conflict with.

Lakatos himself says little about this problem as such.[28] But it is not too difficult to see how his approach can be extended to deal with it. One thing suggested by our earlier discussion of observation reports is that we might in a way conceive of observers themselves as a kind of scientific *instrument*. People use expressions observationally as a result of their having been trained to apply those expressions directly in response to the reception of certain sensory information. Our accepting such obser-vation reports implicitly depends on a certain kind of generalisation: one to the effect that whenever a suitably trained human observer applies the relevant expression, it is as a result of his interaction with the kind of entity that the expression denotes. For instance, if we did not believe that in standard conditions English speakers apply the term 'red' obser-vationally precisely when red things are present, then clearly we would not credit any observational uses of the term they might make; and similarly, if even more obviously, with trained scientists' observation reports about particle interactions, distinctive accents, etc. (Often we will have a fairly sophisticated account of the way that the entities in question relate, perhaps via technical instruments, to the physiology of an observer's sense organs. Our acceptance of observation reports about those entities will then be sustained by our detailed theories of those instruments and our sense organs. But an articulated account of this kind does not seem essential for an expression to have an established observational use, provided that we at least make the general assump-tion that what the expression denotes does have *some* kind of determinate effect on human observers.)[29]

What this means is that we can now extrapolate Lakatos's method-ological precepts to the assessment of observation reports themselves. Our worry was that a scientist defending some version of a research programme might always deal with an unwanted observation report by simply rejecting it. But we now see that doing this will commit him to rejecting certain generalisations about the way human observers interact with the entities he is studying. And so we can require him, if he is going to do this, to do it in a progressive way. That is, he should only reject an observation report if he is in a position to *replace* his previous assumptions about humans' observational abilities with some revised assumptions about how the entities in question can be detected. Thus he might devise some new technical instrument to aid observers, or he might conjecture that observational illusions will arise in certain specific circumstances and suggest ways of allowing for them. But he cannot reject the observation just because it does not fit his theory, and leave it at that.

This requirement, that observational procedures need to be replaced progressively, is thus an effective constraint on wanton disregard of unwanted observations. And it is the more effective the more simple and fundamental the observational abilities in question. To question observers' reports about a pointer reading on the scale of some instrument, for instance, would be to question whether people can in general tell by looking whether two nearby medium-sized physical objects are in close proximity—and this would be admissible only in the unlikely event that alternative procedures could be suggested for all the myriad cases where people currently exercise this apparent ability.

Those brought up in a traditional epistemological environment will no doubt feel most uneasy about the idea that the import of observation reports should be considered dependent on scientific generalisations about the interaction between observers and what is observed. Surely, they will feel, we cannot help ourselves to scientific conclusions in assessing the worth of observation reports, for we can only justifiably come to those conclusions *after* judging that certain observation reports are to be accepted. However, we have now come a long way from the original classical empiricist idea that science starts from a certain basis of observations and proves its conclusions therefrom. There was first the problem of induction—observations cannot prove generalisations. After that there was the problem of unobservables—judgements about unobservables are of necessity only indeterminately tied to obser-vations. And then there was the theory-dependence of observation, which raised doubts about the authority of observation reports themselves. Given all this, it would be irrational to continue to bow to foundationalist scruples and insist that observations should somehow be validated independently of and prior to any scientific theorising. Why should the making of observations not be comprehended *within* our overall scientific theory of reality? Just as we use our theories about instruments to reason from instrument readings to the presence of certain entities affecting those instruments, so we can use our theories about observers to reason from their reports to the presence of what must be affecting them. Of course our coming to judgements about particular bits of reality always involves somebody making an observation report at some point. But that reality always intrudes on our theories through observation reports is no reason in itself to give those reports any special privileged status. As with anything else, we should continue to credit those reports only as long as our general view of reality, including human observers, gives us reason to do so. [30]

6. CHOOSING BETWEEN METHODOLOGIES

I have been suggesting that Lakatos's methodology of scientific research programmes goes some way towards showing how objective decisions between competing scientific positions are possible. But how is this suggestion to be substantiated? Feyerabend claims that any attempt to lay down rules for rejecting theories will only repress scientific advance. Kuhn advocates the dogmatic institution of monolithic paradigms. What shows that Lakatos's procedures for conducting science are the right ones?

As mentioned earlier, Feyerabend, Kuhn and Lakatos all appeal to the history of science to defend their views. Feyerabend insists that Galileo's theoretical innovations were possible only because Galileo ignored every conceivable methodological precept. Kuhn appeals to the success of such sustained traditions as Newtonian mechanics. And Lakatos in various places aims to decide the precise degree of progressiveness required in a research programme by reference to similar historical cases.

This kind of argument presents something of a puzzle. Although the analysis of particular historical examples is often contested, the appeal to history in itself seems perfectly cogent and to the point. If Galileo's practice is indeed at variance with Lakatos's picture of science, then surely this does something to discredit Lakatos's methodology. But why should it? Why should Lakatos's precepts have to fit *Galileo's* practice?

Why should not Lakatos simply decide that Galileo's practice was unscientific? Not everybody who calls himself a 'scientist' merits the title. And even those who do can on occasion do unscientific things. It seems as if we ought to be in a closed circle—trying to decide between scientific methodologies by appealing to examples of good science, when we need such a methodology to know which those are.[31]

Still, the historical arguments in question *do* seem relevant. It somehow looks as if behind the methodological dispute there must be some kind of implicit agreement about what counts as a successful scientific development, as a scientific advance. Yet, again, how is this possible, given that the substance of the dispute is precisely how science should be conducted?

To sort out this confusion we need to consider Lakatos's distinction between a research programme itself and a version of such a programme. A version of a research programme, recall, consisted of a definite set of auxiliary hypotheses conjoined to some 'hard core' of relatively fundamental postulates. The research programme, then, was the continuing tradition consisting of successive variations on the common theme of that hard core. If we keep this distinction clearly in mind, then we can see that on the specific question of what shows the worth of some *version* of some programme there is in fact little room for dispute. Remember that it is a version, rather than a research programme as such, that can give rise to definite experimentally testable predictions. None of the parties to the methodological dispute seriously deny that it counts against the version in question when such a prediction is not borne out. Nobody denies that anomalies have to be *dealt with*—that a version facing an anomaly should if possible be replaced by some other version which avoids that anomaly. Even Feyerabend, when insisting that conflicting observations should not prevent the development of some new theory, does not mean to imply that these awkward 'facts' should just be *ignored*. On the contrary, his point is that it might well in time be possible to *reinterpret* those 'facts' so as to make them *consistent* with the new ideas. And so even he recognises that anomalies need to be removed, by revising the hypotheses which lead us to credit the awkward 'facts'. Similarly, there is, I think, no real disagreement that, given two sets of specific generalisations, two definite versions of research programmes, it is the one which covers a wider range of phenomena, that accounts for a greater range of empirical detail, that is in that respect superior.

It is only when we move on to the conduct of research programmes as such that the methodological disagreements arise. For then we are no longer asking about the worth of some specific and testable conjunction of generalisations that we might accept at a given time, but asking how best to develop our ideas over time. It is on this level that such questions arise as to how long it is worth sticking with certain basic assumptions in the absence of auxiliary hypotheses to explain awkward phenomena; as to how quickly a programme should expand the range of data it covers; as to whether the most fruitful strategy for science is to concentrate all its resources in one paradigm; etc. And in fact such questions as these implicitly presuppose the agreed criteria for evaluating specific versions of programmes. For when we ask how 'best' to develop our ideas, what we want to know is precisely which strategy will succeed in leading us to general, anomaly-free conjunctions of specific generalisations.

In a sense we can say that the Popperian requirement that scientific theories ought to be *falsifiable* applies perfectly straightforwardly when the unit in question is a specific version of a programme. Considered as a whole the conjunction of the total set of generalisations making up such a version *will* be falsifiable, in that it yields definite predictions, and is to be rejected if such predictions are not borne out. And such a version is the more satisfactory the more falsifiable it is,[32] the wider the range of phenomena for which it yields definite predictions. Our problems arise only when we shift the meaning of 'theory' ('position', 'view', . . .) and consider as our unit some favoured sub-set of central postulates around which we are going to develop successions of auxiliary hypotheses. It is here that the intertwining of conceptual with factual issues emphasised earlier raises difficulties. For while anomalies can show that a specific version is wrong somewhere, that something needs to be changed, they do not show exactly where. Should the observational procedures involved be re-examined? Should some other auxiliary hypotheses be changed? Or is it even time to give up the favoured central assumptions? Somehow the scientist has to decide whether or not to continue using his terms with a content tied to the postulates in his hard core. But Popper does not help him to decide this. Popper's simple logic for choosing 'theories' breaks down when what is understood by 'theory' is that *part* of a version which can persist as a hard core through successive falsifications.

When we talk about Newtonian mechanics, monetarist economics, Weber's account of bureaucratisation, etc., as *theories*, what we are talking about is not some specific set of generalisations capable of definite empirical refutation, but rather something like a continuing programme of research. This is, I think, the most natural sense of 'theory' (and the one I shall be using henceforth unless specified otherwise). And so we can understand Feyerabend's and Kuhn's initial concern to deny the possibility of objective theory-choice in science as due to their realisation that significant theoretical disputes are not about simply falsifiable Popperian hypotheses, but rather about sets of basic postulates which retain an identity over time as the peripheral assumptions surrounding them are refined and elaborated. However, in emphasising the complexity of theory choices in science Feyerabend and Kuhn have obscured the important and basic point that there *is* unproblematic and objective agreement about what the refinement and elaboration of basic postulates is *aiming* at—namely, to come up in the end with definite, detailed and anomaly-free sets of generalisations to explain what happens. Feyerabend and Kuhn do implicitly recognise this point, even if they do not overtly acknowledge it. For it is what gives their historical arguments the force they have. When Feyerabend appeals to Galileo to discredit any reverence for 'established facts', what he is trading on is of course our common awareness that the theoretical tradition originating with Galileo did eventually and indubitably come up with the explanatory goods. And exactly the same point can be made about Kuhn's appeals to the *success* of Newtonian mechanics and similar programmes.

Perhaps part of the confusion here stems from Popper's classic distinction between the 'context of discovery' and the 'context of justification'. Philosophers in the Popperian tradition (which certainly includes Lakatos and Feyerabend, if not Kuhn) see themselves as concerned solely with matters of *justification*, with questions of how scientific theories are to be assessed once they are actually put forward. Where the theories come from in the first place, how they are *discovered*, is presumed not to be a matter for philosophical evaluation but, if anything, something for social, psychological or psychoanalytic explanation. The idea is that, provided a theory is properly assessed after it is proposed, it is no discredit to it that it might originally have occurred to its proponent because he found it ideologically attractive, or because it came to him in a dream.[33] I suspect that a too unthinking acceptance of this rather simple Popperian dichotomy has done much to obscure the perfectly good sense in which the more elaborate methodological questions of contemporary debate *are* concerned with discovery rather than justification. It has stopped the disputants seeing that their argument is essentially about how best to conduct research programmes so as to *discover* satisfactory versions. It is true that how the research programmes themselves are first discovered still seems predominantly an 'irrational' matter, suitable only for social or psychological explanation. But it is a mistake to infer conversely that because philosophy can have something to say about choices between existing research programmes, those programmes cannot in turn be oriented to the discovery of successful versions.

Whatever the source of the confusion, now that we are clear that theories (in the sense of programmes) are aimed at the discovery of successful versions, it becomes easy enough to understand how historical considerations can be relevant to deciding their proper conduct—the point of looking to the historical evidence is simply to see what kind of strategy has in the past succeeded in coming up with successful versions. I am inclined to the view that the actual history of thought supports the Lakatorian version of things—the view that advances are best achieved by competition amongst programmes, with survival requiring that 'progress' be made, if not immediately, at least within some decent time interval. But this is scarcely the place to adjudicate what the historical evidence actually shows. A couple of brief remarks will have to suffice.

Kuhn is concerned lest competition will lead to perpetual debate about fundamentals and prevent the serious exploration of the empirical worth of theories. There is indeed a danger here. But it seems to have been avoidable without *all* scientists in the relevant area adopting the *same* basic ideas, provided at least that the various individuals or groups within the community each periodically commit themselves to *some* programmes for the time being. That different scientists might have different commitments does not in itself seem to matter, as long as they are each variously serious about their own favoured views.

Feyerabend's work raises questions about the time factor involved in Lakatos's methodology. The point of the Galileo story is that it was an extremely long time indeed before the embryonic programme instituted by Galileo managed, with various stops and starts, to progress past the long-established Aristotelian mechanics it was challenging. Feyerabend's fear is that any attempt to specify a required rate of progress for research programmes would stop scientists such as Galileo persisting with ideas which for the moment seem hopeless. Even if we agree that 'progress' is uncontroversially desirable in the long run, how long is that? Any specific time limit seems arbitrarily restrictive, but to leave the run indefinitely long means we end up without a methodology at all.[34]

Although Feyerabend is raising a serious problem here, it does not follow that anything should go in science. A mineral prospector can never be *sure* that the site he is currently working will not provide a large strike with a bit more persistence. But that would not make it rational for him to continue working on that site for ever. He will know from experience that at a certain point the most efficient strategy is to move on to a new site. Similarly we should be able to learn from the history of science the point at which it becomes generally wise to abandon a degenerate programme (always admitting that the foolhardy might strike lucky in particular instances).

7. SCIENTIFIC REALISM

Can we now construe science realistically? Are we entitled to see science as making claims about an independent reality? We have seen that there are objective criteria for comparing the worth of different versions of scientific research programmes by reference to their relative freedom from anomalies and their relative generality of scope. And these criteria, together with the history of science, allow us to derive rational procedures for choosing between different research programmes as such.

Even so, we still cannot suppose that scientific assertions make determinate claims about independently existing entities in any simple sense. For the content of scientific concepts, the meaning of scientific terminology, is still dependent in essential part on the structure of the theory (programme, paradigm) they are used in. It is relevant here that our choices between theories are always comparative—what a theory promises is to prove itself with versions which are *less* beset by anomalies, *more* general in scope, than those of its competitors. We do not require it to anticipate *the* truth, *the* account which is never going to be superseded by some superior alternative. There is, I suppose, nothing in principle impossible about the idea of an absolutely correct scientific view of some area—a set of interrelated generalisations that will account perfectly for every occurrence that might in any way be detected. But even if this is an ideal, it seems to be quite unattainable, and in any case it is not clear how we could recognise it if we reached it.

What this means is that the concepts we are working with at any time will always be tentative tools for representing reality as it really is. Reality need not be composed of those elements that our current theory supposes it to be made of. And so we cannot consider the parts of our theory, the various interrelated statements that make it up, to be answerable one by one to various bits of reality. Since the way our terminology cuts up reality, so to speak, depends on the structure of our passing and supersedable theories, it would be misleading to view the validity of statements made using that terminology as somehow depending on whether they truly represent relations between the actual elements of reality. Again, the problem is not just that we cannot *know* whether the elements of reality are related as our theories represent them to be—it is rather that the terminology of our theories is not tied tightly enough to the elements of reality to make this a determinate question.

Still, I think there is room to characterise the view of science I have reached here as a realist one. For this view does nothing to deny that there is an articulated reality 'out there', that our scientific theories are trying to represent that reality as it is, and that our scientific practice selects those theories that do this most satisfactorily. That there need be nothing in reality corresponding neatly to the concepts we use does not preclude this. Although even our observations are always described in the tentative terminology dictated by our currently accepted theory, we can still definitely discover that reality is different from the way our current assumptions represent it, by means of our observations failing to turn out in the way our current assumptions lead us to anticipate. And then of course we try to remedy this deficiency by constructing a new set of assumptions to which reality will not similarly object.

So there is a perfectly good sense in which our theoretical frameworks should be taken as answerable to an independent reality. We cannot happily think of each bit of our theory as making claims about separate and determinate objects in reality. But in a sense we can take our whole theory to be doing this. Take the picture analogy seriously for a moment. Suppose a theory is a blurred, or somewhat distorted, painting of reality as it really is. Because of this, it is indeterminate who in the painting is exactly who in reality, which objects in our picture are supposed to correspond to which objects in reality. But in spite of this indeterminacy, it is a picture *of* reality all right, which can be discovered not to fit reality in various respects and then adjusted so as to improve the fit. So such difficulties as we do have with 'realism' should not make us think our theories are not responsible to reality at all, that they are not to be taken as assessable attempts to grip onto an independent and articulated existence.[35]

8. SOCIAL FACTS AGAIN

Let us now finally return to the question of social facts. At the end of the last chapter we left the individualist arguing that since social facts cannot be observed they cannot exist, and the Durkheimian responding that, as with unobservables in physics, the explanatory usefulness of social facts was in itself sufficient justification for allowing them to be real.

At first sight, the Durkheimian might now seem to be on strong ground. The last section's niceties about how far anything we talk about is really 'out there' are not to the point here. Any general doubts raised in the last section do nothing to show that social facts in particular are less real than anything else, for those doubts apply as much to relatively observable phenomena as to entities that we standardly detect only indirectly. So provided the Durkheimian has definite hypotheses about the relationship of his social facts to their more accessible individual manifestations, by means of which he can test claims about those social facts, then he would seem perfectly entitled to suppose they exist over and above those individual manifestations.

But things are not that simple for the Durkheimian. It is important to remember that what is at issue is not just whether social facts exist, but whether they exist *in addition to* facts about collections of individuals. The individualist does not want to deny that there are norms, institutions, economic structures, etc. All he wants to insist is that they do not exist external to individual reality, but only as complex (and perhaps therefore not that easily detectable) aspects of it.

The Durkheimian argument under consideration is that supposing supra-individual social facts to exist will allow us to *explain* regularities on the more manifest individual level. Just as we ascribe an independent reality to light waves because they account for rainbows and similar phenomena, so, the Durkheimian can argue, we should allow a reality to external social facts because they enable us to explain why the members of given societies display common attitudes, behaviour and interactions.

But are external social facts actually required for this explanatory job? It is when we ask this question that the Durkheimian argument finally breaks down. For the burden of much of Chapter 1, and in particular of Section 4 thereof, was that regularities in social behaviour and attitudes can be explained perfectly well without bringing in any supra-individual social facts. As we saw, we can quite satisfactorily understand how certain attitudes and activities are perpetuated within societies by considering the processes of socialisation by which one set of individuals passes them on to another. And similarly we should be able to explain why such patterns change in certain circumstances by examining how normal socialisation processes are disrupted or over-ridden by other influences on individuals. There is no need to invent

Durkheimian social facts to account for social patterns and changes in them.

There is nothing wrong in general with the idea that a reality should be attributed to certain entities because of their explanatory power. We take light waves to exist because otherwise we could not explain why rainbows appear, why sticks bend in water, etc. We take there to be gravitational forces because otherwise we could not account uniformly for the falling of apples, the orbiting of moons, and other kindred regularities. But this is no argument for Durkheimian social facts, precisely because we *can* explain social regularities about human individuals otherwise than by invoking such social facts. There is nothing wrong with multiplying entities when necessary. But here it is quite unnecessary.

It might be objected that I am presupposing a detailed and general social psychological understanding of social developments which far exceed the rudimentary and local accounts which are all that current theory in the subject can provide. I do not want to deny the substance of this objection. Present social psychology is indeed nowhere near yielding a complete explanation of large-scale social patterns. But the present inadequacies of social psychology are not the crucial issue. The important question is where we should look for explanations of social patterns. Even the defenders of Durkheimian social facts are inclined to suppose, like everybody else, that it should always in the end be possible to explain the characteristic attitudes and behaviour of given individuals by reference to such things as their past training by parents and teachers, their interactions with their peers, their experiences in the workplace, etc. My argument is that our accepting this as an admissible programme should remove any remaining motivation for postulating social facts over and above complexes of facts about individuals. For when we *do* have a detailed understanding of how the components of such complexes influence each other we will need nothing further to account for any patterns we find amongst those complexes.

I am not saying that sociology collapses into social psychology. There is no reason why we should not be able to chart patterns amongst features of society in the large, independently of worrying about how to explain those patterns on an individual level. And there are perfectly good reasons for remaining on the macro-level even when we *are* in a position to offer socio-psychological accounts of what underlies those large-scale patterns. These and related matters will be discussed in Chapter 5.

What is more, as long as we remain short of a detailed social psychological underpinning for our macro-theories, it will be perfectly admissible to use a terminology for social facts which is not fully definable in individual terms. As with any theory, our central concepts will be constituted by the structure of our system of postulates as much as by any links with relatively observable phenomena. So there is no reason why a theorist primarily concerned, say, with the links between administrative requirements and forms of administrative organisation as such should need to tie his theoretical terminology definitively to fixed phenomena on the individual level. But this will not make social facts refer to some distinctive non-individual level of reality. That terms for theoretical entities like light waves cannot be defined explicitly in terms of their observable manifestations is indeed a corollary of our construing them realistically as seperate existents which *produce* those manifestations. Any difficulties about defining social facts in individual terms are of less ontological significance. It is not so much a matter of their existing on a separate level from individual reality as of our not yet having decided, so to speak, exactly which bits of individual reality they are to be reduced to. As long as our firmest hold on 'bureaucracy' is that it is that form of administrative organisation which arises when there is a general demand for administrative decisions to be predictable and uniform, then we can perfectly properly rest with a partial and open-ended specification of what 'bureaucracy' consists of for the individuals involved.[36] But if we ever come to develop our understanding to the point of being able to explain fully *why* such demands go together with such organisations (in addition to knowing *that* somehow they do) then, by the nature of the case, we would have been led to adopt some definite notion of the individual substance of bureaucratic organisations.

3 Causes and Statistics

1. SCIENCE AND CAUSES

In the last chapter scientific theories were portrayed as consisting of structures of interrelated generalisations. Can we seriously aspire to such theories in the social realm? An obvious initial objection is that social reality is simply much too complicated to succumb to such analysis. Surely the complex processes of social development will not lend themselves easily to exceptionless generalisations of the form, 'Whenever A, then always B'.

A section of Chapter 5 will be devoted to the question of whether all social developments are at some level determined by prior factors. It would be inappropriate to pre-empt that discussion at this point. But even if there are exceptionless general laws governing social processes, there remains the problem of whether we can ever hope to *know* them. Perhaps there are some plausible formulations of exceptionless generalisations in the social sciences ('all unstratified societies lack division of labour'; 'dominant values always favour ruling class interests'). But anybody who has tried will realise how difficult it is to find many serious examples of such generalisations. It would be foolish not to admit that in most cases any connections we might uncover amongst social phenomena are not going to be invariable. At a methodological level, social reality is just too complicated. However we try to relate any manageable number of different factors, there will always remain yet further influences that might intrude on specific occasions and produce exceptions to any general patterns we uncover. So it would scarcely be realistic to recommend that the social sciences should be restricted to the discovery of exceptionless generalisations about social phenomena. If anything, it would seem more appropriate for the social scientist to aim at such statistical assertions as, 'In most cases A is followed by B', or, 'B happens more often when A occurs than when it does not'.

Still, need this entirely discredit the social sciences' claims to be scientific? Why should social scientific theories not be comprised mainly of statistical generalisations rather than strictly universal ones? Such

50

theories would still be testable against the empirical evidence, even if not in quite the same way as theories comprised entirely of non-statistical claims. Single counter-examples do not disprove statistical hypotheses. But such hypotheses can still be discredited by the results of repeated observations. One example of a Protestant society where capitalism did not develop does not disprove the statistical hypothesis that capitalism is more likely to develop in Protestant societies than in others. But if in the comparative investigation of a number of societies, we find that there has been as proportionately as many capitalist developments in non-Protestant societies as in Protestant ones, then we would have a definite indication that there was something wrong with the hypothesis. There is, admittedly, an indeterminacy about how unlikely (or 'significant') our observations should seem before we should decide to reject a statistical hypothesis. And the underlying logic of such 'significance test' is not at all well understood.[1] But for all that, few would question that the empirical data can, on occasion, require the revision of statistical hypotheses.

Still, is it enough that our theories be testable? There remains a problem with another important feature of science. This is science's ability to identify the *causes* of what happens, something to which we have paid little explicit attention to so far. Science does not just chart testable connections or associations between different kinds of phenomena. It also somehow shows how the presence of one thing can *make* another happen, how it can *bring it about* or *produce* it. When your water pipes burst, you are told it is *because* of the temperatures dropping below freezing. When an eclipse of the moon occurs, it is explained as *due* to the relative positions of sun, moon and earth.

How exactly does science show us what causes what? When your water pipes burst it might not only have been cold, but also raining, and your spouse may just have left you. What entitles us to pick out the cold, rather than some other proximate change like the rain or the desertion, as the cause of the bursting? As we shall see shortly, it is by no means easy to get an exact answer to this question. But on one thing there has been wide agreement since at least the time of David Hume: namely, that one event's being the cause of another is somehow to do with the first's invariably occurring with the second. For instance, we pick out the freezing as the cause of the bursting because we know that it, unlike rain or desertion, is 'constantly conjoined' with full water pipes of certain constructions bursting.[2]

Here we seem to have a serious obstacle to the social sciences counting themselves as 'scientific'. If the attribution of causes is an essential part of science, and if this requires knowledge of exceptionless general-isations, then it seems that any proper science of society is out of the question. It might occur to some to plead that, for the reasons rehearsed in the last chapter, even the natural scientist's knowledge of general-isations is always tentative. But this is no real defence. However tentative, the hypothesising of deterministic connections is not the same thing as hypothesising statistical ones. If the social sciences cannot even *pretend* to deterministic knowledge, then they seem to be disqualified right from the start as a means to the discovery of causes.

Nevertheless I want to argue in this chapter that social scientific theories can tell us about causes. I shall not deny that it is inevitable that such theories will be composed almost entirely of statistical gen-eralisations. Instead I shall try to show that there are perfectly sound procedures for inferring conclusions about causes from statistical data.

It is a common dictum amongst social scientists that 'correlation does not prove causation'. In spite of this, statistically minded social scientists have in recent years developed a number of techniques designed to do just that—to infer causes from statistical correlations between various social phenomena.[3] These techniques, which involve the simultaneous analysis of the statistical relationships amongst a number of different factors, do have an intuitive plausibility—they do seem able to give us some grip on the causal connections amongst the factors involved. What is less clear is the fundamental logic of the processes involved. In particular, there is no good account, so far as I know, of how the leap is made from what remain essentially statistical premises to conclusions about deterministic causal relationships. My aim in this chapter will be to show exactly how, and in what circumstances, this leap can be justified.

2. CAUSES AS SUFFICIENT CONDITIONS

We first need to examine in some detail the way in which full knowledge of exceptionless generalisations is supposed to show what causes what. Even in this apparently more favourable case it is by no means clear what shows one event to be the cause of another.

Suppose we say that one event is *sufficient* for another if *whenever* the former occurs the latter occurs too. (One event will be *necessary* for another if it is *only* when the former occurs that the latter does.) Then we could try, as a first approximation, the principle that one event is a cause of another if it is a sufficient condition of it. For example, sub-zero temperatures are sufficient for full water pipes of certain constructions to burst.

On this principle, then, the relation between a cause and its effect consists solely in the existence of a generalisation saying the effect always follows the cause. This is in accord with Hume's analysis of causation. Hume's main concern was to make it clear that the sense in which an effect *must* follow its cause is simply that there is a generalisation which says it always does. There is no further necessity behind such a regularity, no intrinsic connection between the cause and the effect. The regularity simply obtains, and prior to any evidence it would have been equally conceivable that it should not.

The suggested principle can equally well be put in the form of an analysis of what it is for one event to *explain* another. Suppose we wish to explain some event (the 'explanandum'). We can specify that what this requires is the production of an 'explanans' from which the explanandum can be logically deduced. Given our suggested analysis of causation, this is effectively to say that events are explained by their causes. For it is precisely knowledge of a sufficient condition for some event, together with the generalisation stating that it is so sufficient, that enables us to deduce that that event had to occur.[4]

To digress briefly, it is worth comparing this kind of explanation, the causal explanation of a particular event by reference to another particular event which is sufficient for it, with the explanation of a generalisation itself, such as was at issue in the last chapter when we wondered why it is that rainbows always form in certain conditions, and when we considered the possibility of explaining general patterns in social attitudes and activities. The contrast is between asking why your downstairs water pipes burst yesterday, and asking why it is that water pipes in general burst at sub-zero temperatures. Just as with causal explanations of particular events, explanations of generalisations can also be considered to require the production of premises from which they can be logically deduced. But in this latter case those premises will not contain descriptions of any particular events or circumstances, such as that the temperature dropped below zero in your downstairs on some particular date, but only other universal generalisations of a wider scope than the one to be explained. Thus we explain why water pipes always burst when the temperature drops below 0°C by showing that this regularity is logically implied by generalisations about the expansion of ice between 0°C and −4°C, about the pressures such expansions produce, and about the behaviour of such pipes under such pressures.

If we explain a generalisation in this way, there is a sense in which we get a deeper understanding of its truth—we see how it is a logical consequence of other more fundamental laws. However, it would be a mistake to insist, as some are inclined to do, that we cannot use a generalisation in an explanation unless we have an explanation of it in turn. For, if we stuck to this dictum seriously, we would then need an explanation of the generalisation which explains the generalisation which explains . . ., and so on, *ad infinitum*, whenever we wanted to explain anything.

Let us now return to the idea that for one event to cause another is for it to be a sufficient condition of it. An immediate difficulty to be faced is that we often quite happily take occurrences to be caused by earlier events which manifestly are not sufficient conditions for them at all. For instance, we might quite correctly explain a house's burning down by the occurrence of a short-circuit in it, even though it is clearly not true that houses burn down whenever short-circuits occur in them. Indeed, on reflection, it seems that in nearly all the actual causal explanations we give the cause is simply not a strictly sufficient condition of the effect.

Perhaps we should require that causes are necessary for their effects. Consider the example again. We would not have had a fire had the short-circuit not occurred. This suggests that it is not ensuring the effect, but being required for it, that makes something a cause; that is, that the effect occurs *only* when the cause is present.

But this cannot be right either. Short-circuits are not, in our sense, necessary conditions of houses burning down. Lots of other things, like dousing it in petrol and setting a match to it, will do the trick equally well without any short-circuit being present.

To get out of this tangle we need to return to the initial idea that causes are sufficient for their effects. But we need to realise in addition that such causes will generally consist of the joint presence of a number of factors, which together are sufficient for the effect. Our problem arises because in normal discourse we do not usually bother to mention all the relevant factors. So the ones we do draw attention to will as a rule not by themselves be sufficient conditions for the effect.

A short-circuit by itself does not suffice for a fire. But a short-circuit, plus the absence of fuses plus faulty insulation plus, say, the proximity of polyester curtains do together constitute a sufficient condition. To attribute the fire to the short-circuit is implicitly to claim that it was one of a set of factors which together were sufficient for the fire. If we discovered there were adequate fuses, or adequate insulation, or no inflammable materials near the wiring system, we would know that it was not the short-circuit that started the fire.

Which, amongst a set of factors which are jointly sufficient, we pick out as 'the' cause in normal discourse will depend on particular features of the conversational situation, such as what is mutual knowledge amongst the conversers, what they find most interesting, what they think could (ought to) have been avoided. For present purposes the details of these conversational conventions are irrelevant. Henceforth I shall simply use 'cause' to refer to *any one* amongst a set of conditions which are jointly sufficient for some event; when it is necessary to refer to the total set of conditions I shall speak of the 'full cause'.

We are now in a position to see in exactly what sense a cause can be said to be 'necessary' for its effect. It is not that the cause has to be there in general whenever the effect occurs. Fires happen without short-circuits. Rather it is that without the cause in question the circumstances present on the particular occasion under examination would not have added up to a sufficient condition for the effect. If the short-circuit had not been there, the absence of fuses, insulation, etc. would not have added up to a sufficient condition for a fire. What we require of a cause is that it be *necessary-for-the-factors-present-to-be-sufficient*.

We can put the point like this. We do not allow as a full cause just any set of conditions which are jointly sufficient for the effect. In addition, it needs to be a *minimally* sufficient set; that is, a set which would cease to be sufficient if any of its members were removed. From this it follows that if any part of a full cause had been missing on some actual occasion, what remained would not have sufficed for the effect. If the short-circuit had not occurred, the other factors would not have been enough to bring about the fire.[5]

The requirement of minimal sufficiency also means that we will be prevented from including as causes irrelevant factors, such as, say, there being a change of Pope when the house burnt down. While this factor is one of a set which is jointly sufficient (the set which also includes the short-circuit, no adequate fuses, no insulation, and polyester curtains) this set is not minimally sufficient, for it would remain sufficient even if the condition about the change of Pope were dropped.[6]

3. SIDE-EFFECTS AND ECLIPSING

We have now arrived at the view that a cause is one amongst a set of factors which are jointly and minimally sufficient for the effect. But even this will not quite do. Whenever the barometer falls, and there is a certain amount of water vapour in the atmosphere, and the barometer has not been fiddled with, and various conditions for the formation of water droplets are satisfied, it rains shortly afterwards. We have here a perfectly good sufficient condition for rain, which would not remain sufficient if the barometer's fall were subtracted. But we would not want to say that the barometer's fall was a *cause* of the rain. On the contrary, our intuitions are that this and the rain are both independent effects of an earlier factor, namely, a fall in the atmospheric pressure.

This difficulty is quite general. Given our analysis of 'cause' so far, if one event A, has two successive effects B and C, then it will as a rule follow that B is a 'cause' of C.[7] But we do *not* always want to say, whenever something has two successive effects, that the first is a cause of the second.

To be sure, it *can* well be the case that the successive effects of something are related as cause and effect, that the original event causes the second effect *by* causing the first. Apart from affecting the barometer, a fall in atmospheric pressure also causes a condensation of water vapour before the rainfall. In this case, the first effect, the condensation, *is* a cause of the second, the rain. But the point is that not all cases are like this. What we lack is some way of distinguishing these latter cases, where an initial cause produces some later effect *by* causing some intermediate effect (graphically A→B→C), from those cases where an initial cause produces the two effects independently $(A \lessgtr^B_C)$. For in both cases B will as a rule be part of a minimal sufficient condition for C.

Recall the earlier mentioned dictum that 'correlation does not prove causation'. This is normally intended as a warning that a statistical association between two factors might not reflect a 'genuine' causal relationship but merely a 'spurious' connection due to their both being independent effects of some unknown prior cause. But we now see that even when we have full knowledge of invariant relationships amongst the factors involved it is by no means clear how we are supposed to distinguish cases where one event causes another from those where the former is merely a 'side-effect' of the real cause of the latter. In fact there is an intimate connection between the problem of distinguishing side-effects from causes given deterministic knowledge and the difficulty of deciding whether or not statistical associations are causally spurious. The solution to the former problem will prove a crucial preliminary to an understanding of how causal conclusions can be derived from statistical data.

Our natural intuitions are that a side-effect like the barometer's drop is in itself *irrelevant* to the effect, the subsequent rain. In the circumstances, rain would have followed the drop in atmospheric pressure even if the barometer had not fallen. With an intermediate cause like the condensation of water vapour we feel on the contrary that the effect's following the initial cause depends precisely on the presence of the intermediate cause—the rain would not have followed the drop in pressure if condensation had not occured.

Can we make this intuitive distinction more precise? I think we can. Note that whenever a barometer fall occurs together with the other factors (the barometer's not being manipulated, high humidity, etc.) which add up to a guarantee for rain, it will also be true that a drop in atmospheric pressure and some of the same factors (high humidity, etc.) are also present, and also constituting a sufficient condition for the rain. And this latter set will also occur, and suffice for rain, on occasions when no barometer fall occurs—such as, for instance, when there are no barometers around. This seems to be characteristic of examples where B is a side-effect of A's causing C. That is, such a B manages to be part of a minimally sufficient set for C only by virtue of standing proxy for A, which would be able to manage perfectly well by itself. Or, to be more precise, whenever such a B occurs as part of a minimally sufficient set for C, there will also be present another minimally sufficent set for C, which contains A but not B; and this latter set will sometimes be present even when the set containing B is not.

This seems to be the basis for our intuition that whenever a side-effect B 'guarantees' C something else is also present which would have sufficed for C anyway even if B had been absent. In a sense A *eclipses* B as a cause of C. The fact that in certain circumstances a fall in the barometer gives us a guarantee of rain is shown to be of no real significance, insofar as on all such occasions a drop in pressure is there to ensure the rain anyway. So I would suggest that for B to be a real cause of C, and not just an irrelevant side-effect, not only does B need to be part of a minimally sufficient set for C, but in addition, there should be no other factors which 'eclipse' B as a cause of C; that is, there should be no other set not containing B which:

(i) is present whenever the set containing B is, and

(ii) is sometimes present even when the set containing B is not.

This definition can be illustrated by means of a Venn diagram. Suppose we depict the fact that B (together with other factors) is sufficient for C by this diagram:

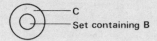

To require that nothing eclipses B as a cause of C, is then, to require that there is no A satisfying the diagram:

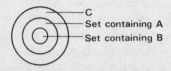

The kind of case where B is indeed causally intermediate between A and C contrasts sharply with the cases where it is only a side-effect. When it is really an intermediate cause, B does seem to be crucially relevant to C's occurrence. A fall in pressure (A) suffices for rain (C) only insofar as it is accompanied by condensation (B); while condensation can suffice for rain even in the absence of a preceding drop in pressure, as when potential nuclei for droplets are introduced either artificially or naturally into a supersaturated atmosphere. Indeed in this case, it is B that 'eclipses' A as a cause of C. Diagrammatically:

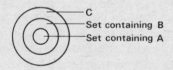

But does this mean that in such cases A is not a cause of C at all? Even if A suffices for C only when B is present, while B can do the trick without A around, our intuitive understanding of the situation is that A *does* cause C, through causing B. The pressure change causes the rain all right, albeit via causing water condensation. Yet our definition would now seem to mean that condensation 'eclipses' the pressure as a cause of the rain.

We can sort this out with the following definitions. B, say, is a *direct cause* of C if, as above, it is part of a minimally sufficient condition for it, and there are no other factors eclipsing it as a cause of C. One event is a *causal ancestor* of another if it is a direct cause, or a direct cause of a direct cause, or . . ., etc. Then we can allow that causal ancestors other than direct causes are also causes, albeit *indirect* ones. So, when A causes C through B, B will eclipse A as a direct cause of C—but nevertheless A will be a causal ancestor of C, through causing B which in turn causes C. On the other hand, when A causes C and has B as an independent side-effect, B will not be a causal ancestor of C—for A, which eclipses it as a direct cause of C, will not be an effect of B.

There is one further awkward case for the 'no-eclipsing' requirement as a way of distinguishing genuine causes from spurious ones. Consider again the case where A and B are both parts of minimally sufficient sets for C. If A eclipses B then it is a direct cause of C and B is not. If B eclipses A the converse holds. If the sets containing A and B can each occur in the absence of the other, then of course *both* A and B are direct causes of C. But what if the two sets always occur together, if their Venn diagrams actually coincide? Suppose there is a certain virus which is standardly followed by a certain kind of skin infection and then by a certain kind of fever. And suppose that the virus is never found without the skin infection, nor the skin infection without the virus. Then we will apparently have no way of telling whether the virus causes the fever directly with the skin infection as a side-effect, or whether on the other hand it is precisely by producing the skin infection that it manages to produce the fever. For, by hypothesis, there are no cases to show whether the virus will suffice for the fever in the absence of the infection, nor whether the infection can do it in the absence of the virus.

Still, we do feel there is a real difference between the two possibilities, even in this difficult case where the virus and the skin infection always occur together. If pressed I think most of us would want to account for the difference by reference to the possible *explanation* of the co-occurrence of the virus, infection and fever. If, for instance, the skin infection erupted because the virus lodged in the skin, and this then produced some chemical which, when it entered the bloodstream and was carried to the brain, precipitated the fever, we would say the virus caused the fever *by* causing the infection. If on the other hand, there was no chain of events leading from the infection to the fever, but it was when the virus itself got to the brain that the fever started, then we would see the infection as merely as a side-effect of the virus's presence.

What is the logic behind this? I think it is best seen as an elaboration of the idea behind the 'no-eclipsing' requirement. When we have an explanation of a generalisation we see how it is a consequence of other more fundamental generalisations of wider scope. When we explain the observed conjunctions of virus, skin infection and fever, we see how they result from principles governing such things as the formation of chemicals, the behaviour of brain cells, etc. And what this enables us to do is to see whether the (theoretically impossible) breakdown of underlying generalisations which would be required for the virus and the skin infection to occur separately would in themselves disrupt the processes in virtue of which each is followed by the fever. Thus, for instance, if we do know that it is a chemical produced by the skin infection that triggers the fever, then we are in a position to judge that if *per impossibile* we did get the skin infection other than from the virus this would still be followed by the fever, while if we got the virus without the skin infection following we would not get the fever. This is an elaboration of the 'no-eclipsing' idea in that what it amounts to is effectively a new way of judging what eclipses what when direct evidence is not available. For what we are doing is imagining theoretically deviant contexts in which the virus occurs without the infection and vice versa, and using them to show whether the one would still suffice for the fever anyway even with the other absent. [8]

4. CAUSES FROM STATISTICS—THEORY

I now want to examine the possibility of extracting conclusions about causes from statistical data. At first sight this might seem a quite misguided project. If two events are only statistically related, then it is perfectly possible that the first might occur without the second following. Even if on a particular occasion they occur together, the presence of the first in itself leaves it open that the second might be absent. So how can we claim to have shown *why* the second did in fact occur? For all we have said, it might not have occurred. Surely we need knowledge of a *determining* condition before we can speak of one event causing another.

But consider an everyday and therefore fairly uncontentious example. Little Johnny comes down with measles. We judge this to have been caused by his having been in contact with another child with measles. However, we cannot, even when pressed, identify a set of factors present which, together with the contact, *ensured* that Johnny was going to come down with the disease. It is not like the short-circuit case, where we merely do not bother to mention all the factors which together with the short-circuit inevitably guaranteed that the fire would take place. We do not know of any such set of factors. Our grounds for the causal explanation seems rather to be that there is a statistical relationship between being in contact with someone with measles and getting it yourself—being in contact with measles makes it more *likely* that you will get it, even if it does not make it certain.

In the face of such examples as this a number of philosophers have decided that causes are not determining conditions after all. On their view, all a causal explanation has to do is show how the probability of the explanation depends on earlier factors. A determining cause is then simply the limiting case, in which the effect is made certain by earlier factors. This is not the line I shall take, though I shall have a bit more to say about it later. It still seems to me that if an event was caused then it *had* to happen. So I am going to stick with the idea that if one event causes another then there are exceptionless laws in virtue of which the first is part of a minimal and uneclipsed sufficient condition for the second. What I want to show is how statistical associations can give us *indirect grounds* for concluding that one event is part of a sufficient condition for another even when we do not know in full detail the laws which make it so. Roughly the idea will be that it can only be because being in contact with measles is part of a full sufficient condition for getting it that we find the disease more often amongst those who have had a contact than amongst those who have not. Then, even if we do not know the other factors making up the full sufficient condition in question, we can at least infer from the statistical association that contact with the infection must be part of that full condition. On this view, for one event to cause another is indeed for it (together with unknown other conditions present) to determine the latter's occurrence. The role of their statistical association is then merely that it gives us indirect evidence for the existence of the deterministic connection in which the causal relationship really consists.

Let us consider in more detail the kind of inference involved here. Suppose we want to explain a certain kind of event, Z. For example, we might want to explain why certain individuals enter manual occupations. Suppose further we discover a statistical association between Z and some other event Y; that is, that Z is more likely where Y is present $(\text{Prob}\,(Z/Y) > \text{Prob}\,(Z))$. Thus, for instance, we might discover that the chance of a manual occupation is higher amongst people from non-academic schools than amongst those who attended academic schools. Can we then conclude that Y is a cause of Z, that some people enter manual occupations *because* of their type of schooling?

The obvious difficulty is that there might be hidden factors confounding the true relationship between Y and Z. That is, Y might be statistically associated with Z purely through being a side-effect of some real cause of Z. It might be, for instance, that the occupation of one's parents is a real influence on one's own occupational category, and that given parental occupation, the type of school attended has no real influence at all. But, nevertheless, if type of school attended is another effect of parental occuation, if more children of parents with manual jobs attend non-academic than academic schools, then we will still find a higher proportion of manual jobs amongst those from non-academic schools.

It is just this danger that most people have in mind when they warn that 'correlation does not prove causation'. But let us suppose for a moment that Y is *not* itself associated with any other causes Z might have. Given this supposition, and supposing also that Z is caused somehow whenever it occurs, then it is possible to prove rigorously that Prob (Z/Y) >Prob (Z) if and only if Y is a direct cause of Z. A detailed demonstration is best left to the Appendix to this chapter. But the idea is simple enough. If Y is a direct cause, then when Y occurs we will get Z if *either* one of Z's other causes is present *or* if the factors which in conjunction with Y suffice for Z are present; while in the absence of Y we will get Z only when one of Z's other causes is present. So if Y is a direct cause of Z then Prob (Z/Y) > Prob (Z). Conversely, if Y is not a direct cause of Z, then its occurrence will not increase Z's likelihood. But we need to be assured, in drawing these conclusions, that Y does not occur more often in the presence of any other direct causes Z may have, for this would produce a statistical association between Y and Z even though the former was not a cause of the latter. Nor do we want Y to occur less often in the presence of Z's other direct causes, for this might just lead to an absence of any statistical association between Y and Z, even though the former *was* a direct cause of the latter.

Can we now say anything about the case where Y *is* associated with other causes of Z? In our example these other causes would be sets of factors which would ensure a manual job whatever the schooling. These might include combinations of such things as parental occupation, geographical location, inherent abilities, etc. We are concerned about the possibility that these things also affect type of schooling, thus producing a 'spurious' association between school and occupation. To deal with this possibility what we need to do is look separately, as it were, at classes of individuals which are all similar in respect of any other causes of Z that Y is associated with. Then if Y still makes Z more likely *within* such classes we can conclude that it *is* a real cause of Z; if it does not, then we can conclude that the original association was only a 'supurious' one, produced by Y's independent association with Z's real causes. If we 'hold constant' or 'control' parental occupation, geographical location, inherent abilities, and so on (which in this context simply means looking separately at classes of existing individuals similar in these respects, and does not in any way imply active manipulation of anything), then we can be sure that any remaining association between school and occupation indicates a genuine causal connection. If type of school still affects the chance of a manual occupation, even amongst individuals equal in all associated respects which have any influence on type of job, then it must be that schooling has some real effect on occupation. The detailed substantiation of this principle is once more best left to the Appendix. But again the idea is simple enough. We can go through just the same reasoning as before, only now within those categories where we 'hold constant' all those influences that might be confounding the association between Y and Z. By restricting ourselves in this way we so to speak ensure that Y is not associated with any other 'remaining' causes of Z. So we can now be sure that any remaining association between Y and Z does show Y to be a direct cause of Z.

It is worth noting that the analysis of causation in terms of 'eclipsing' is crucial to our substantiating the principles of inference involved here. Unless we had added the eclipsing requirement to the standard idea of causes as sufficient conditions, we could not show why the disappearance of an association when we control for confounding influences should rule something out as a real cause. The point can be illustrated by considering the barometer case once more. There is a statistical association between barometers falling and subsequent rain. This association disappears when we control for prior drops in atmospheric pressure—given a change in atmospheric pressure, a falling barometer does not make rain any more likely. But recall that a falling barometer can be part of a perfectly good minimally sufficient condition for rain. What it fails to be is part of an uneclipsed such set. This shows that it is only because causes are specifically *uneclipsed* sufficient conditions that we can take absence of statistical association to show an absence of causation. The point is that a sufficient condition that is eclipsed ceases to be associated with the result in question when we control for those factors which eclipse it. It is precisely those sufficient conditions that are not eclipsed by anything else that remain associated with the effect even after we have controlled for all other prior factors. (This principle, that it is precisely uneclipsed sufficiency that entails statistical association, is given a more detailed substantiation in the Appendix.)

5. CAUSES FROM STATISTICS—PRACTICE

Are the results of the last section of any interest to the practising social scientist? We have seen that statistical associations imply causal connections when there are no confounding influences, or if such as there are have been taken into account by 'controlling'. But do these abstract principles have any practical use?

It is quite out of the question here to deal with all the difficulties that arise in connection with statistical research in the social sciences. But we can make some comments on those problems that are most directly relevant to the possibility of inferring causes from statistics. In particular we can consider whether the necessary provisos about the absence of residual confounding influences are ever met. Consider the position of a social scientist who has carried out a typical sample survey. He will have, for some set of factors, evidence supporting certain conclusions about their statistical associations. Thus, to persist with our earlier example, he could have looked at individuals in western industrial societies with respect to their type of occupation, schooling, parental occupation, geographical location, etc., and derived a table of pairwise associations between these factors, showing how likely each of these will be for an individual given how he comes out on the others. Or he could have surveyed 'primitive' societies, and similarly found statistical relationships between kinship terminology, type of economy, form of religion, etc.

Now if we could be sure that for any pair of features in such a study (F_1 and F_2, say) we had also included any further causes of F_2 that F_1 might be associated with, then we could certainly tell whether F_1 was actually a direct cause of F_2. All we would have to do would be 'control' for all the causes of F_2 that F_1 might be associated with, and see whether F_1 and F_2 were still associated.

But without further qualifications this is far too much to ask for. If any of our factors do cause any of the others, then for at least some pairs F_1 will actually be an *effect* of F_2. If economic system is a cause of religion, then religion is an effect of economic system. And if F_1 is actually an effect of F_2 then it will as a rule be associated with all of F_2's causes—for in general, the presence of any of these will make F_2 more likely, and F_2 in turn will increase F_1's chance of occurrence. So we would have to include all F_2's causes in our analysis before we could show that F_1 did not have an influence on F_2. This would defeat our purpose, for what we are trying to do is show that certain phenomena are causes of others *without* having to identify the full complements of factors which make up strictly sufficient conditions.

What we need to cope with this is a kind of initial ordering of the variables in our study. We need to know, for any F_1 and F_2 which might be causally connected, which would be the cause and which the effect, if they actually were.[9] If we knew beforehand that any causal influence would be from F_1 to F_2, rather than vice versa, then we would be in a much more satisfactory position. For, if F_1 is agreed not to be an effect of F_2 to start with, we can reasonably dismiss the possibility that it is associated with *all* of F_2's other causes. For it will then only be associated with those of F_2's other causes with which it happens to have some common causal ancestor, and there is no *a priori* reason why these at least should not be included in our analysis.[10]

It is important to be clear about what we are asking for here. We are not asking for prior knowledge of *which* factors are causing which. That is supposed to be the outcome of the procedures under discussion. But without prejudging that outcome we can well ask which would be the cause and which the effect, *if* one of F_1 and F_2 turned out to cause the other. Perhaps the best way to explain the point is to illustrate how we might initially derive such a potential causal ordering of our factors. The simplest way would be to let time tell us. For example, if there is a causal connection between school and innate ability at all it must be the latter that is the cause and the former that is the effect, for an individual has his innate abilities before he goes to school. A similar judgement can be made about any pair of factors where one occurs before the other—it must be the earlier that causes the later, if anything, not vice versa. Unfortunately the temporal ordering of our factors will not always be decidable. Do people get geographical locations before or after their parents get occupational categories? Does a society have its religion before or after it has its economic system? These questions scarcely make much sense. When the time sequence is unclear in this way we can sometimes use semi-intuitive considerations to give the required initial ordering. We can easily enough imagine how parental occupation *might* affect school attended (not of course yet knowing if it *does*), but is far less obvious how school could affect parental occupation. But even this kind of reasoning does not always help. *A priori* it seems quite as likely for economic system to affect religion as for religion to affect economic system. Even worse, why should there not be a two-way influence, with certain religions fostering certain economic systems, which economic systems in turn support those religions? The possibility of such reciprocal causation undermines the whole idea of ordering our factors in terms of unidirectional influences from one to another.

When we fear the possibility of reciprocal causation amongst our factors or are otherwise unable to give them an initial ordering, we will for the reasons outlined above simply not be in a position to decide what, if anything, is causing what. But nevertheless we can deal with this problem easily enough if we are in a position to *extend* our analysis, by 'time-lagging' the awkward factors involved. What we need in the above-mentioned case, for example, is information about religion and economic system at successive points of time in the development of our societies. In effect, we need to break down religion and economy each into a number of different factors—religion at stage 1, religion at stage 2, and so on; and similarly for economy. Once we have done this, then of course we can be assured that the state of religion or economy at any stage will, if anything, be a cause of later states and an effect of earlier ones.

Let us now turn to a further problem. Even if we can establish a potential causal ordering amongst those pairs of factors in our analysis that might be causally related, we are scarcely out of the woods. Suppose we know that, if anything, it is F_1 that causes F_2 rather than vice versa. In order to infer that F_1 *does* cause F_2 from a statistical association between them, we still need to consider all those other causes of F_2 that might be producing this association spuriously. Even if we do not have to consider *all* F_2's causes, we still need to consider any that happen to be statistically associated with F_1. How can we ever be sure that we have done this? How can we tell, when we still find an association between school and job after controlling for a number of factors, that there is not still some hidden influence (perhaps parental attitudes, or ethnic group, or . . .) still affecting both and producing a spurious association? We do not have to consider everything, but we do need to be sure we have not left out something that *is* relevant.

One way of circumventing this problem would be by the use of quasi-experimental techniques. By this I mean the kind of investigation where we *introduce* some factor to the kind of set-up we are studying, rather than wait for it to happen. Suppose for instance that the social researcher could actually *decide* which schools certain children went to. Then he could randomly select two groups of children, and send one group to academic schools and the other to non-academic ones. Unless he has especially unlucky samples, the random selection of the two groups means they will have approximately the same proportions of any occupation—relevant characteristics *other* than schooling. And so the researcher could conclude that any significant association between the experimental 'treatment' (that is, type of school attended) and category of subsequent occupation definitely indicates that the former exerts a real causal influence on the latter. [11]

The point here is that by 'randomising out' any confounding influences, by assigning children to type of school in some random way independently of any other characteristics those children may have, we can artificially ensure that the type of school attended is not statistically associated with any other influences on occupational category, *whatever* those other influences might be. This contrasts with the position in a purely survey-type piece of research, where we cannot assign the putative cause we are interested in to subjects at random, but just have to wait and see where it comes up. For then there always remains the possibility that the putative cause under examination comes up more often in the presence of the other causes of the effect in question than in their absence. And so, in analysing surveys we need to *know* what those other causes are, so that we can explicitly 'control' for them to see whether our putative cause has any independent influence on the effect.

It is commonly supposed that techniques of active experimentation are especially suited to the discovery of exact deterministic laws, where all factors relevant to the effects under study are explicitly incorporated in our conclusions. But this is something of a misconception. If we were in a position to identify all the factors that might be needed in the formulation of exceptionless laws, then we would have no essential need of active experimentation. In principle there is no reason why we should not be able to delineate all the operative causes by sitting back and waiting to see which factors turn up with which. We might of course be able to speed up the process by actively setting up certain combinations of circumstances and seeing what happens. But with patience we should be able to discover such combinations turning up by themselves. It is precisely when we do not know all the factors that might be of relevance to the result that experimental manipulations become most useful. For they are just what we need in order to arrange things so that we can stop worrying about the possibility of unknown confounding influences. [12]

But be this as it may, it does not really solve our problem. For in nearly all cases it will be both impracticable and morally indefensible for the social scientist to intervene in the processes he is studying. There are any number of reasons for not foisting schools on selected children, let alone religions on primitive societies. So we will still in general be left with the problem of telling whether our survey has taken explicit account of all possible confounding influences. And here I think we finally do have to admit that there can be no certainty. In the end there is no further court of appeal other than a tutored intuition that there are no further hidden factors which might be producing spurious associations between the factors we are studying.

6. THE WORTH OF STATISTICS

Does this admission discredit the possibility of inferring causes from statistical premises in the social sciences? Compare our situation with that of somebody trying to establish causal connections directly without bringing in statistical relationships. Mill's methods of eliminative induction, in particular his 'method of difference', show us what is involved in doing this. What we need to assume is that there is always some cause for the result in question, and also that we have a complete list of all the possible factors that might singly or jointly function as the cause of that result. Then a simple 'difference observation' will enable us to identify a given factor as actually being a cause: we need to find a pair of cases in the first of which the presence of that given factor is followed by the result and in the second of which the absence of that factor is followed by the result's absence, while all the other possible causes do not vary between the two cases. If we do find such a pair of cases then we can be certain that the factor in question is a cause, for otherwise the result would have had to be present or absent in both cases.[13]

But note that this procedure requires that what must remain constant between the two cases is *all* other possible causes whatsoever of the result in question. The inference involved is secure only as long as we are sure that there is no other difference between the two cases to account for the variation in the result. What this shows is that inferring conclusions about causes from statistical associations in fact requires us to assume *less* than if we are to do it by directly establishing deterministic connections between events. A Mill-type difference observation to show that schooling affects occupation, for instance, would require us to know that two people are exactly alike in *all* other respects which can affect occupation, even in respects such as, say, foot size, which are statistically quite independent of schooling. The statistical mode of reasoning only requires us to consider specifically such other possible causes as might for some reason be statistically associated with schooling.

Of course in either case our judgements about what might possibly function as a cause of a given result cannot but be tentative. Given the problem of induction it could not be otherwise. Even if we can take for granted that the result in question is always caused *somehow*, nothing can conclusively demonstrate that only a certain range of antecedents could possibly be responsible. Our current ideas about the possible causes of a given result will derive from what our general conceptual framework leads us to expect about the kinds of elements and relationships that make up the world. When such conceptual frameworks change, so will our ideas about what could possibly be causes. But this does not affect the point at issue. If we are ever to use our observations to move from ideas about what *might be* causes to ideas about what *are* causes, then we have to make an assumption about what influences might be affecting our results in such a way as to undermine our inference. And, however we look at it, this will be easier if we proceed statistically, when we only have to worry about those other possible causes that are somehow statistically associated with the one we are interested in, than if we are going straight for deterministic connections, when *any* causes unaccounted for can confound the reasoning.

There is a kind of cost to the advantage we get from the statistical mode of reasoning. Given the assumptions required by Mill's method of difference, we can move with certainty from the difference observation to the identification of our cause. But with the statistical procedure there is an intermediate step, which introduces a further possibility of error. That is, we first have to decide whether our observations really do indicate a serious statistical relationship between the factors we are interested in, that they are not just an artefact of an unusual or unlucky sample. And, as explained at the beginning of the chapter, such decisions involve the non-deductive logic of significance tests. These decisions arise specifically for the statistical method of deriving causes because even when, as we hope, all associated confounding influences have been taken into explicit account, there still always remains the possibility that the other statistically *un*associated causes might turn up in disproportionate numbers in our sample.

But we need not worry too much about the inconclusiveness of significance tests here. Their verdicts can certainly be taken seriously, even if there always remains an abstract possibility that those verdicts are mistaken. And, in any case, it is not as if the difficulty is especially one that arises when we try to derive *causes* from statistical associations. On the contrary, it is there whenever we want to know whether or not an observed association of two factors is just a matter of a lucky sample, whatever we might want to make of it if we conclude it is not. Suppose we have a randomly drawn sample of school leavers in industrial countries, in which we find proportionately more manual workers amongst those from non-academic schools than amongst those from academic ones. Quite independently of any worries about causes, we can ask whether this really reflects the fact that manual jobs are more common amongst alumni of non-academic schools, or whether, on the other hand, it is merely a chance feature of our sample. It is this question that significance tests try to answer. Once we have agreed there is a real association, *then* the different question we have been discussing all along arises—is this association due to a causal influence of school on job, or is it a matter of some further hidden factor influencing them both? An association can perfectly well be 'significant', in the sense of not being a sampling accident, and yet be causally 'spurious', in the sense of resulting from hidden confounding influences. [14]

So any problems involved with significance tests as such are irrelevant to worries about the possibility of confounding influences misleading us about causes. Insofar as we are concerned specifically with this latter worry the earlier point remains that it will be easier to work with statistical associations than to look directly for deterministic relationships. There does, it is true, remain some room for doubt about the social sciences' ability to get at causes. Even if it is easier to get at social causes by statistical than by deterministic methods, it might still not be easy enough. The natural realm seems simple enough even for Mill's direct deterministic techniques. The social world might be too complicated even for the less demanding statistical approach.

But this seems to me unduly pessimistic. It would be foolish not to allow that that society is too messy for explicit deterministic analysis. But we have now seen that allowing this by no means rules out the possibility of getting causal conclusions altogether. We can know of social causes without knowing in detail the laws by which they operate.

In the next chapter I shall start considering a quite different reason for thinking that social developments are not susceptible of causal analysis—namely, that there is something distinctive about human actions which prevents their being explained in causal terms. But first a couple of short sections will round off our discussion of statistics and causation.

7. REGRESSION ANALYSIS

So far, the examples and procedures discussed have involved only qualitative factors. Characteristics such as being rural, Protestant or patrilineal do not come in numerical degrees. They either apply to a given person or situation or they do not. However, readers are more likely to be familiar with techniques of controlling for confounding influences and so on from examples where the statistically related variables being analysed are quantitative rather than qualitative. What relevance does the preceding discussion have to the possibility of inferring causal conclusions from, say, a correlation between such numerical variables as *duration* of education and initial *salary* on entering an occupation?

In fact procedures for dealing with numerical variables can be seen as a kind of special case of the methods discussed so far. We cannot go into details here about the quantitative case and the extra assumptions it involves. But a few basic observations will give the idea.

The standard tool for dealing with numerical variables is linear regression analysis. This is applicable when one quantity is an approximate linear function of another. Suppose for instance that Z is initial salary, Y is duration of education, and that on average $Z = a + bY$ for some a and b. This 'line of regression of Z on Y' is an approximate relationship in that for any particular person the initial salary will vary by some random amount from the exact value indicated; but it nevertheless specifies what the average initial salary will be amongst those with a given number of years of education. The analogy with the qualitative case is that we can see such a relationship as showing that the chance of Z being in a given interval is made more likely by some values of Y than by others. And so, just as before, we can take such a relationship to present a *prima facie* case for thinking that Y is part of what *causes* Z to have the value it does. The 'error' by which Z differs from the exact value indicated by Y would then represent the influence on Z of causes other than Y.[15]

But again just as before we have to watch out in drawing such an inference that such other influences on Z are not themselves statistically related to Y. If there were a systematic tendency for these other causes to have a positive influence on Z whenever Y happens to be high, and a negative influence when it is low, then we would find that there was an approximate linear relationship of the required kind between Y and Z, even though Y was not in fact really a cause of Z.

The way to deal with this is of course to identify the influences that might be producing such a spurious association and 'control' for them. For instance, we might be worried that duration of schooling is correlated with starting salary only because they are both affected by X, the level of parental income, say. We would then need to see whether we still found a relationship between years of education and starting salary even amongst people who are equal in respect of parental income. We speak here of the *partial* regression of Z on Y, given X. The use of partial regression analysis to test whether a relationship between two quantities remains after possible confounding influences have been taken into account raises exactly the same issues as our earlier discussion of 'controlling'. In particular, if we are to use such methods to identify causes, then as before we need (a) to start with an initial ordering of our variables with respect to potential causal relationships and (b) to be sure we have taken explicit account of all the other causes with which the one we are examining might be associated.[16]

8. INDETERMINISM AND CAUSATION

I mentioned in passing earlier that it is possible to give a quite different account of the connection between statistical associations and causal relations from that offered here, namely one according to which statistical associations are themselves the actual substance of causal relationships rather than just evidence for the underlying deterministic relationships in which causal connections really consist.

The foremost proponent of this view in recent years has been Wesley Salmon.[17] Roughly speaking, Salmon holds that for one event to be the cause of another *is* simply for the former to affect the latter's probability. A full cause making its effect *certain* is thus for Salmon just the limiting case of causation.

Salmon of course has to avoid counting all statistical associations as causal connections. He does not want barometer readings causing rain simply on the grounds that they make it more likely. To deal with this Salmon specifies further that the explanatory factors we adduce should not only affect the result's probability but should also comprise a 'homogeneous reference class'. By this he means that there should be no further factors which added to that set alter the probability of the explanans. Thus barometer readings are no good for causing rain, in that adding in atmospheric pressures gives a higher probability of rain; but atmospheric pressures are not so ruled out, since when we add barometer readings to them it makes no difference to the chance of rain. In such cases he says that the atmospheric pressure 'screens off' the barometer as a cause of rain.[18] Clearly this is similar to our analysis where the disappearance of a statistical association when 'controlling' for some prior factor was taken to show that this prior factor eclipsed one of our original variables as a cause of the other.

Nevertheless, there remain fundamental differences between

Salmon's approach and mine. Consider a case where some result is fully determined. For Salmon we will not have a 'homogeneous reference class' for this result until we have included all the determining factors. Anything less will be ruled out as an adequate explanation for Salmon on the grounds that the probability it gives the result can be increased, up to certainty, by adding further of the determining factors. Thus for Salmon we only have distinctive statistical causation when the result in question is not determined—when the statistical relationship between cause and effect reflects an actual indeterminacy in the explanandum's occurrence. [19]

My approach as developed so far is by contrast concerned specifically with inferring causes from probabilities when the result *is* in fact determined. This is rather puzzling. We have two superficially similar systems of conditions on legitimate explanation, both relying on the possibility of 'controlling' for prior factors and seeing whether they 'eclipse' or 'screen off' spurious causes from their apparent effects, yet applicable to mutually exclusive sets of situations. What are we to make of this? I think it should make us suspicious of Salmon's approach. My arguments in this chapter have been to the effect that causes can soundly be inferred from such statistical associations as merely reflect our incomplete understanding of what determines the events under study. As these arguments explicitly and essentially assumed the events under study *did* have deterministic causes, they will not do to justify what Salmon has in mind, the application of similar procedures in non-deterministic cases. Nor does Salmon have some independent justification for such applications. He simply puts them forward as intuitively plausible. In itself this would not necessarily dismiss his approach. Argument has to start somewhere. But given that the procedures in question undoubtedly have an initial plausibility also in cases where our statistical understanding clearly does reflect incomplete knowledge, and given that we have *derived* an independent justification for those procedures in such cases, then it becomes very tempting to conclude that Salmon's analysis gains its plausibility only because of the superficial similarity of what he has in mind to the methods discussed in this chapter, that he is trading on the implicit fact that his procedures *would* make sense if the statistical associations involved were, contrary to his specifications, only partial reflections of underlying deterministic relationships.

What then of those events which really are undetermined? I have been assuming throughout this chapter that the world is at bottom deterministic, or at least that the bits of it under investigation are. It is time to relax this assumption somewhat. Modern physics suggests that at bottom the world is not deterministic. And, less cosmically, there is certainly nothing absurd in the idea that certain social events are never made certain by the totality of antecedent factors, but if anything, are only given a certain probability by that totality. However, if there are indeed such social events then I think that the right view is that they are simply not caused, and that as such their occurrence is consequently not explainable. In just the same conditions, the event could well not have occurred. How then, can we possibly take those conditions to tell us why it *did* occur on this occasion? To be sure, we can speak in such cases of the antecedent conditions affecting the *probability* of the event's occurrence. But that is something different. In such cases, we can treat an event's probability as a thing, as a real feature of what occurs, and ask what caused the event to have that probability. Indeed, the discussion of causation in this chapter will apply perfectly straightforwardly to this question. But why the event itself then actually occurred, given that it had the probability it did, must remain a further question, and one that lacks an answer.

Neatly enough, it is precisely in the case of abslolutely undetermined events that we can speak meaningfully of the probability of a particular event as a real occurrence capable of a causal explanation. When we speak of a particular event which is in fact determined as having a probability less than one relative to certain circumstances, all we can mean is that in general events like that turn up with a certain frequency in such circumstances. This is not a feature of the particular event itself so much as of the general class in which we find the relevant frequency. Considered in itself a particular determined event will, so to speak, 'have' a number of different such probabilities, depending on which of the circumstances actually present on that occasion we consider it relative to. It is this general frequency notion of probability I have of course been assuming throughout this chapter. But when we come to a particular event that really is undetermined, we are no longer forced to think of its having a non-unitary probability as simply being a matter of some general class displaying some frequency. Since now *all* the circumstances present on the occasion in question leave the event with a chance of occurrence less than one, we can see this number as giving a real measure of how likely it actually was for that event to occur on *that* occasion. And then we can quite sensibly ask what *caused* there to be that chance of that event on that occasion.[20]

Appendix to Chapter 3

The first thing to be shown is that if Z is always caused and Y is statistically independent of any other direct causes Z may have, then Prob (Z/Y) > Prob (Z) if and only if Y is a direct cause of Z.

Let us express the disjunction of Z's full direct causes in the form YW or X, where X is the disjunction of those full direct causes that do not contain Y as a part, and W the disjunction of those sets of conditions which together with Y give full direct causes of Z. Our question is now whether W has any members—*are* there any sets of conditions which together with Y make up full direct causes for Z?

Since, by hypothesis, Z occurs if and only if one of its full direct cause does,

$$\mathrm{Prob}(Z/Y) = \mathrm{Prob}(YW \text{ or } X/Y)$$

$$= \frac{\mathrm{Prob}(YW \text{ or } YX)}{\mathrm{Prob}(Y)}$$

$$= \frac{\mathrm{Prob}(YW) + \mathrm{Prob}(YX) - \mathrm{Prob}(YWX)}{\mathrm{Prob}(Y)}$$

And so, since Y is independent of X,

$$\mathrm{Prob}(Z/Y) = \frac{\mathrm{Prob}(YW) - \mathrm{Prob}(YWX)}{\mathrm{Prob}(Y)} + \mathrm{Prob}(X)$$

Now,

$$\mathrm{Prob}(Z) = \mathrm{Prob}(YW \text{ or } X)$$
$$= \mathrm{Prob}(YW) - \mathrm{Prob}(YWX) + \mathrm{Prob}(X)$$

So, given that Y does not have a probability of 1, which would mean it always happened and so was ineligible as a cause to start with, Prob(Z/Y) > Prob(Z) if and only if Prob(YW) > Prob(YWX).

If Prob(YW) > Prob(YWX), then Y must be a direct cause. For, if it were not, YW and *a fortiori* YWX would be impossible, and so both would have zero probabilities. So if Prob(Z/Y) > Prob(Z) then Y must be a direct cause of Z.

If, conversely, Prob(YW) ≤ Prob(YWX)—that is, if Prob(YW) = Prob(YWX)—then either Y is not a direct cause and both sides of the equation are zero, or X is certain once YW obtains. But if the latter were the case then X would eclipse YW as a cause anyway. For X and Y are statistically independent and given that YW's being certain is ruled out to start with this means that X will sometimes occur without YW. So in either case if Prob(Z/Y) is not greater than Prob(Z) then Y cannot be a direct cause of Z. (It is here that the 'no-eclipsing' analysis of causation is crucial. If eclipsed sufficient conditions could be causes, then we could not argue from an absence of association to an absence of causation).

That was the first thing to be shown. I now want to consider the situation when Y *is* associated probabilistically with X. Let $V_1, \ldots, V_n$ be those parts of the disjuncts of X which are either singly or jointly associated with Y. Then T, the disjunction of sets of factors 'left' after we 'remove' $V_1, \ldots, V_n$ from X, will be statistically independent of Y. What we now need to know is whether the presence of Y makes Z more likely *within* any category of instances which are all similar in respect of $V_1, \ldots, V_n$. That is, is Prob(Z/YV) > Prob(Z/V), for any V which a combination of the presence and absence of the various $V_1, \ldots, V_n$?

If it is, then we can definitely conclude that Y is a cause of Z. For we can go through exactly the same reasoning as before within the class of instances given by our V. Except now we have assured ourselves that Y is probabilistically independent of T (the 'other causes' of Z 'within' our V). So if Y does make Z more likely it must be that together with certain other factors, which might include elements of V, it makes up a full direct cause of Z.

If Y increases the chance of Z within some combinations of $V_1, \ldots, V_n$ but not within others, then this shows that relevant elements of such combinations are themselves part of full causes containing Y. If, however, Y does not make Z more likely for *any such* combination—if Prob(Z/YV) = Prob(Z/V) for all possible Vs—then we can in general conclude that Y is *not* a direct cause of Z. Again we can apply our earlier reasoning 'within' each V, with the assurance that Y is now independent of Z's 'other' causes: and so we can conclude that there is nothing which together with any combination of $V_1, \ldots, V_n$ can be added to Y to give a full cause of Z.

There is however one exception to this last principle which needs mentioning. Suppose Y *is* in fact a cause of Z, but that whenever it occurs it is made *certain* by a given combination of other causes, V. Then there is no question of its increasing the probability of Z within that V. Technically $Prob(Z/YV) = Prob(Z/V)$, since the condition YV will be effectively equivalent to the condition V. In the simple case where we assumed that Y was independent of Z's other causes this difficulty did not arise because if Y were absolutely certain it would be ineligible as a cause. But now we have to worry about a certainty-relative-to-V, which cannot be so ruled out. This is in effect a version of the difficulty which arose with the virus — skin infection — fever case. We can not tell if Y (skin infection) is eclipsed by V (virus) because they always occur together. And so, analogously with the earlier discussion, we need to admit that further considerations will be needed to distinguish genuine from spurious causes in such cases.

4 Actions, Rules and Meanings

1. REASONS AS CAUSES

In everyday life we characteristically seek to explain actions by giving the reasons for which they are done. That is, we attempt to account for actions by attributing certain internal mental states to the agents performing them.

How adequate is this everyday mode of explanation? We can distinguish two standard responses to this question.

On the one hand there is what I shall call the 'materialist' answer. This denies that reasons can explain actions. The 'materialist' feels that if we are to conform to the standards set by the natural sciences we must disavow 'subjective' mental entities in our explanations. Instead of dealing in such ineffables we should try to elaborate testable theories relating behaviour to such objective material phenomena as physiological processes or patterns of past conditioning.

On the other hand there is the 'interpretativist' response. This repudiates any approach to human action based on models of explanation drawn from the natural sciences. 'Interpretativists' urge that human action is a distinctive phenomenon, not to be seen as determined by prior causes according to invariable laws, but rather to be *interpreted* and *understood* by uncovering the reasons or purposes behind it. In their view the materialist perspective substitutes a blind and unthinking automaton for the autonomous, self-reflective agent man actually is. [1]

It is widely assumed that these are the only two possible views on the explanation of action—that if you are against the interpretative view you must be for the materialist. In this chapter I am going to argue that this assumption is mistaken—that the correct approach to action explanation is neither materialist nor interpretativist. Common to both these views is the assumption that reason explanations are not causal explanations. I intend to show that the account of scientific theorising developed so far gives us good reasons for doubting this assumption.

That is, I shall argue that reason explanations *are* causal explanations. In a sense I shall be granting the materialists that the explanation of action should conform to the natural scientific model, but denying that this requires disavowing reasons; conversely I shall be following the interpretativists in wishing to retain the everyday mode of explaining actions in terms of reasons, but demurring at their claim that this removes human action from the scope of scientific explanation. By being clear about the real requirements of scientific method we get the best of both worlds. We can satisfy the desire for coherent standards of explanatory success without being artificially restricted to talk of nothing but neurones or contingencies of reinforcement; conversely, we can help ourselves to the sophisticated structure of everyday thinking about behaviour without making something mysterious of our explanatory methods.

Reason explanations of actions have a quite definite structure. Consider the following examples:

(1) Q. Why did your great-grandfather leave Scotland for London?
    A. He wanted work.
(2) Q. Why did Harold Wilson call an election in October 1974?
    A. He thought Labour would get an increased majority.

In such explanations there are two explanatory factors involved. First there is the agent's *desire* for some state of affairs; and secondly, there is his *belief* that his action will be conducive to that state of affairs. In practice it is usual to mention only the desire, as in (1), or only the belief, as in (2). But a moment's reflection will show that any reason explanation implicitly attributes the other related attitude to the agent as well. To see this, consider what would happen to the above examples of explanations if it were accepted that your ancestor did *not* expect there to be work in London, or that Wilson did *not* want an increased majority.

So the reasons behind an action involve a desire, plus a belief that the action will contribute to the satisfaction of that desire. My claim is that such reasons *cause* the ensuing action. (From now on I shall use 'reasons', or 'attitudes', when I wish to refer indiscriminately to beliefs and/or desires.) As explained in the last chapter, the claim that reasons cause actions requires that there be some generalisation showing an agent's reasons to be part of a minimal and uneclipsed sufficient condition for his action. Can the existence of such a generalisation be demonstrated?

One possibility would be to show some kind of statistical connection between the having of reasons and the performance of the indicated action, and to infer the existence of the required generalisation by the kind of reasoning discussed in the last chapter. But I shall not attempt this. The requisite statistical data do not exist, and it is by no means clear how one might go about establishing such an abstract and general association in practice. Instead I shall argue directly for the necessary general connection between reasons and actions, by actually producing and defending a generalisation which relates them as cause and effect.

The simplest attempt at such a generalisation would be 'Whenever an agent believes a certain action will produce a result he wants, he performs that action'. But this obviously will not do. Often an agent will believe that a certain action will produce a desired result, and yet not perform it, because he anticipates it will have other consequences which he dislikes more than he desires that result. I often have a desire to stay in bed all day, but of course usually do not, for in general I know that doing so would preclude other things more important to me.

This suggests the following modification: 'Whenever an agent believes a certain action, X, will produce some desired result, Y, *and* there is no state of affairs Z whose avoidance he prefers to Y and which he believes will also result from X, then he will perform X'.[2] But it is easy enough to generate counter-examples even to this more elaborate formulation. For one thing, on any method of counting results, it may well be that there is no *one* Z the avoidance of which the agent prefers to Y, yet he may still fail to do X because the totality of the unattractive side-effects he envisages outweighs the attraction of Y for him. And another difficulty is that people's actions are not influenced only by beliefs as to what will *certainly* follow from their actions, as the above generalisation assumes. They are also swayed by judgements that a certain action will make a certain result *likely*, even if not certain. On occasion an agent might do something even though there is no desirable result he is *sure* will follow, provided only that he attaches a high probability to some such results following his action. We can speak here of an agent having a *partial* belief that a given action will have a given result. The strength of such a partial belief can be equated with the agent's subjective estimate of the probability of the result following if he performs the action.[3] A partial belief will weigh more with the agent, so to speak, the stronger it is.

If we are to deal with these difficulties we need somehow to conceive of an action as depending simultaneously on all the various different consequences it is envisaged as having, and also on the different degrees to which it is supposed that these consequences will follow. It will be helpful at this point to introduce the idea of an agent's 'decision scheme'. This will depend on the various ends that the agent desires and the relative strength of his desire for each end, a list of the possible actions open to the agent, and, for each combination of a possible action and a desired end, the degree to which he believes that end will be satisfied if he performs that action. So we can conceive of an agent's decision scheme as a matrix, or grid, in which the rows represent alternative actions, the columns represent desired ends, and the elements his subjective estimate of the probability of the end for that column being achieved given that he performs the action for that row.

Now, such a decision scheme will indicate, for each of the alternative actions open to an agent, how far it seems to him likely to satisfy his desires. More precisely, we can take the 'expected desirability' of an action for an agent to be the sum, for all his different ends, of the strength of his desire for each end multiplied by his subjective probability of that end being achieved if that action is performed.

This then suggests a possible generalisation about the connection between reasons and actions: namely, that agents always perform those actions with greatest expected desirability. It is this generalisation I shall defend as showing reasons to be causes of actions.

Of course, if I succeed in this it will mean that, strictly speaking, it is *all* the beliefs and desires which contribute to an action's having greatest expected desirability that make up the full cause of the action. But there is then no difficulty in seeing the everyday practice of giving a specific desire or the partial belief relating the action to that desire in explanation of an action as a special case of our general tendency to mention only that part of a full cause which is most surprising, least generally known, most morally significant, etc.

2. DECISION SCHEMES, COMMON SENSE, AND RATIONALITY

It might seem that an awful lot has to be swallowed if we are to see reasons as causing actions. Am I really claiming that people always compute what to do by working through some array of numbers in their heads?

At first sight the interpretativist story appears far more plausible. The interpretativist will agree that to explain an action by reasons is to show that the agent believed it to be conducive to some desired aim.

But he will deny that an agent's beliefs and desires somehow quantitively *determine* what he does. His picture will rather be that an agent's various different beliefs and desires will indicate any number of alternative actions as reasonable, as possibly conducive to some desired result. It is up to the agent himself to decide which reasons to act on, whether to act morally or selfishly, whether to be prudent or to go for immediate satisfaction, etc. The autonomy of human agents consists essentially in the fact that they themselves choose freely amongst such alternatives, independently of any constraining generalisation. And so all that can be required of an action explanation is that it shows how the agent had some rationale for what he did, not that he was determined so to act.

Plausible as this picture is, it is not difficult to show that it is inadequate. Consider the following case. A man removes all his clothes while travelling on a hot train. In explanation we are told that he wanted to feel cooler, and believed that being naked would help. Even if we did accept that he had that belief and that desire, we would scarcely be satisfied. Our natural response would be that, while we have in a sense been shown *a* reason the man had for his action, there must be more to be said. Normally such a reason would not be strong enough to override the reasons he would have had against so acting—the disinclination to exposure, the fear of ridicule and imprisonment, etc. Of course we might come to be satisfied with the explanation if we could be shown that the man lacked these normal aversions, or stood to win some money, or that the heat was quite unbearable, or something along such lines. But this merely supports the basic point I am making—that we cannot just accept *any* reason the agent might have had as satisfactorily explaining his action. We need in addition to be shown that this reason, in conjunction with the agent's other beliefs and desires, was such as to give the agent *sufficient* reason to perform the action.

What this kind of example indicates is that something like the notion that people perform those actions with greatest expected desirability is in fact part of our everyday thinking about human behaviour. The idea of a decision scheme and the associated apparatus is thus not something I have plucked out of thin air, but something that seems to be implicit in our commonsense theory about the antecedents of action. For it is difficult to see how the everyday requirement, that the reasons offered in explanation of an action should be *sufficiently* strong to account for the action, is to be captured without eventual recourse to something like the decision scheme approach.

The idea that this approach is implicit in common sense might occasion some initial scepticism. The idea that people always do what has greatest expected desirability seems to imply that humans are supremely calculating, selfish and rational beings. Surely this extreme picture of human motivation is no part of commonsense. However, the inconsistency is only apparent. Let us take calculation, selfishness and rationality in turn.

It is not part of what I am claiming that action is always preceded by a process of conscious computation. Clearly it is not. The thesis is rather that the actions people perform will as it happens, be those which *would* be selected by such computations. No doubt something like conscious calculations are sometimes performed by people prior to their decisions. But this is not essential to the picture I am presenting. I take people to be *choosing* the course of action their more or less conscious beliefs and desires indicate as best, precisely insofar as the action they perform *is* the one with greatest expected desirability, whether or not they have deliberated on the matter beforehand. So the conscious experiences sometimes involved in reaching decisions play no particular part in my account of the antecedents of action.

Secondly, I do not at all wish to imply that people always act for selfish reasons. Though 'desire' is the most convenient term for people's attitudes to their ends, it is perhaps slightly misleading in this connection. For I do not want to assert that everybody's actions are always directed solely towards their personal gratification. There are certainly cases where people are moved to act by their concern for the well-being of their friends and relations, or the benefit of humankind in general, even when they are sure they themselves will not enjoy the results in any way. So 'desire' should be understood to cover whatever it is that moves people, including any altruistic or moral concern for the welfare of others they may have. (A similar if less defensible misunderstanding would be to suppose that 'desires' are always innate. There is nothing in what I have said to rule out desires being produced by social or other environmental causes.)

Thirdly, it is important to realise that the amount of 'rationality' presupposed by the decision scheme approach is quite minimal. This approach does, it is true, assume precisely that people are 'rational' in that they do what their beliefs indicate to be most likely to satisfy their desires. But it does not at all assume that those beliefs or those desires are themselves in any way rational. The decision scheme approach says nothing at all about where an agent's desires and beliefs should come from. This account is perfectly consistent with the fact that people can on occasion have very odd reasons indeed for their actions.[4]

3. ATTRIBUTING BELIEFS AND DESIRES

That decision schemes and so on are implicitly part of common sense is not entirely to the point. This may make them seem less outlandish than they first appear. But it scarcely shows that they amount to a full-fledged scientific theory which might yield properly causal explanations. 'Common sense' contains all kinds of ideas which fail to satisfy the standards of scientific acceptability.

Indeed it seems that the 'theory' of action I am defending will fall at the first hurdle. For how can we tell what beliefs and desires people have? Clearly if explanations by reasons are to be anything more than arbitrary exercises of imagination, it must be possible to establish that an agent actually *does* have the desires and beliefs attributed to him.

It might seem sufficient that we can identify our own attitudes by introspection. But this is not an adequate response. For one thing, many philosophers, following Wittgenstein, doubt whether judgements about phenomena in principle only accessible to single individuals are a coherent possibility at all.[5] And in any case, if reason explanations are to be backed by a general scientific theory, there needs to be some way of attributing mental states which will not necessarily restrict any investigator to an unrepresentative sample of one.

The way we can, and do, deal with this problem is by inferring the attitudes people have from other things we know about them. We do this on the basis of our general assumptions about how people's having certain beliefs and desires relates to other facts about them. In this respect beliefs and desires can be seen as akin to any of the relatively unobservable entities investigated in the natural sciences. As we saw in Chapter 2, there is nothing in science that requires that we describe things only in directly observable terms.

So, for instance, we might work out what someone believes from our knowledge of what situations he has been in. If I know of a normal person that he, say, works as a fruit-picker, I do not need anything further to tell me that he knows that the pay for that work depends on the amount of fruit picked. In general, and in less trivial cases, we can similarly reason from what we know someone to have experienced to his having the obvious beliefs a normal person would form therefrom.

Again, we might work out some of someone's inner states from seeing what he does. Given our general assumptions about the link between someone's attitudes and their actions, we will in certain cases be able to reason backwards, as it were, from their behaviour to their mental states. Of particular importance will be what someone *says*. We take certain expressions to express certain beliefs and desires, in a way to be discussed later, and so we can on occasion move from an individual's utterances to conclusions about his internal attitudes.

Obviously there is more to be said about these procedures. There are questions about their general reliability. But the principle is clear enough. Given any individual, the idea is that we take what we know of his experiences and his behaviour, and from this reconstruct a specification of his decision scheme, subject to the constraints that the beliefs and desires we attribute to him are ones that (a) would have been produced by his experiences and (b) would have led him to act as he did.

Exactly how reliable are the principles of inference involved? One objection might be that we are not in general entitled to assumptions about what beliefs it is natural for people to come to in given situations. Perhaps this seems plausible with members of our own culture, but can we simply assume that the concepts in terms of which people from different cultural traditions organise experience and formulate beliefs are the same as ours? A similar point can be made about inferring attitudes from linguistic utterances. Once we move outside an ethnocentric context it becomes clear that our ability to tell what certain sounds mean cannot be taken for granted. These are serious (and, incidentally, related) objections. But it would take us too far astray to pursue them at this point. I shall return to the issues involved in Chapter 6.

What about the quantities involved in decision schemes—the *degrees* of belief and desire? Remember that actions are being supposed to depend not only on *what* is believed and desired, but also on *how much* they are believed and desired. It might seem quite unclear how the procedures I have outlined could ever succeed in attaching precise numbers to an agent's attitudes.

However, there are in fact circumstances where even this requirement can be satisfied. Suppose we know that a man thinks there is an even chance of a certain proposition, p, being true. Then, if he is indifferent between certainly getting some outcome A and getting B if p turns out true, it is not hard to see that he must desire B twice as much as A. (We could establish his indifference by getting him to choose between the certainty and the gamble and, making sure there are no extraneous influences on what he does, observing that a marginal incentive on either side will swing his decision.) How can we ever be sure that a man attaches a probability of $\frac{1}{2}$ to some proposition? One way is to take two things the man desires to different degrees, say C and D, and get him to choose between the two gambles: *C if p, D if not* and *D if p, C if not*. Again, a moment's reflection will show that if he is indifferent between these two gambles, and nothing else is influencing his choice, then he must think there is an even chance of p being true. In fact, it is in principle possible to attach numbers on suitable scales to all an agent's desires and all his partial beliefs by these kinds of procedures. There is no question of demonstrating this here, but the basic idea is to offer the subject a succession of choices between gambles, at each stage using what has previously been established about him to infer further of his degrees of desire and belief.[6]

It might seem that these methods of attaching numbers to an agent's attitudes are somewhat artificial. They can only be applied in quite special and contrived circumstances. Can they really underpin a *general* account of human action? But compare the situation with that in mechanics. All changes of motion in any matter whatsoever are held to depend on the precise masses of the bodies involved and the forces acting on them. This is supposed to be true of everything from the motions of the stars to the flight of birds and the flow of rivers. But we only have precise knowledge about the forces and masses involved in a tiny proportion of cases—those where the interactions are relatively simple and where, moreover, we can apply our instruments (magnetometers, beam balances, etc.). I do not of course want to push this analogy any distance, but it should serve to show that a quantitative account of the determinants of action by no means requires that we *always* know in full numerical detail *all* the factors behind every action. Of course we cannot. But this does not mean we cannot *sometimes* tell *enough* about an agent's decision scheme to compare the expected desirabilities of his actions.

4. TESTING THE THEORY

It is one thing to show we can sometimes tell what beliefs and desires people have. It is another to show that the claim that people always do what has greatest expected desirability is a proper scientific generalisation. Many will want to argue that this generalisation is quite untestable—that it is only a kind of conceptual tool for representing agents as comprehensible beings. The 'materialist' and the 'interpretativist' might well join forces here, differing only in the subsequent inference they draw—while the materialist says, 'So much for explanations by beliefs and desires', the interpretativist concludes that actions are not caused.

Why should the generalisation in question be thought scientifically empty? One argument might be that we presuppose it whenever we test it. This is not a serious objection. It is true that some of the methods outlined above for detecting people's attitudes from what they do take it for granted that people do what is, in the relevant sense, rational for them—it was precisely because we took people to choose that action with greatest expected desirability that we could move backwards from their choices to their degrees of belief and desire. But there is nothing wrong with this. What we do is use the theory once to infer somebody's beliefs and desires, and use it again to anticipate his action. If success is not guaranteed when we use the theory once, it is certainly not going to be made certain by using it twice. Provided we do not include the action we are trying to account for itself in the data from which we infer the agent's attitudes, there is in principle no reason at all why people should not act so as to confute our predictions.

But *do* we always observe the proviso just mentioned? It is not at all clear that we do. Indeed, it could be complained that if only we did, we would soon have to admit that it is quite false that people always act rationally. For there are in fact plenty of cases where people do things that seem irrational given what we can infer of their beliefs and desires from their past behaviour and experience. But we do not regard these as counter-examples, falsifying our theory. Instead we decide in such cases that we must have got the agent's beliefs and desires wrong—we might conclude, for instance, that the agent must have somehow changed his mind in respect of those attitudes indicated by his previous behaviour and experience.

So the accusation would be that we can retain the theory that people always act rationally only because we refuse to treat it falsifiably. Whenever we come across a counter-example we renege on any commitment to falsifiability and use the action in question itself as a basis for inferring the beliefs and desires behind it, legitimising our ploy by such ideas as that people can change their beliefs and desires over time.

How damning is this? According to Popper this kind of defence of a theory is the essence of scientific bad faith. But, as we saw in Chapter 2, Popper's picture of scientific development is far too simple. In reality scientific theories are articulated structures of interdependent assumptions, not isolated hypotheses that can be tested one by one. It is as a rule quite legitimate to defend the more central assumptions in such a structure against an apparent counter-example by revising some of the more peripheral assumptions responsible for the anomaly. I would suggest that this is just what happens with our everyday theory of human behaviour. The core of this theory is the idea that people always do what has greatest expected desirability. We relate this central idea to the data by means of our various auxiliary assumptions about how to tell what beliefs and desires people actually have. The notion that people's attitudes can change over time then merely indicates one way in which we are prepared to rethink these latter assumptions when they lead us astray. But this preparedness does not condemn the overall theory as unscientific—none of the most revered theories in the history of science would ever have survived if their proponents had not been similarly prepared to defend their central tenets from the phenomena by revising auxiliary hypotheses.

Indeed, the admission that people can change their minds is by no means the only ploy by which our sophisticated everyday thinking about human action is ready to defend itself against unwanted results. For instance, we allow that people do not *always* form the beliefs which should be obvious given the situations they experience. They can be distracted or not paying attention for some reason. Again, we recognise that even sincere assertions by linguistically competent speakers are not *always* accurate guides to their attitudes. For people will on occasion deceive themselves about what their real motives are, in cases where those motives are somehow disreputable. What is more, there is even room in our thinking for limited exceptions to the central principle that people always perform those actions with greatest expected desirability. People are sometimes beset by strong emotions, or have to act on the spur of the moment, or are faced with choices involving a number of complex considerations; and we allow that in such circumstances they might well be led to do things which are less than 'rational' whatever their desires and beliefs.

In fact, it has to be admitted that our everyday thought is very well stocked indeed with ways of explaining why people sometimes act in an unexpected manner. Is this not after all too much of a good thing? Even the liberal view of scientific developments outlined in Chapter 2 did not give the scientist *carte blanche* to invent *ad hoc* escape clauses for every possible anomaly facing his theory. He was at least required to revise his set of assumptions in as 'progressive' a way as possible; that is, in ways which led to new and independently testable predictions.

But even here it is not clear that our thinking falls short of the requirements of scientific propriety. If we were *always* prepared simply to say, 'He must have changed his mind', when someone acts in a way inconsonant with our previous information about his attitudes and leave it at that, then our theory of action would indeed be completely degenerate, in that nothing that anybody did would ever leave us puzzled. But in fact, we are not thus completely agnostic about how people's ideas change over time. Far from taking beliefs and desires to be completely volatile, subject to unaccountable variation, we have reasonably clear views about what kind of ideas in what circumstances will be subject to change, and what ideas will remain constant from occasion to occasion. Similarly, we have fairly definite assumptions about what can distract someone's attention sufficiently to make him miss some salient aspect of his situation; about what motives are sufficiently disreputable for certain people to deceive themselves about them; about when people will be emotional, rushed, or insufficiently incisive, and about what they will do then. Insofar as these elaborations are definite they can be compared with what people actually do and say, and further modified where necessary.

Still, even given all this, is there not *some* difference between the decision scheme approach to action and, say, the scientific study of electromagnetic phenomena? Even if the former responds to some extent to such anomalous behaviour as succeeds in attracting our attention, this scarcely seems to be on the same level as the elaboration of electromagnetic theory by directed and controlled testing of precisely formulated hypotheses. In the end, I do not want to continue denying that there are real dissimilarities here. But what I hope I have shown is that this is merely a quantitative matter of degree of rigour and precision. For if this is accepted, then it follows that the scientific acceptability of our everyday theory of action should be decided, not by whether it is more progressive than electromagnetic theory, etc., but by whether it is is more progressive than competing theories of human behaviour. That *other* disciplines might have more admirable theories is no reason for discarding our best going account of human action. And there seems to me little room for dispute that the decision scheme theory is the best such account. There is no serious competition to speak of. Behaviourism tries to explain actions by past experience without bringing in internal mental states at all. As such it is merely an emasculated version of our everyday theory needlessly deprived of the coherence and explanatory power the latter gets from invoking such theoretical entities as beliefs and desires. What fruitful research there has been in the behaviourist psychological tradition has involved the more or less implicit adoption of various tenets of everyday thought about action: it would be far more fruitful if this were explicitly recognised and the findings elaborated *within* everyday thinking. Physiological accounts of human behaviour are scarcely off the ground.

Perhaps at some future date we will have an understanding of human action which unifies mental and physiological categories. Insofar as the physiological mechanisms involved failed to match up neatly with our present ideas about the mental antecedents of action, this eventuality would no doubt involve some modifications of our current mentalistic theory. (For that matter, it would no doubt involve changes in current physiological theory too.) But this is no reason for repudiating our current theory *now*—if the possibility of a superior future theory required rejecting the best extant one, we would never believe anything about anything. [7]

5. RULES AND ACTION

So far in this chapter I have said nothing about *rules*. For many 'interpretativists' this will have made my arguments so far largely irrelevant—there is an influential school of interpretative thought which holds that it is precisely because human actions conform to rules that it is inappropriate to explain them causally.

The foremost English-speaking representative of this view in recent years has been Peter Winch. In his influential *The Idea of a Social Science* Winch argues that the relevance of rules to all human actions introduces into the explanation of action a normative element which precludes any causal approach. To explain an action is for Winch to evaluate it against the standards current in the society in question. Thus when we refer to the traffic regulations to account for Englishmen driving on the left, or to the conventions of marriage ceremonies to explain why a groom places a ring on his bride's finger, or to religious taboos to illuminate why Hindus do not eat beef, we are not giving the causes of the actions in question, but showing what justification or rationale they have in the social context in question, showing how they make sense in that context. [8]

In support of this view it can be pointed out that a rule admits of exceptions in a way that a scientific generalisation does not. A principle of the form 'In circumstances X, Y should be done' can obtain in a given society, and yet there can be cases where Y is not done in circumstances X. Such deviations do not necessarily show that the rule does not exist, merely that people do not always do what they should. By contrast, if we were to accept that there were counter-examples to a scientific generalisation ('In circumstances X, Y happens') we would have to abandon the generalisation. It seems that explaining an action as conforming to a rule does not imply that it *had* to happen, as is done by a causal explanation.

However, an emphasis on exceptions to rules does raise one difficulty for the Winchian view. How are we to explain deviance? If what is socially appropriate is the same for both conformists and deviants, it is rather obscure how reference to rules is by itself going to account for the differences between them. Nor is it even clear that even conforming actions can always be explained by the applicable rule. Suppose a man is quite ignorant that it is *de rigueur* in certain circles to compliment one's hostess on her table linen when invited to dinner. Nevertheless, when first introduced into this milieu, he does so anyway, because the linen is indeed fine. While his action is just what is required by social propriety, it is clearly no part of its explanation that it is so appropriate. He would have done just the same even if (as he in fact supposed) there were no such rule.

To deal with these problems and the Winchian view in general we need to take a closer look at the notion of a 'rule'.

Winch says that 'the notion of following a rule is logically inseparable from the notion of *making a mistake*'.[9] For him this shows that rules are for evaluating actions and not for causing them. I want to draw out some different points. If certain actions are deemed correct and others incorrect in a given society, it must be that the members of that society discriminate between the two categories by reacting positively to correct actions or negatively to incorrect ones. These reactions might range from definite rewards or sanctions to vague signs of approval or disapproval. But a people who divided actions into two groups, but did not display any consequent negative or positive reactions whatsoever to the actions so classified, could clearly not be held to be distinguishing *correct* from *incorrect* actions.

However, if we did come across such a set of reactions we would not feel we had the whole story. We would want to know about the source of these reactions—*why* do certain actions evoke sanctions? (As the difference between 'positive' and 'negative' reactions is of no significance in the present context of discussion, I shall consider only negative reactions from now on.)

The standard answer will be that most of the members of the social group have some kind of moral disapproval of actions deviating from the rule in question. It is because they find it somehow wrong that they chastise transgression. (The interesting question of exactly how principled disapproval has to be for it to count as *moral* will not be pursued here.) So for any individual the rule has both an 'internal' and an 'external' aspect. 'Internally' the rule is present insofar as the individual disapproves of and reacts negatively to behaviour which fails to conform to it. 'Externally' the rule is there for the individual in that he is aware that others will react similarly to his transgressions.[10]

We might press still further. Why do the people have these attitudes of moral disapproval in the first place? And to this the standard answer will be that the presence of the rule itself is the source of these attitudes. On introduction to the social group an individual finds that certain forms of behaviour incur negative reactions. This characteristically leads to his 'internalising' the rule—he himself acquires an attitude of disapproval to the behaviour in question. And this means that there is a general tendency for the kind of rule in question to be self-perpetuating, to itself produce those attitudes which will constitute its continued existence.

It would, I think, be a mistake to think the above analysis captures all social phenomena describable as 'rules'. The existence of a self-perpetuating moral attitude common to a social group which conduces both internally and externally to a regularity in behaviour is indeed a central case. But it is not the only one. I shall use the term *norm* to distinguish it from other cases.

To introduce another species of the genus 'rule', consider the question of how norms get started in the first place. It is natural to think, given some norm, that the attitudes which produce the reactions which produce the attitudes etc. would never have arisen in the first place unless the society in general, or some powerful sub-section, had at some time recognised it to be in their interests that a certain form of behaviour for evaluating actions and not for causing them. I want to draw out some therefore instituted sanctions against it. Legislation would be the paradigm of such a development. This need not in itself amount to a *norm* as defined, in that the discouraged behaviour need not be morally disapproved of in itself but discouraged only because its prevention has come to be seen by the relevant group as a means to the satisfaction of ends that they independently have. I shall use the term *regulation* for this kind of case, where some standard is instituted by deliberate design as a means to some further end.

Regulations, then, are distinct from norms. But, given the earlier discussion, it is clear how a regulation can *lead* to a norm, with the sanctions against the behaviour getting internalised as attitudes of moral disapproval to transgressions in themselves.

To digress briefly for a moment, it is worth observing that this does *not* mean that norms and the attitudes behind them will always serve the pre-social interests of the population in general or some dominant group therein. For one thing, we have been given no reason to suppose that the institution of a regulation is the only way a norm can originate. And even when a norm does start in this way, it may well continue to perpetuate itself after circumstances have changed so as to make it irrelevant to the end originally intended. In the long run, no doubt, norms disappear when they come into actual conflict with the satisfaction of other independent aims. But these other aims will generally themselves be social products, so even here we have no reason to see societies as generally tending towards arrangements which will satisfy their members' pre-social motives.

Another kind of rule deserves mention at this point. The institution of money is a good example. We all accept metal and paper tokens of little intrinsic value in exchange for valuable goods and services. We do this, not because of threatened sanctions, nor out of moral feeling, but simply because we assume we can use the tokens in turn to get valuable goods and services from others. And we are right in this assumption precisely because other people make it too, and so *do* accept the tokens from us. We have here a regularity in people's behaviour which derives from the fact that it is in each individual's interest to conform, given that (nearly) everybody else is going to conform too. Other examples of this phenomenon would be customary meeting places, certain kinds of signals, and perhaps, language in general. Loosely following David Lewis, I shall call regularities of this kind *conventions*.[11]

I have mentioned norms, regulations and conventions. It is difficult to find any characteristics common to all three categories. Norms and regulations both involve sanctions; but conventions do not. Conventions and norms both share the interesting property of tending to perpetuate themselves without further ado once established; regulations, however, persist as such only as long as those upholding them continue to see it as in their interests to do so. Regulations and conventions are both regularities deriving from conformers' anticipations of others' reactions; but this is not essential to norms, insofar as the internalisation of the associated values will lead individuals to conform anyway.

6. RULES AND REASONS

In a way this casts doubt on the intuitive notion of a social 'rule'. All that seems to join the cases we have looked at is the vague and question-begging idea of a regularity in behaviour which somehow depends on the contingencies of the social set-up. Perhaps we ought to invoke here

Wittgenstein's notion of a 'family resemblance' property, which has a continuum of instantiations each sharing features with certain others but without any overarching characteristic common to all. No doubt we could find further intuitively plausible examples of social 'rules' which were neither norms, regulations nor conventions.

Fortunately, there is no real need to continue worrying about what really counts as a 'rule'. One thing that the last section should have made clear is that there is after all no distinctive mode of rule-explanation of action requiring its own elucidation—to cite a 'rule' in explaining an action is merely a special case of accounting for the action by reference to the agent's beliefs and desires. Thus to explain an action as conforming to a norm is merely to say it is done because an individual has internalised a certain moral desire, or because he believes others will react to deviation in a way he wants to avoid, or both. Someone whose behaviour is explained by a regulation is acting as he does because he anticipates that disobedience will incur unwanted sanctions. Conventions are conformed to because individuals see conformity as conducive to their desires, given their beliefs in others' conformity.

In general, we can see the presence of a rule as simply a matter of the members of the society in question having certain interrelated beliefs and, perhaps, desires, which tend to produce a certain conformity in their behaviour. When we explain an action as 'conforming to a rule' it is not so much the rule itself as what I shall call these *associated attitudes* that explain it. Thus the relevance of rules to actions gives us no special reason to think our explanations of actions are not causal. Insofar as explanations in terms of beliefs and desires are causal, so then are rule-explanations as a special case.

To corroborate this view of rule-explanation I shall return to the two problems that were posed for the Winchian view earlier. Consider first the case of the 'lucky dinner guest'. It is now obvious what is wrong with explaining his compliment in terms of its social appropriateness. For while there is a rule about such compliments, and corresponding associated attitudes amongst most members of the social group in question, the dinner guest himself lacks those attitudes. *His* reasons for paying the compliment cannot be the attitudes associated with the rule. It is precisely because attributing his action to the rule is to implicitly claim that his action is caused by those standard attitudes that we reject the attribution.

Conversely, the fact that someone *deviates* from a rule might similarly be attributed to his not having socially normal beliefs and desires. He may lack the value behind some norm; or he may be ignorant of those beliefs which sustain general conformity to other rules. Not that all deviance need result from this kind of 'inadequate socialisation'. Even somebody who does have the attitudes associated with some rule will invariably have many *other* beliefs and desires which will weigh with him in deciding whether to conform or not. The associated attitudes will incline him towards conformity, but his other reasons may well weigh on the side of deviance. Even the man who has properly internalised our values against stealing, say, will not therefore always and automatically refrain from doing so. For he will characteristically also have desires for the benefits he believes he might get from successful larceny. So there might well be occasions where need presses and opportunity offers to a degree sufficient to override his moral disinclination to theft.

Again, the integration of rules into the decision scheme approach to action explanation deals in obvious and satisfying ways with a case which is problematic for the view that rules explain actions in a distinctively non-causal way. As it happens, this last point also goes some way towards answering a worry central to the contemporary school of sociological thinkers known as 'ethnomethodologists'. This movement is in part a reaction to the way the notion of a 'norm' is wielded by orthodox sociologists committed to a Durkheimian disavowal of considerations of individual psychology. Such sociologists tend to assume that by definition anybody who has been properly socialised will conform willy-nilly to the norms of his society. Ethnomethodologists quite reasonably complain that this makes man out to be a 'cultural dope', a puppet manipulated from without by external forces not of his making and beyond his control, when in fact he is a reflective and conscious being who can and does create his own strategies for action.[12]

The view developed in the last few sections accounts for the relevance of norms to action without making such a monkey of man. Even the man who has successfully acquired the attitudes associated with some rule is by no means thereby determined always to act in conformity to it. For he will inevitably have other fish to fry. His actions will flow from a whole complex of beliefs and desires, including attitudes associated with other social rules, innate attitudes, and attitudes resulting from idiosyncratic and perhaps unrecoverable features of his personal background. No two people will be the same, and each will be led to their decisions by their own ideas. These might or might not involve conformity to any particular norm. To allow that all actions depend in part on socially inculcated attitudes is not at all to say that all actions will automatically conform to existing standards.

7. ETHNOMETHODOLOGY

It needs to be conceded immediately that these last remarks will scarcely satisfy the ethnomethodologists. Even though it is difficult to pin down any one set of doctrines common to those who share this label, one thing that is clear is that their iconoclasm does not stop with their complaint that traditional sociology leaves man no room to order his own actions.[13] For one thing, they also share a suspicion of the prior assumption, which I have not questioned so far, that the rules of a given social group always have a clear and unambiguous existence.

The ethnomethodologists point out that the upholding and observance of a rule requires that the people concerned be able to decide what exactly constitutes conformity to a rule. They object to this ability being taken for granted. Consider the rule, 'Be respectful to your elders'. What is to count as 'being respectful'? Addressing them as 'Sir' or 'Madam', not interrupting, not swearing . . .? Are jokes allowed? Can one contradict? Even with an apparently more definite case like 'Do not steal' there are problems. What about someone who removes goods from a shop but says he did it by mistake, or that he intended to pay later?

The ethnomethodologists argue here that the application of social rules standardly requires judgements about the *meanings* of particular actions.[14] It is only after we have somehow decided on the meaning of an action that we can decide whether it conforms to the rule or not. But for the ethnomethodologists there are no objective and unambiguous procedures for arriving at such judgements—the meanings of particular actions are always *indexical*. By this they mean that the meaning given to an action will always depend somehow on features of the particular context in question, rather than on any invariant general principle or rule specifying its meaning in any situation. They see the fixing of meaning as something actively *done* by the participants in a particular social interaction. The participants give 'accounts' or explanations of their actions. Others query these accounts and ask for further elucidation. Eventually some agreed meaning for those actions is 'negotiated'. Thus someone taken to have behaved 'disrespectfully' might try to show how his action should be construed differently—say as 'over-enthusiastic', or 'absent-minded'. The others concerned might accept his account. Or they might question it as inconsistent with other of his actions or with what he must have known. Eventually some common understanding is settled on, and social interaction proceeds from then on on that basis.[15]

Thus the ethnomethodologists are dubious about the whole idea of social rules setting up any definite guidelines for action. If rules require judgements about the meanings of actions, and if such meanings are always actively and independently negotiated by the individuals involved on each particular occasion, then in what sense can those rules be held to exert an objective influence on behaviour?

Much more generally, ethnomethodological considerations about meanings also seem to undermine the whole idea of looking for a general scientific theory of the causes of human actions. Generalisations are about classes of events objectively sharing some common property. If the meanings of actions are not objectively fixed independently of the interpretation of those actions by the individuals involved, it seems quite misguided to attempt to formulate generalisations about actions.[16]

Even more disturbing conclusions can be drawn. Given that scientific generalisation is out, the appropriate task for the sociologist is to study the *methods* by which societal members do decide the meanings of actions and thereby establish some sort of order in their continuing social interaction. Of course the sociologist himself is also, in doing this, using certain methods to attach meanings to human activities which do not have a fixed meaning independently of the application of some such methods. So if the sociologist is to have any pretensions to objectivity he needs to step back and investigate the methods which he himself uses to attach meanings to others' activity. And then, of course, he will need to detail the methods with which he conducts *that* investigation; and so on.[17]

Not all ethnomethodologists go this far towards making an impossible regress of sociology. On the other hand, some go even further. No matter. For I intend to show that there is no real substance to ethnomethodological doubts about whether actions have definite meanings apart from what the individuals involved in the particular context decide. To dispel those doubts we must examine the notion of *meaning* itself.

8. ACTION-MEANINGS AND WORD-MEANINGS

What exactly is it for something to have a *meaning*? Sometimes we speak of the reasons (beliefs, desires) behind an action as its meaning. I shall call this *action-meaning*. At other times something rather different is intended: namely, the established communicational content of a type of expression, sentence or similar sign. I shall call this *word-meaning*. As we shall see, these two senses of 'meaning' are not unrelated, nor are they the only possible ones. But it is important for us to start by keeping them separate.

Let us first concentrate on the idea that the reasons behind an action constitute its 'meaning'. Now, the ethnomethodologists are indeed right in their initial observation that the application of rules involves judgements about action-meanings. For social rules are almost invariably concerned with actions individuated in terms of reasons; what counts as conformity or deviance is not just a matter of the physical characteristics of what is done (if it is at all), but also depends on what effects the agent envisaged would result from what he did. 'Being rude', 'stealing', 'paying', 'working' and 'lying' are all descriptions which impute reasons to the agent over and above any specification of his brute bodily movements. What is more, in such cases the action description will often imply specifically that what the agent does is oriented to some wider context of social rules. For instance, someone cannot be held to be 'paying' for something unless he is acting with an awareness of a more general set of rules which make up institutions of property and exchange. In such cases the action being described is said to be *constituted* by the context of rules to which it is oriented, in the sense that the description in question can only apply to things done in such a context of rules.[18]

But what is not so clear, however, is why action-meanings have to be 'indexical', if this is supposed to imply that there is no definite answer to the question of what reasons were behind an action except whatever happens to be decided by particular negotiations on the matter. If all that is intended by the 'meaning' of an action is the motives behind it, then why should we abandon the conclusion reached in Section 3 above that it is in principle a perfectly determinate matter what beliefs and desires an agent has and is acting on? The point that these beliefs and desires might include attitudes associated with some wider context of rules makes no essential difference here. The beliefs and desires associated with rules are still beliefs and desires. What reason have we been given for rejecting the idea that there is a determinately right answer to what somebody's motives are, independently of what individuals discussing the issue happen to conclude?

It seems to me that the ethnomethodological position is at least partly due to a confusion about the nature of the 'meaning' in question. It is all too easy to fall into the following line of reasoning. 'If actions have determinate meanings, it must be in virtue of certain principles or rules which allow us to read off from the observable features of the action what it signifies. These principles would specify that each physically distinct type of action would have a certain fixed meaning whenever it occurred. But in fact we are not in error when, on different particular occasions, we ascribe different meanings to actions of the same physical kind. So there cannot be any invariant principles of the kind required to give actions objective meanings. The meaning of an action becomes fixed only when those involved in the particular context happen to reach a decision on the matter'.[19]

The mistake here lies at the beginning, and involves an erroneous assimilation of action-meaning to word-meaning. We can only scratch the surface of the theory of linguistic meaning here. But let us consider what is probably the central case, the word-meaning of assertions (that is, those utterances for which questions of truth and falsity can arise). It will be accurate enough for our purposes at this point if we take it that an assertion has the word-meaning it does in virtue of some established rule according to which someone is expected to utter a certain string of sounds only if he has a certain belief. It is because of such a rule that the sounds 'I-am-her-father', say, have the word-meaning they do in English, and that in general assertions express the beliefs they do express.

What this means is that the word-meaning of an assertion *does* depend on a rule which enables us to read off from its observable (accoustic, visual) characteristics the belief that it standardly expresses. If there were no such rule about the sounds or marks in question they would have no such determinate meaning. But it is simply a mistake to suppose that for actions in general to have determinate meanings, in the sense of motives, there must be some comparable rules laying *that* down. If I hurry home to watch the Cup Final on television, it is not some contingent social standard that makes that the reason behind my haste. Nevertheless that *is* the reason.

The point is that the action-meaning of my haste depends, not on any general agreement about the import of such behaviour, but on the actual structure of my particular motives on that particular occasion. This explains why the action-meaning of a certain type of physical behaviour can vary from context to context. People can do the same things from different motives. To find out what someone's motives are thus requires a consideration of all kinds of features of the particular context—in the above example you would need to attend to what I said about what I was doing, to what I knew about dates and television programmes, to what my past and future behaviour showed me to be interested in, etc. Given a different person in a different context the action-meaning of his hurrying home might be something quite different. But this does not show that we lack appropriate rules for reading off the action's meaning from its physical features, and are therefore somehow actively creating meanings for it by contextual negotiation. Action-meanings, unlike word-meanings, do not derive from such rules at all, so there is nothing untoward about a given physical movement varying in 'meaning' from context to context. If there is a sense in which action-meanings are 'indexical' it is simply that the methods outlined in Section 3 for uncovering the beliefs and desires behind someone's action will always require us to look at a number of features of the context in addition to the action's physical characteristics. But this does nothing to show that these methods fail to produce a determinate answer to a proper question, that we are somehow creating the meaning of the action rather than discovering it.

9. AND GRICE-MEANINGS

Any number of complications conspire to obscure the fundamental point just made. We can deal with some of them by introducing an idea due to H. P. Grice. According to Grice an agent 'non-naturally means' something by an action if he intends to produce some effect in an observer, by means of the observer recognising that that is his intention. I shall say that the intended effect in such a case is the *Grice-meaning* of the action.[20]

The point of Grice's definition is that it picks out those actions by which an agent intends to communicate some information to an observer *overtly*. We can bring this out by considering a kind of action which fails to fit Grice's definition in this respect. People often 'put on a front'—act in a certain way because they want people to take them to have certain attributes, certain traits of character, beliefs, desires, values or whatever. Thus someone may spend freely in order to suggest that he does not particularly care about money; or he may ignore slights so as to conceal he is aware of them. Given that we generally care what people think of us, and generally have ideas about what our actions will make them think of us, such motives cannot but be involved in very many of our actions. In a sense, such actions are designed to 'communicate' something to our audience. But we do not 'non-naturally mean' anything by them in Grice's sense, for the communication, such as it is, is intended to be *covert*— we do not want our observers to recognise that our intention in so acting is to get them to believe something. Indeed, if they did, it would probably defeat our object—if someone sees that your reason for spending freely is to convince him you are unconcerned about money, it will not work.

What is the connection between Grice-meaning and our earlier notions of word-meaning and action-meaning? Grice-meanings are in certain respects closely related to word-meanings. But in the end they will turn out to be essentially a special case of action-meanings.

To see the relation between Grice-meaning and word-meaning, suppose someone utters an assertion the word-meaning of which is given by a rule according to which he is expected to have a certain belief if he utters that sentence. Then, as a general rule, he will Grice-mean his hearers to take him to have that belief. For he will standardly assume that members of his own linguistic community will take him to be conforming to the rule which gives the sentence its word-meaning, and will also standardly assume that they will know he assumes that. So in so speaking he will intend that his hearers should attribute to him that belief that the sentence officially expresses, and that his hearers should do this because they realise that is what he is trying to communicate.

It is often supposed that the classic cases of covert communication—conspicuous consumption, bravado, etc.—are performed according to something like linguistic rules. But we now see this cannot be right. For if there were such rules, then people would generally have to intend the communication overtly. To essay a covert communication you must assume that others will take there to be a non-communicational basis for your action. This might still be something to do with social rules ('Well brought-up girls do not act informally with mere acquaintances'), but not rules which are recognised as making certain actions vehicles of communication. Of course, if a certain type of action is particularly suitable for putting on a front, then people will in time come to realise that it is so used. Thus with spoked hub-caps, college sweat-shirts, and various modes of social informality. But then the behaviour in question ceases to be any good for covert communication, and, if anything, becomes used for the overt expression of often rather different messages. There are various intermediate cases which complicate the picture, such as where some people but not others realise that certain actions are standardly performed with a covertly communicational intent.[21] But the basic point still stands. If an action has a definite word-meaning then it will standardly be overtly Grice-meant to convey that meaning; and, conversely, if its standard communicational content is covert then this cannot be a matter of word-meaning.

But in spite of these affinities, it would be a mistake to identify Grice-meaning with word-meaning. A number of considerations demonstrate that these are in fact quite different notions, and that it is action-meaning to which Grice-meaning should really be assimilated. The most striking is that in certain special circumstances people can use assertorical expressions to overtly communicate something quite other than those expressions' established word-meanings. People can make puns, create metaphors, and commit various other linguistic deviations. Thus people sometimes expect their audience to grasp that they are playing on the acoustic similarity of the word they actually use with some other word. Or they can invoke other kinds of associations between words. Sometimes a speaker is mistaken about the word-meaning of his utterance; or expects his hearers to be so mistaken; or expects his hearers to think that he is so mistaken. In all these cases he will use words with a certain literal word-meaning, but expect to be understood as asserting something different from that word-meaning. These are deviant cases, which is why we pick them out as *puns, metaphors* or as involving *mistakes* at all. But notwithstanding their deviancy these are all clearly cases of communication where the speaker expects to succeed because he expects his audience to recognise what he is trying to say. This shows that the Grice-meaning of an action does not have to be the same as its word-meaning.

A rather different argument to the same conclusion is that it is on occasion perfectly possible to Grice-mean something by an action which does not have any generally recognised import established by rules at all. Imagine that Sherlock Holmes unexpectedly ceases walking constitutionally with Dr Watson and settles himself next to a man on a Regent's Park bench, not as a pre-arranged signal, but because he knows that Dr Watson will be able to work out from this that he has somehow deduced that the man is the criminal they are seeking. Holmes intends that Watson will be led to see what he has concluded by recognising that this intention must be behind his, Holmes's, action. So Holmes's communication to Watson is overt in Grice's sense (even if it is hidden from the criminal), but it is not in virtue of any established rules, even private ones, that it tells Watson what it does.

In fact, there is a far more significant class of cases where people Grice-mean in the absence of any relevant word-meanings. So far I have concentrated on cases of Grice-meaning where the intention is simply to get the audience to recognise that the speaker has a certain belief. But the simple conveying of beliefs is not the only kind of effect that an action can be Grice-meant to produce. Commands, questions, wishes, requests, entreaties, warnings, promises, offers, and so on, are all kinds of actions intended to produce quite specific effects in an observer, by means of his recognising that that is what the agent is aiming at. To take just one example of a so-called 'speech-act', to communicate a warning to someone is to alert him to some potential danger by getting him to see that that is what you are trying to do. In general, people can perform such speech-acts perfectly well without invoking any special word-meanings. To adapt an example from P. F. Strawson, someone saying to a skater, 'The ice over there is thin', would be the paradigm of someone Grice-meaning his action as a *warning*.[22] But the only linguistic rules involved are those that relate to the use of those sounds as an assertion and make it express the straightforward belief it does. What makes those sounds function additionally as a warning are simply the features of the particular context (it is a potential skater who is being addressed). In different contexts the same words could without any linguistic deviation be overtly intended as an entreaty, say, or as a command (consider a child who wants his father to let him go fishing, or an army officer who thinks his men need a winter swim). We do, it is true, have special word-meanings in English which can be used for the general categories of interrogations and imperatives, namely the interrogative and imperative moods. We also, just about, have an optative mood for expressing wishes as such ('Oh for a pint of bitter'). In addition, we have special forms of words for situations where it is especially important for instutional reasons that it be absolutely clear what speech-act is being performed (as when the jury's foreman says, 'Guilty'). No doubt all languages have some similar devices. But nevertheless it would be a mistake to think that all speech-acts on all occasions only manage to have the Grice-meanings they do by virtue of invoking suitable word-meanings for that purpose.

We have now seen that while Grice-meanings have certain affinities with word-meanings, there are various significant cases which de-monstrate that Grice-meanings by no means always derive from word-meanings. The point of all this is that it enables us to better understand the possibility of falling into the ethnomethodological error. The closeness of Grice-meanings to word-meanings makes it very easy indeed to suppose that if an action has a definite Grice-meaning this will have to be fixed by a rule which gives the action a word-meaning readable off from its observable physical characteristics. But then the cases where Grice-meanings turn out not to be so derived make it tempting to conclude that the actions in question cannot have any fixed content except what people discussing the matter decide to give them. And then perhaps some such thought as that all actions are somehow communicational suggests that this conclusion ought to be extrapolated to actions in general.

But the right way to read the puzzle, such as it is, is to realise that Grice-meanings are at bottom just a special case of action-meanings. By definition the Grice-meaning of an action is to do with the reasons for which the agent performs it. So to find out the Grice-meaning of someone's action, if it has one, what we have to do is uncover the actual structure of his motives in the old way. Does he intend to produce a certain response in his observers by means of their recognising that he intends to produce this response? There is still no reason to think there is not a perfectly determinate answer to this question, even if arriving at it still requires a consideration of many complex features of the particular context.

Nor is there any special puzzle about Grice-meanings sometimes corresponding to word-meanings and sometimes not. The easiest way to convey something overtly by an action is of course to get oneself to be taken to be conforming to a rule which gives that action an established word-meaning. But that is not the only way. An action's word-meaning, if it does have one, can be viewed as a kind of abstraction from the way it actually is used by particular people on particular occasions. This abstraction is given by a rule which lays down how the action *ought* to be, or is *expected* to be, used, and which thereby specifies its word-meaning as an invariant function of its physical characteristics. But, as with all such rules, there are deviations. So, as with puns, mistakes, etc., people can quite determinately give an action a Grice-meaning which is at variance with its established word-meaning. And, apart from this, there is the possibility, as with Holmes and as with non-basic speech acts, of Grice-meaning by an action things which do not conflict with any word-meanings involved but which simply transcend them.

Perhaps it is worth quickly mentioning here a couple of further ways in which word-meanings relate to action-meanings, but which still do not give us any reason to doubt that the latter have a determinate existence. Firstly, as I shall discuss in Chapter 6, people from different cultures have different concepts for ordering and describing their natural and social environments. Conceptual variations across cultures undoubtedly derive in the first instance from the different linguistic trainings to which people in different cultures are subject. And one consequence of such conceptual variation is that the kinds of motives a given people can have, the ends they can adopt and envisage, will vary from culture to culture. So there is a sense in which the reasons behind people's actions, the action-meanings of what they do, will always depend on the word-meanings their language is able to express. But even this connection between action-meaning and word-meaning (quite different from those discussed so far) does not make the attribution of reasons arbitrary. As Chapter 6 will make clear, it is perfectly possible in principle to overcome cross-cultural conceptual divergences and decide objectively on an alien people's motives. Secondly, and rather less seriously, there is the point that whenever we use words to describe an action, alien or otherwise, we avail ourselves of the word-meanings of *our* language to do so. However, if this truism is in itself supposed to somehow make the 'meanings' of *actions* indeterminate, then it would seem to follow that anything we ever speak of, including such things as sticks and stones, must have indeterminate 'meanings'. Perhaps there is some sense in such a thought, to do with the general way in which the conceptual schemes behind languages vary across time and culture, but it can scarcely be something which raises any distinctive problem about the study of human action.

So, all in all, we have found no reason to accede to the general ethnomethodological worry that the meanings of actions are indeterminate. We can continue to maintain the view that there are objectively existing reasons behind what people do. Even communicative actions themselves turned out to require understanding in terms of their issuing from definite desires (to produce a certain response in an audience) and beliefs (that a certain utterance or action will achieve this). So there is no reason to abandon the idea of a scientific theory showing human agents' reasons to be objective causes of their actions. Having argued this at some length, it is worth acknowledging that the ethnomethodologists *do* raise some important issues about the more particular question of whether social rules have a definite and unambiguous influence on what people do.

For one thing, it needs to be admitted that in practice people often do 'negotiate' with others about the meaning of their actions. They will often try to convince sceptics that their motives were admirable or reputable. Without in any way going back on the idea that it is an objective matter what people's motives really are, we can recognise that what is publicly decided about such motives will often depend on how particular negotiations on the matter turn out. (This might depend on such things as the relative power of the participants,[23] their success at deceiving others by 'putting on a front', etc.) And insofar as whether a given rule is deemed applicable to a particular action depends on whether or not the agent is agreed to have had the motives under negotiation, then we can allow the ethnomethodologists that the socially effective import of that rule will be affected by the possibility of entering negotiations on whether one transgressed it or not.

Then there is a rather different sense in which people can on occasion 'negotiate' about rules. So far we have been supposing that any indeterminacy in the application of rules arises from difficulties about telling what motives people acted from. But even if this is not under dispute at all, there can still be disagreement about whether a rule was broken or not. Suppose it is absolutely clear and agreed on all sides that someone taking goods from a shop intended to pay later. We might still have a problem in deciding if he was *stealing*. Here it is the content of the rule as such, rather than the content of his action, which needs clarification. We need to decide whether such-and-such motives condemn someone as a thief; this is quite separate from the earlier problem of deciding whether somebody actually has such-and-such motives. But it is easy enough to see how here too people might 'negotiate', and somehow settle the issue by persuasion, bargaining, bullying, appeal to precedent or whatever.

Whether the existence of either of these kinds of 'negotiation' is sufficient to justify the ethnomethodologists' thoroughgoing distrust of social rules as determinate influences on people's behaviour is another question. We can allow that people can on occasion deceive others (and perhaps themselves) about the motives behind their actions, without giving up altogether the idea that social rules guide actions in the definite kind of way discussed in Sections 5 and 6 above. For it remains an open question how far such deception is an exceptional case, by contrast with those instances where people know full well what others will make of what they are up to. And the fact that social rules themselves can be vague even where the motives behind given actions are uncontentious might well similarly be argued to be an essentially deviant case. Even if we admit that all rules have some periphery of vagueness, it seems likely that most at least will have an unambiguous core where it is clear whether an action with given motives constitutes a transgression or not.

In any case, the extent to which ethnomethodological doubts about social rules as such are justified is irrelevant to the more general thesis of this chapter. For even if they were fully justified, it would not follow that people's actions do not flow from determinate motives. It would simply mean that the motives in question are never the simple kind of rule-oriented 'associated attitudes' discussed in Sections 5 and 6. Even if people never take social rules for granted, but always think in addition about what interpretation is likely to be put upon their actions, and about how any unclarity in the relevant rules is likely to be resolved, it still remains the case that they are acting on the basis of definite thoughts, albeit more complicated ones than is standardly supposed.

In this chapter I have argued that human actions can be explained causally. What exactly has the explanation of individual human actions got to do with social scientific explanation in general? Many will wish to object that social science proper proceeds on a quite different level from the realm of individual action. Indeed a common response to the work of the ethnomethodological school is that, interesting as it is about the niceties of how people manage their personal interaction, it is irrelevant to the explanation of large-scale developments in social structures. In the next chapter I shall turn to an examination of the relationship between explaining individual phenomena and the explanation of large-scale social development as such.

On a more specific level it might be observed that, insofar as social science does involve analysis on an individual level, it is unlikely that there will be much interest in detailing the connections between people's motives and their consequent behaviour. Surely the more pressing question will always be why people have the motives they do—that they act as they do given their motives can generally be taken for granted. I would not want to contest this observation. My concern in this chapter has been more metaphysical than methodological, namely to show that there is nothing about the nature of human activity in itself that precludes the application of causal notions. Still, the discussion of various kinds of rules in Sections 5 and 6 did go some way towards indicating, on a general level, how certain desires and beliefs can get instilled in people. This kind of question will be further covered in the last two chapters. In Chapter 6 I shall consider how the different systems of abstract beliefs found in different cultures might be accounted for. And the discussion in Chapter 7 will include various further observations about the way in which dominant social values might affect the beliefs people adopt.

5 Men and History

1. THE WHY AND THE WHAT OF SOCIAL FACTS

In Chapters 1 and 2 I argued that social facts did not involve any level of reality other than that comprised by aggregates of individuals and their characteristics. This amounted to a defence of an 'individualist' position against the 'Durkheimian' view. But I took pains there to point out that I was concerned purely with the 'what' and not with the 'why' of social facts. That is, I was asking only what social facts *are*, not how they should be *explained*.

As we saw, these two kinds of questions are certainly different. To decide that a norm against exogamy *is* nothing more than a shared attitude against marriages outside the group, or that inflation *is* simply people being able to get less goods in exchange for a given monetary unit, does not tell us what *explanations* are appropriate for the presence of such a norm, or for a change in the value of money. We know *what* must obtain for a certain description to be true, but not *why* that obtains, if it does.

This difference is often obscured by the terminology of 'holists' and 'individualists'. It is conventional to apply this same 'holist — individualist' terminology both to debates about the constitution of social facts and to controversies about the explanation of social facts. It was partly in order to resist this conflation that I chose 'Durkheimian' rather than 'holist' to describe the anti-individualist position on the constitution of social facts.

There are a number of reasons why it is important to remain clear about the difference between the 'what' and the 'why' questions. For one thing, as was pointed out in Chapter 1, there seem to be some perfectly good senses in which one might be an individualist on the 'what' question, as I am, and yet a holist on the 'why' question. I even suggested that it could make sense to be a holist (Durkheimian) on the 'what' question and a kind of individualist on the 'why'. So it is a mistake to simply assume that answers to the 'what' question have obvious implications for the 'why' question. What is more, once we do take care to distinguish these two questions, it is possible to show that there are a number of seperate strands to the 'why' question itself, all of which require independent treatment.

In this chapter I am going to distinguish and analyse three different views that an 'individualist' about the explanation of social facts might be concerned to defend, and a 'holist' might wish to deny. Firstly there is the claim that in explaining a social fact it is essential to give an explanation of all the individual facts that make it up. (This will be dealt with in Sections 2 and 3.) Secondly, there is the view that social facts are often historical accidents, to be explained, if at all, not by other social facts, but by the occurrence of coincidences or the actions of socially exceptional individuals (Section 4). Finally, there will be the thesis that social facts and their development are in general to be accounted for by the exercise of human free will, and not by the influence of impersonal forces beyond human control (Section 5).

As we shall see, these three claims each raise rather different issues. There is no uniform way of answering all three simultaneously. Roughly speaking, I shall show the 'holist' to be right on the first question, and the 'individualist' to be right on the last two. But this is only very roughly speaking: there is a nest of philosophical problems behind the conventional formulations of these questions which ensures that any simple answers will be misleading. (For instance, I shall show that, despite appearances, an individualist position on either of the last two issues is quite consistent with determinism, the view that every event has a cause.)

One last preliminary point: I have argued that, however they are to be explained, social facts consist of nothing more than aggregates of individuals and their characteristics. Perhaps the most interesting amongst such social facts are those that, so to speak, have the property of perpetuating themselves, like the norms and conventions discussed in the previous chapter. However, I shall not restrict the term 'social fact' to these cases, but shall use it to refer to any large-scale feature of society whatsoever. So the average age of a social group will be a 'social fact', as much as its property system. While this obviously introduces a certain arbitrariness—there is no obvious point at which the scale becomes 'large' enough to move from the individual to the social—nothing I shall argue for will depend on exactly how this distinction is drawn.

2. DIFFERENT ASPECTS OF SOCIAL HAPPENINGS

The first question is whether social facts necessarily have to be explained by means of explaining their individual components. Of the three questions distinguished above, this is perhaps the one that most concerns professional sociologists. For if sociological explanations did always so have to be 'reduced' to explanations of individual facts, it would become unclear what made sociology a distinct discipline separate from individual psychology.

Perhaps this is part of the attraction of the Durkheimian view on the 'what' of social facts. For if social facts involved something more than their individual components, then of course explaining such social facts would of necessity be more than a matter of explaining their individual components—there would always be what happened on the distinctively social level of reality to explain as well.

But fortunately for those sociologists concerned with academic demarcation disputes the reduction of explanations of social facts to explanations of their individual components is not essential, even given that we must reject the Durkheimian view of the constitution of social facts. At first sight this may seem puzzling. If social facts are made of nothing more than the totality of their individual components, then surely to explain one is simply, *per se*, to explain the other?

But consider. An increase in the suicide rate in some society is fairly obviously definable in individual terms, as the change in the proportion of people committing suicide in successive time intervals. Now take the general proposition that increases in social mobility lead to increases in the suicide rate. It would seem that this generalisation would enable us to explain the particular fact that the suicide rate in a certain society increased in a certain period, given that we could establish that social mobility had increased there (and that other relevant factors did not vary). But notwithstanding the obvious definability of suicide rates in individual terms, such an explanation clearly does not derive from or involve explanations of the individual facts in question. For the individual facts involved are individuals committing suicide; yet the explanation at hand will clearly not tell us why *those* people committed suicide, while others did not—why, that is, it was the unfortunate Jones, but not Smith, who contributed to the rise in the figures. All that is explained is why the rate as a whole went up, not why the particular people involved did what they did.

There seems to be something of a paradox here. If a particular suicide rate *is* nothing but Jones, Brown and some specified others committing suicide, how can we explain it without explaining of Jones, Brown, etc., why they committed suicide? To resolve this we need to consider the basic structure of scientific explanations. At its simplest, we invoke a generalisation of the form 'All Fs are Gs' to explain of a particular thing, *a*, which happens to be an F, why it is also a G. Now, in doing this we clearly do not explain *all* the properties of *a*. Our generalisation, and consequently our explanation, deals only with one specific aspect of *a*, namely its being a G. In general, whenever we explain any occurrence we only explain one *aspect* of what happens, never, *per impossibile*, the event in all its 'concrete particularity'.

In the example at hand there being an increase in the suicide rate is one aspect of what happened on that particular occasion; the increase being 'fulfilled' by those particular individuals who did commit suicide rather than by others was a different (though not unrelated) aspect of what occurred. And so there is no reason why the generalisation which explains the former aspect should automatically yield an explanation of the latter.

To explain why a social phenomenon is 'fulfilled' by the relevant things happening to certain definite individuals rather than to others we need, not some generalisation about the overall situation which gives sufficient conditions for a social phenomenon of that kind, but generalisations about *individuals*, stating factors which lead individuals to have the relevant individual characteristics. Thus to explain why that particular batch of individuals, rather than others, committed suicide, we need to know not simply that overall increases in social mobility produce, *ceteris paribus*, overall increases in the suicide rate, but something along the following lines: that certain kinds of individuals will commit suicide if they move upwards socially; or that certain kinds of individuals will commit suicide if they move downwards socially; or that certain kinds of individuals will commit suicide if their acquaintances are socially mobile while they are static.

It is true that if we explain, of the particular individuals who did so, why they committed suicide, by means of whichever of these latter generalisations is supported by the evidence, then we will also along the way have explained the more general aspect of the matter, namely, why there was an overall increase in the suicide rate. For the 'individual' generalisation invoked will, roughly speaking, have the 'social' generalisation as a consequence. But this does not mean that we cannot give an explanation of a social phenomenon at all unless we have an explanation of the way it is individually fulfilled. For we might well be in the position of having the 'social' generalisation required to explain the social fact as such, without knowing what the appropriate 'individual' generalisation is. As illustrated above, there will *a priori* be a number of different possibilities for what is going on at the level of the individual components of a social fact, for any given generalisation which allows us to explain it merely as that kind of social fact. This is because the description of a particular occurrence simply as a certain kind of social phenomenon will as a rule leave open the more specific matter of exactly which individuals in the society in question had the relevant character-istics. Since we need to explain more in explaining the latter matter, we need more in the way of general knowledge to do it.

Even when we *do* have individual generalisations which would allow us to explain the individual details of a social fact, in addition to explaining just why the social fact itself occurred , we might well not be concerned to do so. As a rule the sociologist will be interested in large-scale social facts as such, and not concerned to explain why some definite individuals and not others played certain parts in those social phenom-ena. If someone was concerned to explain, say, urbanisation in nineteenth-century Britain, it would merely hide the wood for the trees to have to demonstrate, for every actual person who moved townwards, the circumstances in his individual situation that led him to do so. But of course there is no necessity for this. Now that we are clear that the occurrence of a social fact and the way it is individually fulfilled are distinct aspects of what happens, and therefore call for different explanations, we can see how we can explain the former without explaining the latter, even in those cases where it is in our power to do both.

3. REDUCTION TO TYPICAL INDIVIDUALS

I have so far argued that the 'holist' answer to our first question is the right one: there is no necessity, in explaining a particular social phenomenon, to do so via giving an explanation of its individual components. But there are still strong arguments against this holist answer. So far I have been implicitly taking it that generalisations about social facts will be cast in a precise deterministic form. But I am scarcely entitled to this. As pointed out in Chapter 3 it is inevitable that almost any available generalisation relating social facts will be statistical in form. It would be surprising indeed if on every occasion that social mobility had increased in any society there had been a corresponding increase in suicides. What we find rather is that on *most* such occasions the suicide rate increased.

Some writers argue that this gives us reasons for rejecting the holist answer to our first question. [1] The difficulty they raise is one discussed in Chapter 3. The fact that two factors are statistically associated does not guarantee that one is the cause of the other. It might well be a 'spurious' association, due to the two factors both being independent collateral effects of some yet further factor. Even if there is a well-established statistical relationship between social mobility and suicide rates we have no warrant for taking the former to be the cause of the latter, rather than, say, their both being the common effect of a higher level of education. So, since it is only genuine causes that explain, we will be quite unable to substantiate our putative explanation of the increased suicide rate. And this problem will be quite general, given the inevitably statistical nature of social scientific generalisations.

The argument of these writers is that the only way to deal with this problem is to explain our 'macro-generalisation' in individual terms. The idea is that, unless we know what interactional and psychological processes lie behind our gross statistical correlations between large-scale social facts, we will not be able to check whether or not that correlation does indeed reflect an explanatory connection of the required kind. [2]

It is worth being clear about this argument. It is not based on some general notion that it is invalid to use a generalisation in an explanation unless we have some explanation of that generalisation itself. As pointed out in Section 2 of Chapter 3 this principle leads quickly to an absurd regress. The idea is rather that the unavoidably statistical format of social scientific macro-generalisations gives us a specific problem about the possibility of spurious causation; and it is specifically this latter difficulty that requires us to have individual explanations for social scientific generalisations before we can use them in explaining social facts.

Now it is true enough that such explanatory reductions of macro-generalisations to underlying individual processes can help with the problem of 'spurious' causes. As when we explain any generalisation such a reduction shows us in more detail the underlying chains of events which so to speak 'link' up the originally related phenomena. And this can give us a check on our specifically causal assumptions. For instance, if we know that what lies behind the social mobility – suicide association is the fact that a movement up the social scale will in certain kinds of individuals initiate a psychological process which can lead to suicide, then we will have grounds for rejecting the idea that the correlation between social mobility and suicide is merely a matter of their both being collateral effects of increased education or some other such factor. For we will have reason to suppose that there are circumstances in which increased social mobility will initiate processes which will suffice for increased suicides, quite independently of whether or not there is any antecedent alteration in educational level or whatever. (Compare the argument at the end of Section 3 of Chapter 3, where I showed how an explanation of what underlies the general virus-infection–fever conjunction would show whether the infection was a cause of the fever or merely a side-effect. The problem there was the rather different one of sorting out causes in the specially awkward kind of deterministic case, but the principle is the same.)

It would be a mistake, however, to now abandon the 'holist' position defended in the last section. There are two reasons for this. Firstly, the kind of individual reduction now being recommended is rather different from that the necessity of which was denied in the last section. And, secondly, there are grounds for doubting whether a knowledge of underlying processes is essential for resolving difficulties about spurious causes anyway.

I shall take these points in order. The demand that we understand the individual processes behind some 'macro-generalisation' is a far less strict requirement than that we should always explain social facts by explaining their individual components. The reason is that we are not necessarily being asked to apply our understanding to the specific individuals involved in any particular case. We can know what kind of psychological and interactional chains link social mobility and suicide rates in general, without, so to speak, having to 'localise' the process whenever we apply the generalisation; that is, without actually identifying the specific individuals who committed suicide and showing the actual sequence of events leading up to their doing so.

To be sure, we would have the general information required to give such a detailed account if desired—to show, of each of the individual components of the social phenomenon, what led to *it* being as it was. But, as pointed out at the end of the last section, even if we have the ability to explain the individual components of some social fact in this way we will not as a rule be concerned to do so, for our interest will standardly be focused on the social fact as such.

To have the kind of explanatory understanding which helps with difficulties about spurious causation, all that is needed is that we be *able* to trace out the individual histories involved in the social fact, not that we should actually do so in any particular case. Thus we can judge that increased social mobility actually causes increased suicides, rather than merely being associated with it, if we know how social mobility initiates, in certain individuals, psychological processes which can lead to suicide, even if we do not utilise this knowledge in any particular case to show why it was Jones, rather than Smith, who killed himself.[3]

Characteristically we will manifest our knowledge of the underlying processes leading to the occurrence of social phenomena by elaborating the sequence of events which a 'typical individual' will undergo in the kind of situation in question. That is, we will consider in the abstract a kind of person satisfying certain conditions, and then trace out a process of development; but we will standardly not apply this story in accounting for what happens to any *actual* individual.

The difference between reducing sociological explanations to explanations in terms of actual individuals and reducing them to explanations in terms of typical individual is often found puzzling.[4] The solution to this puzzle is that these two kinds of reduction are directed to different ends. Explanation in terms of actual individuals is appropriate when we wish not only to explain why a social phenomenon of a given kind occurred, but in addition to explain why it was 'individually fulfilled' in the way it was. Explanation in terms of typical individuals serves a quite different purpose—it tells us what *accounts* for general macro-correlations between social facts, and thereby helps to assure us that there really is a *causal* link involved. So even if typical individual reductions of social scientific explanations are necessary, this does not affect the conclusion of the last section that reductions to actual individuals are not. But *is* it necessary to have even typical individual reducations?

The argument was that typical individual reductions are essential if we are to be sure that sociological correlations reflect that right kind of causal link. I have admitted that typical individual reductions are one way of helping with this problem. But if we return to the arguments of Chapter 3, we will see that they are not the only way. For it was shown in Chapter 3 that there are perfectly good statistical techniques for checking whether an association between two social factors really does indicate a causal connection, which can be applied without explaining that association in individual terms.

In outline, it will be recalled, these involved 'controlling' for other factors which might be producing a 'spurious' connection. Thus, for instance, if we were worried that the association between social mobility and suicide rates was spurious, owing to their both being affected by educational levels, we should investigate whether the association disappears *within* sets of cases all coinciding with respect to educational advance. If it does disappear, the association is spurious; if it does not disappear, then it is not simply a matter of the influence of educational levels.

Of course the use of such techniques to demonstrate that a statistical association really does reflect the required kind of causal connection has to involve a number of further assumptions. As shown in Chapter 3, we need firstly to know, of any two factors which enter into our analysis, which would be the cause and which the effect, if there were a direct causal connection between them. And secondly we need to be sure that we have included in our analysis all the other causes of our putative effect that our putative cause might be associated with.

But as we saw earlier the need for these assumptions did not suffice to discredit the statistical techniques in question. The first requirement, that we have an initial ordering of the factors in our analysis, can be dealt with by considering the time sequence of those factors, or where necessary, by extending the analysis and using 'time-lagged' versions of the original factors. The second requirement was admittedly less easy to satisfy. But the crucial point was that *any* procedure for getting at causes requires some assumption to be made about the range of possible influences confounding our observations. This applied even if we avoided statistics and used Mill's methods of eliminative induction. And it would apply to analysis of the individual level as much as to analysis on the macro-social level. There is, so far as I can see, no obvious reason why it should be any more difficult to satisfy when we are working with statistical connections between macro-facts than anywhere else.

I have now argued that neither reduction to actual individuals nor reducation to typical individuals is essential for social scientific explanations. It is perhaps worth distinguishing my defence of a 'holist' answer to the first question of this chapter from that which would be mounted by a traditional Durkheimian. I am not saying we *cannot* have individual reductions of social scientific explanation on the grounds that the explananda of such explanations exist in some supra-individual realm. On the contrary, I would hold that it is in principle always possible to give an individual reduction (of either kind) for any sociological explanation. Insofar as social facts are in the end constituted by aggregates of individual facts and nothing more, it should always be possible, in long-term principle at least, if not in foreseeable practice, to uncover the underlying connections between the individual components comprising those social facts which would enable us, if we so wished, to give typical or actual individual reducations. The point I have been making in these last two sections is simply that such knowledge about the individual level is by no means an essential prerequisite for using macro-sociological generalisations in explaining why a social fact of a certain kind occurred on some particular occasion.

What is more, while the Durkheimian will see the search for such individual knowledge as essentially misguided, I would argue that it is for a number of reasons perfectly desirable even if not absolutely essential. It is our ability to give typical individual reductions that is of interest here. As pointed out, actual individual reduction generally only serves to obscure the social wood with the individual trees. But there are real advantages to typical individual reductions. We have already seen how they can be of some real help in distinguishing genuine from spurious causes. It is also undeniable that we in some sense will have a deeper understanding of what is going on when we can explain our macro-generalisations: we will see how they are expectable conse-quences of individual truths which are applicable in a wider range of contexts than the specific kind of social circumstance under exam-ination.[5] Moreover, and related to this, there is also the important point that we will attach greater warrant to those macro-generalisations for which we can give a typical individual account. The historical and comparative evidence for social scientific generalisations will often be extremely fragmentary, and even with statistical generalisations we will often be concerned about the validity of extrapolating from our sample to further cases. However, if we can show how such a generalisation is a consequence of various socio-psychological truths of more general application, then that generalisation will receive the extra empirical support which accrues to those socio-psychological principles in virtue of that wider application.

But none of these considerations show that we cannot get by at all without individual reductions. We certainly have some reasons for wanting such reductions, but none are conclusive. We have other ways of sorting out genuine from spurious causes. We can survive without the deeper satisfaction of knowing why the macro-generalisations we use in social explanations hold good. And there is no reason to dismiss altogether the possibility that the direct evidence might on occasion provide adequate corroboration for some macro-generalisations. In concert the various reasons for wanting individual reductions might account for the gut feeling of some thinkers that we have not *really* got a social explanation until we can back it up with a typical individual story.[6] But there is no sound basis for this feeling.

Now we are clear about all this we can see why most social scientific explanations in fact involve a mixture of purely macro- with individual generalisations; why, that is, we standardly offer some kind of idea of some of the individual processes behind the macro-connections we invoke, even though these are nothing like enough to give a complete explanation of why those macro-connections hold. The reason of course is that while we can get by without individual reductions, they do have a number of attractions. So even though there is fortunately no compulsion to account completely for sociological explanations in individual terms, we will have good reasons to make such gestures in that direction as we can.

4. HISTORICAL DETERMINISM

In the last section I took it for granted that social facts can be explained causally. My concern was solely with the question of how, if at all, such explanations needed to relate to the individual components of social facts. So I implicitly assumed that social facts can be determined to occur by prior sufficient conditions. True, I have allowed that we might often not be able to *state* such conditions, and would have to settle for statistical associations. But I have taken it that in basing explanations on such statistical associations we at least assume that there *is* a deterministic generalisation which makes the explanans part of a sufficient condition for the explanandum.

But *are* social events determined by prior sufficient conditions? Many readers will have felt uneasy about this idea. It seems to suggest there is a prearranged plan to the whole of history, with each stage inevitably following the one before according to invariable laws. And this seems to be at variance with the intuitively plausible idea that historical developments are often 'accidents', depending on odd confluences of factors or on unpredictable decisions by influential individuals.

In this section I am going to examine the idea of historical determinism and the uneasiness it gives rise to. But there is one aspect of the matter I shall ignore for the time being. This is the resistance to historical determinism which stems from our conviction that we are free to affect the course of history. The argument that history cannot be determined since we can alter what is going to happen by the exercise of our free will will be considered in the next section. For the moment I wish to evaluate the claim that history is determined without bringing in any intuitions we may have about our freedom to change it.

Let us take it that an event is determined if it has a cause. This requires that there were prior conditions which according to some general law are always followed by an event of the kind in question. If this was so then in an obvious sense we can say that it was laid down that that event was going to happen as soon as those prior conditions occured.

We can say that a process is a deterministic one if each stage is determined by some features amongst the previous stages, back to some starting point. Once a deterministic process has started the whole course of the process is fixed.

Universal determinism is the thesis that the whole history of the universe forms a deterministic process: that everything that happens is an inevitable outcome of prior events, and so on backwards—to the beginning of time, if there was one, or for ever if there was not.

Now clearly *historical determinism* is not the same as universal determinism. One obvious difference is that it is narrower in scope—it asserts not that everything in the universe follows a preassigned programme, but only that the specific sequence of events starting with the beginnings of human society, and comprising its subsequent development on the social level, are all determined. But this is not the only difference. Even if we restrict our attention to human macro-history, what is normally understood by 'historical determinism' is a quite special kind of determinism. The historical determinist is not just saying that every large-scale development in human history is de-termined. It would be quite consistent with this latter claim to allow that an 'exceptional individual' had influenced the course of history, provided only that we simultaneously allowed that his unusualness was determined by, say, his idiosyncratic upbringing or his rare mixture of genes, which in turn were determined by his parents' characteristics or the mechanics of his conception, ... What the advocates of historical determinism are normally concerned to defend is the far more specific idea that the causes of social events are themselves always to be found amongst prior *social* events—that no essential part is played in the causation of the large-scale features of society by anything other than the prior large-scale features of that society. Thus the view of the historical determinist would be that it is in principle possible to predict the future state of a society from knowledge of such large-scale characteristics alone, without ever having to bring in such things as the presence of exceptional individuals, etc. In this respect historical determinism is a far stronger claim than universal determinism, one which might well be false even if every event, including every social event, is determined. For universal determinism could well remain true even if the causes of social events were not always other *social* developments. [7]

Some historical determinists in the Marxist tradition propose the even stronger thesis that all large-scale developments in any society can be accounted for solely by reference to the *economic* features of that society. The criticisms I have of historical determinism in general will apply *a fortiori* to this special version of it. [8]

Historical determinism implies that it is in principle always possible to predict the future large-scale features of a society from its present ones. An objection that immediately offers itself is that the development of a particular social system is often subject to the influence of factors entering the system from without. Conquests, the spread of religious ideas from neighbouring societies, or changes in the natural enviornment, to mention but a few such factors, have manifestly made a great difference to the development of many societies on many occasions. This would seem a knock-down argument against the idea that the development of any given society depends on nothing but the prior large-scale set-up in that society.

However, there is a reasonable enough defence open to the historical determinist here. Even the most uncontroversially deterministic system, such as a number of celestial bodies interacting gravitationally, is subejct to interference from extraneous factors, as when a new body enters the system from without. The claim that a given system is deterministic with respect to certain features—that the states of those features at one time determine their states at any later time—is always made subject to the *caveat* that the system remains 'closed' (that is, isolated from interference from without the system). Of course the *usefulness* of viewing something as a deterministic system, or, for that matter, as a system at all, depends on its actually remaining as a rule closed for appreciable stretches of time. If it is never closed for long then we can achieve a deterministic perspective on its behaviour only by seeing it as part of some larger system which does standardly remain closed. But if we are to dispense with *caveats* about closedness altogether even the most thoroughgoing determinist will need to include the whole universe in his analysis. For only when all possible intruders have already been included in the system we are analysing can we guarantee there will be no interference from outside.

So the historical determinist would be justified in making his thesis the claim that earlier facts about a society determine its later ones *only as long as* it remains free from interference by outside factors. When such factors do operate they can well make a difference to subsequent developments within the society, and so to view those developments as determined we will have to step back and consider the society under investigation as part of some larger system.

But even given this refinement historical determinism still seems open to easy refutation. It scarcely seems open to dispute, for instance, that post-war economic developments in Western industrial nations would have been different if we did not have the economic theories formulated by Keynes; or that inflation under the Wilson—Callaghan British Labour government in the nineteen-seventies would have been higher if the leaders of the trade union movement had not been prepared to co-operate with the government (leaving aside the question of whether it was their supporting an incomes policy or acquiescing in monetary stringency that was more significant in this respect). Surely here we have cases where large-scale social phenomena depend essentially on small-scale developments. And, since social systems are not something different from the sum of their individual components, we cannot admissibly argue here that these small-scale developments are intrusions from outside the system under study.

At this point the historical determinist can adopt a different ploy. While accepting the existence of such examples, he can deny that they in fact refute his position. For he can allow that the small-scale developments mentioned were in a sense prerequisites of subsequent social developments, but accommodate this by arguing that they were themselves inevitable consequences of other large-scale social factors operative at the time. He can admit that social things would have been different *if* Keynesian economic theories had not been formulated, but argue that neverthless the general intellectual and social situation in the nineteen-thirties made it inevitable that such theories *would* be formulated. And in support of this he can point to the existence of a number of other writers with similar ideas at the time. Similarly, he can accept that *if* trade union leaders did not co-operate inflation would be higher, but argue that this is only to say that if the general state of the trade union movement were different so would inflation be, since the decisions of those leaders depends not on any individual whim but on the relevant features of the general social situation.

In this way it would be possible for the historical determinist to insist that such significant individual decisions etc. are always simply part of large-scale social processes, in the precise sense that a proper understanding of the relevant generalisations would always allow us to predict social developments without bringing them in. (He can then allow that we could predict such small-scale developments too, if we were interested; but for him this is simply because such developments are ensured by general socialisation processes, or by perceptions of the situation that would be adopted by anybody in the relevant position, or by the nature of the procedures by which people are selected for positions of power, etc.)

Nonetheless, now that we are reasonably clear about what is at issue, it is in the end difficult to see what good arguments there could be for accepting historical determinism as so far characterised. Why should the kind of defence just outlined work in all cases? Take Lenin's early death, for instance. This was surely not entirely determined by large-scale social factors. Yet there are grounds for thinking that if Stalin had not come to power at that point some large-scale aspects of the subsequent history of the Soviet Union would have been different. Perhaps this particular judgement would be a mistake—perhaps a better analysis would show how Lenin himself would have been constrained to act as Stalin did even if he had survived. But why should *any* such judgement be a mistake? The historical determinist has to claim that, given any putative counter-example where a large-scale development apparently depends on some small-scale change, either

(i)   despite appearances, the small-scale change was not *significant*— other macro-social factors would have ensured the large-scale development even if the small-scale change in question had not occurred (Lenin had survived), or

(ii) the small-scale change was not an *accident*—while the large-scale development would indeed not have eventuated without the small-scale change, the small-scale change (Keynesian theories, trade union co-operation) was itself an inevitable consequence of other macro-social factors.

In any particular case, the validity of one or the other of these diagnoses requires that a generalisation of a quite specific kind applies to the situation. The point I am urging is that there seems no warrant whatsoever for supposing that such generalisations will always in principle be available. Perhaps it would be wrong to dismiss historical determinism out of hand—it is abstractly possible that in the end careful investigation of problematic examples and comparison with relevantly similar situations will always show putative counter-examples to be either not historically significant or not historical accidents. But in the absence of any specific arguments to the contrary it seems far more reasonable to allow that at least some changes in some of the large-scale features of some societies have on occasion depended in some part on historical accidents.

There is one final retreat the historical determinist might try at this point. He could admit that some social developments do indeed depend on accidents at the micro-level. But he could suggest that this is only true insofar as we are looking at the *details* of a society's large-scale development. The idea would be that only, say, the timing of certain changes, or the specific form they take, depend on factors not themselves socially determined. If we step back from the details, the historical determinist might say, and look instead at the broad sweep of history, then we will appreciate the determinism of the process. Thus it might be that the emergence of certain kinds of new social classes in certain circumstances is always independent of historical happenstance, even if the precise timing of their appearance and the details of their relationships are not predictable on the basis of macroscopic factors alone.[9]

In effect this is a claim that a certain number of abstract sociological factors form a deterministic set, even if this is not the case for *all* large-scale features of society whatsoever. Such a qualified historical determinism could well be true even if the all-encompassing formulation discussed so far is indefensible. But, even so, its truth would be a matter of its fitting what actually happens, and not something that could be assumed dogmatically prior to any examination of the relevant evidence. To justify such a perspective we would first have to specify clearly exactly what abstract aspects of societies history is supposed to be deterministic with respect to. And then we would require the historical and comparative evidence to bear out in fact the claim that no development in any of those aspects has ever been a result of some micro-level accident. While some such qualified version of historical determinism might be valid, a tolerant scepticism would seem appropriate until such time as a definite proposal has been empirically substantiated.

It is worth repeating at this point that denying historical determinism does not commit us to a rejection of universal determinism. Even if some social facts are not caused by social facts alone the small-scale 'accidents' which are necessary to account for them might well be the deterministic outcome of such things as idiosyncratic genes or odd childhood experiences, as suggested earlier. So from a wider viewpoint it might well still be that social facts, along with everything else, are always determined. The point to grasp here is that what we count as an *accident* depends essentially on what we have in mind as 'normal' causative factors. From the viewpoint of the social scientist or the social historian events which are not predictable on the basis of prior social factors alone are 'accidents'. But such 'historical accidents' need not be undetermined in any absolute sense—it is simply that they are undetermined by the kind of large-scale social factor in terms of which social analysts are wont to give explanations. ('Coincidences' can be considered as special cases of accidents, namely, as those accidents which involve two things *sharing* some feature, such as their time and place of occurrence, or—a different kind of concidence—the same name. So what counts as a 'coincidence' will also depend essentially on what frame of reference is being adopted.)

Universal determinism is equivalent to the thesis that there are no absolute accidents or coincidences. Modern micro-physics suggests that universal determinism is false. But the critique of historical determinism developed here is quite neutral on this cosmic question. For I have worked with the implicit idea that if some social fact is not determined by other social facts, or by intrusions from without the society in question, it will nevertheless be explicable in terms of micro-features of that society. So I have done nothing to suggest that social developments, or anything else, can just happen, independently of *any* prior causes.

To conclude this section I wish to point out a number of things that are *not* implied by the claim that historical determinism is false; that is, by the claim that certain events are (a) not determined entirely by prior social factors, and (b) necessary parts of what suffices for subsequent social developments. Firstly, the claim that a certain event is not historically determined does not imply that social factors play *no* part in the determination of that event, that the event would have occurred even if the social situation had been different. Thus, if someone claims that Hitler's idiosyncratic personality and what resulted from it were historical accidents he is not saying that Hitler would have turned out the same if he had grown up in Ancient Greece—merely that the general social conditions operative at the time do not by themselves suffice to explain his character. Secondly, the claim that a historical accident has a significant effect on subsequent social developments does not require that it had that effect independently of concurrent social conditions, that it would have had that effect in a different social set-up. Someone who argues that Hitler's idiosyncrasies affected Germany's conduct of the war does not have to show that Hitler would have been able to ensure just those policies whatever the social situation in Germany at the time—merely that those policies would in those circumstances have been different with a different leader. These two points show that it is no defence of historical determinism to show that significant individuals are always 'products of their time' and never able to do more than 'harness the broader forces of history'—historical determinism is adequately refuted if we show that 'the time' leaves certain aspects of individuals unexplained, and that those aspects affect how 'the forces of history' are harnessed.

Furthermore, while the denial of historical determinism does imply that we cannot give complete explanations of social developments on the basis of social factors alone, it does not mean that analysis on this level is ruled out entirely. For one thing, we might well be able to formulate sound *statistical* generalisations involving only large-scale social factors. This will be possible when certain social factors ensure certain developments given the presence (or absence) of other 'accidental' conditions, and there is some kind of statistical regularity governing the presence (or absence) of those conditions.

Finally, it is important to realise that the insistence that there are significant historical accidents does not imply that there are *no* processes in which social developments are entirely determined by social factors alone. It might well be that certain sequences of events are, as it were, instances of 'local' historical determinism. For instance, it is plausible that an increase in the money supply in a capitalist economy running at full capacity will ensure inflation, quite independently of whatever else is going on in the society in question. And this could be so even admitting that whether there is an increase in the money supply can depend on 'accidental' events. The historical determinist is wrong to say that accidental factors never matter. It seems equally indefensible to say that they always matter, that no social developments are ever determined by social factors alone. The right view is surely that historical accidents matter, sometimes.

5. FREE WILL

Let us go back once more to the idea of explaining given social developments causally. Implicit in this idea is the supposition that such developments will always occur given certain prior conditions. Many get worried because this kind of supposition seems to imply that men are never free to bring about or prevent social developments—if social developments are determined, then surely men cannot affect them.

There certainly seems something absurd about such an implication. If, as we have agreed, social phenomena consist of nothing more than complexes of facts about individuals, then must not the occurrence of such phenomena depend on the decisions and actions adopted by those individuals?

This kind of reasoning has led many thinkers to doubt whether we can ever be entitled to the kind of generalisation required for the causal explanation of social facts. Such a generalisation would have the import that whenever certain situations arise certain social facts follow. But it seems as if it should always be possible for people in those situations to act on occasion so as to make the generalisation false. Often adduced as instances of this possibility are 'self-defeating prophecies'—cases where it is precisely because a certain social event has been predicted that people act so as to prevent its occurrence.

These 'libertarian' reactions to the possibility of sociological explanation are standardly made most vehemently in response to the historical determinist notion that there is a prearranged scheme for the overall course of human history. ('Are men merely pawns of the historical process?')[10] But it would seem equally appropriate to react in this way to the weaker claim which allows that social developments are on occasion determined in part by non-social 'historical accidents'. For the important issue is surely whether social phenomena are determined at all—not what *kind* of determining conditions might be involved. There is no obvious reason why determination by micro-factors should allow men more freedom than determination by large-scale social factors.

In fact the problem at hand is not really one peculiar to sociological explanation. For at bottom it is nothing more than a special case of the general difficulty about determinism and free will, which arises as soon as we suppose human actions to be the deterministic outcome of any prior conditions whatsoever.

Broadly speaking, we can distinguish two schools of philosophical thought about determinism and free will. There are those that hold, straightforwardly enough, that an action's being determined is incompatible with its being an exercise of free will. We can call these thinkers *incompatibilists*. But incompatibilists do not hold the floor unchallenged. There are also *compatibilists*, who argue that an action's being determined is in itself no bar to our deeming it free. On the compatibilist view what makes an action free is merely that it in some sense results from the decision of an agent—even if that decision is itself determined by prior conditions.

Perhaps the clearest way of formulating the compatibilist view is as the claim that someone's behaviour is freely willed precisely insofar as it is caused by his beliefs and desires, even if these are determined in turn by prior factors. The test is thus 'Would the agent have behaved differently if he had wanted something different?' If the answer is yes, as it normally will be, then the action was free—for his wanting what he actually did was a necessary part of what sufficed for his behaviour. On the other hand, if we decide that someone would have been caused to behave as he did *whatever* he wanted, if he *could not* have done differently whatever his aims, then he was not free. His behaviour was, so to speak, something that happened to him, rather than something he *did*. Paradigm examples would be where someone is physically constrained in his activities, either by external force or the limitations of his natural abilities; or where he has some pathological compulsion which drives him along a certain course quite independently of what aims he adopts.

So the compatibilist does not require absence of determination for free action. Instead, what he asks for is determination of a certain kind, namely, determination through the agent's beliefs and desires. That an action depends on what the agent wants ('He would not have done it if he *had* thought differently') is, the compatibilist will point out, in no way inconsistent with the agent's being determined to want and so do what he actually did, any more than 'It would not be wet if it had not rained' is inconsistent with the actual rain and subsequent wetness being the deterministic outcome of prior conditions.

The debate between compatibilism and incompatibilism interacts with the topic of the last chapter. In a sense the point of compatibilism is that it gives someone who thinks that actions are caused a way of making some sense of our immediate intuition that we have free will. Conversely, anybody who cannot help feeling that freedom must somehow be incompatible with determinism is likely to be attracted to the interpretativist view that actions are not caused, that human agents contribute to their choices in a way not capturable in any scientific theory. But notwithstanding these affinities the issues are distinct. There is nothing incoherent in accepting simultaneously that human actions are caused and that this is indeed incompatible with the existence of human freedom, that any immediate experiences of 'free will' we may have are a kind of illusion.

I shall not try to adjudicate the relative strengths of compatibilism and incompatibilism here.[11] Given my view that actions are caused there are the obvious attractions in compatibilism. But it is hard to get rid of the feeling that there is something *ersatz* about the 'free will' that compatibilism offers us. ('How *can* we really be free, if our past always makes it completely inevitable that we will act just as we do?')[12] Even so, I shall use the rest of this chapter to elaborate what a compatibilist would say about sociological explanation. For even if there is something eventually suspect about the compatibilist version of 'free will', there is undeniably something in the distinction between behaviour that results from someone's beliefs and desires and behaviour that he is constrained to, willy-nilly. And so it will still be worth seeing how far social developments can be viewed from within a deterministic perspective as things men *do*, rather than as things that happen to them.

The compatibilist will regard the 'libertarian' argument with which I introduced this section as invalid. For it is only if we implicitly take for granted an incompatibilist line on free will that we can move immediately from a social development being determined to the conclusion that it did not depend on anybody's free actions. Once we adopt compatibilism we have room to allow that social developments are determined, without being driven to the counter-intuitive conclusion that nobody is ever free to affect such developments by their actions.

However, even the compatibilist cannot suppose without further ado that *whenever* a particular social development is determined by certain prior conditions the free actions of men are involved in its coming about. He has to find out whether or not the process by which those prior conditions determined the development in question actually did include as an essential component certain men acting on the basis of their beliefs and desires. In this connection the kind of individual reduction of social scientific explanations discussed in Sections 2 and 3 becomes crucial. For it is specifically what happens on the individual level that will show whether or not the sequence of events on which some social development depends includes people having certain beliefs and desires and acting accordingly.

An individual understanding of the way a given social development is determined could lead to one of a number of different conclusions about its dependence on men's free actions. (For ease of exposition I shall identify myself with compatibilism from now on.) In the first place it might turn out that the prior conditions in question determined the subsequent development quite independently of anybody's free will. That is, it might be that the sequence of events by which those prior conditions ensured that development did not involve anybody acting on the basis of their beliefs and desires after all. Consider, for instance, the way in which overpopulation relative to agricultural resources ensures an increased death-rate, or the way in which general illiteracy guarantees that any system of administrative organisation will be a non-bureaucratic one. In such cases the path from determining conditions to consequent result does not involve the people concerned having certain attitudes and acting accordingly; given the prior conditions the result follows quite independently of what anybody involved might think or do. So there is no part of the process to which we can point and say, '*If* they *had* been inclined to act differently the result would have been prevented'. And consequently there is no part of the process by reference to which we can attribute the result to the exercise of free will.

Whether the prior conditions involved in such cases (the relative shortfall in resources, the illiteracy) can in turn be attributed to what anybody freely did is a further question, requiring further analysis. Even if someone deliberately and freely chose to bring about the shortfall, the point remains that once the shortfall occurred there was *then* no possibility of anybody doing anything to prevent the increased death-rate. This illustrates a point of some general significance. Whenever we raise the question of whether anybody's free actions are involved in the way some social development is brought about, it will be necessary to consider it relative to some specification of the conditions which are being taken to have initiated the process culminating in that development. Otherwise we would have to count as a product of free will any development which eventuated, however distantly, from some historical free action. While this would make a kind of sense, it would simply obscure the distinction we are after.

Let us now consider the case where the exercise of free will *is* involved in the process by which certain conditions bring about certain social results. This will be when it is an essential part of the process in question that certain people have certain beliefs and desires and act accordingly. Thus, for instance, when an increase in demand leads to an increase in price in a competitive market, it is precisely in virtue of sellers wanting a higher revenue and realising that they can get it by putting up their prices that the result comes about. In this case we can attribute the development to what the people involved (the sellers) freely did. For we can see that *if* they *had* not realised there was chance of a higher revenue, or *if* they *had* not wanted it, they would have acted differently, and the price would not have gone up. Of course—this is the point of compatibilism—this in no way denies that the increase in demand made it inevitable that the sellers would realise, via the presence of queueing buyers, etc., that there was a chance for increased income, and consequently, given also the natural inevitability of the sellers wanting more money, made it inevitable that they would up the price.

It is worth noting that when human free will is involved in the determination of some social result it can either be a matter of a large section of society acting collectively on the basis of certain common beliefs and desires, or a matter of a single individual or small group acting on the basis of theirs. The actions of sellers in a competitive market would be a case of the former kind. A similar example would be the collective rising of a revolutionary proletariat against the forces of the established regime. But if we had a single monopolistic seller raising his price because of a rise in demand for his goods, the basic point would remain the same—the rise in demand would produce a rise in price only via his acting in accord with his motives.

It is also worth noting that this distinction, between collective choices affecting social developments and a single individual's or small group's choice doing so, cuts across the distinction discussed in the last section between the large-scale determination of social developments and the determination of such developments by significant historical accidents. For to say that the causation of some social development involves a single individual acting on his beliefs and desires is not to deny that his choice is the determinate outcome solely of prior large-scale social conditions. Thus we might with perfect consistency both attribute the rise in price to the monopolist's acting on his beliefs and desires, and maintain that it was quite inevitable given the large-scale social situation that any such monopolist would think and act in that way. Conversely, the common resolve of the proletariat to rise might well be a historical accident in the relevant sense, resulting in essential part from some such historical happenstance as the death of an individual in a violent demonstration.

Perhaps there remains something puzzlingly counter-intuitive about the compatibilist view of the determination of social developments. How can we think simultaneously of some event that we are free to affect it and that its occurrence is predetermined? If it is laid down that some development will take place, then how can there possibly be room for us to make a difference?

But we must beware here the fallacy of fatalism. The fatalist argues that, since it is true of future events that they are going to occur, our activities can make no difference to what will happen. ('Whatever will be, will be'.) What he forgets is that many future events occur precisely *because* of our present decisions and activities. We should not allow any dependence of those decisions and activities on prior factors to obscure this truism.

More specifically, for the compatibilist the determination of social developments does not mean that such developments do not frequently depend essentially on certain individuals or groups choosing to engage in political action. He can allow that our choices, deriving from the hopes we have for our programmes and our fears of what political quietism will bring, will often be crucial in producing subsequent changes. For, according to the compatibilist, this will simply be a special case of social events being determined *through* what people freely do.

A similar case will be the aforementioned 'self-defeating prophecies'. When people act so as to confute some prophecy it is precisely because they believe that, if they do not so act, the prophecy will be borne out. That the making of the prophecy is what draws people's attention to what is required to prevent it, does not show that their preventative action is undetermined—on the contrary, it is often quite clear that once a prophecy has been promulgated it is inevitable that people will confute it. Nor, incidentally, does the self-destruction of particular prophecies show that there are never deterministically sufficient conditions for social events. All it shows is that in such a case the prophesier was wrong if he thought he had identified such sufficient conditions. For, as it turned out, the event in question required at least that people did not hear of the prophecy and act so as to defeat it.

6 Alien Belief Systems

1. THREE APPROACHES

In this chapter I am going to discuss the interpretation and explanation of what are often called 'alien belief systems'. Roughly speaking, these are those systems of beliefs about primitive gods, ancestral spirits, magical powers, totemic creatures, witches, sorcerers, and so forth, which are found amongst traditional peoples, and which inform their magical and religious practices and the explanations they offer for various natural and human events. As such, 'alien belief systems' are to be distinguished from modern world religions, which have given up altogether to science the attempt to control and explain the natural world. As a recent writer has put it, modern religions are almost exclusively 'anthropocentric' in being concerned solely with the moral status of man in his relation to God, while traditional thought has a 'cosmocentric' focus on the explanation and anticipation of natural and human events.[1]

It will be convenient to distinguish three broad lines of approach to the study of alien belief systems. What might be called the 'common sense' approach runs as follows. Traditional beliefs are quite without foundation and in conflict with the empirical evidence. To explain them we should therefore not consider any reasons that might be proffered in support of them, but rather look for some special factors which will explain why the people in question are irrational in this way. Thus we might explain a traditional thought system as an ideology accepted only because it is consonant with the values prevalent in the society in question. Or perhaps we could see certain social settings as particularly conducive to irrational fears and superstition. And, of course, though not popular nowadays, there are those accounts which attribute the adoption of irrational beliefs by members of traditional societies to some inherent intellectual deficiency on their part.

This 'common sense' view is by no means uncontested. Another school of thought disputes the initial judgement that alien belief systems are indeed irrational. They ask whether we are entitled to dismiss as irrelevant the reasons that the people concerned themselves advance in support of their beliefs, and argue that if we only take the care to find out we will discover that native thinkers often work within an articulated and sophisticated intellectual context which gives coherent support to the particular beliefs which seem absurd in isolation. Once we allow that within their intellectual frame of reference there are good reasons for many alien beliefs there seems to be no further need to look for out-of-the-way distorting factors to explain those beliefs. The native beliefs are as much a product of their reason as ours are of ours, and no more in need of special explanations. This 'alternative rationalities' approach thus sees Western scientific rationality as just one rationality amongst others, each in its own way perfectly adequate to account for the beliefs of those who think within it, without any recourse to 'irrational' influences.[2]

The third view to be distinguished is the 'symbolist' approach. This shares with the last-mentioned view a refusal to account for the apparent inconsonance of alien belief system with the objective evidence in terms of the intrusion of 'irrational' distorting influences. But rather than seeking to instate some wider notion of 'rationality' which will accommodate traditional thought as well as modern science, the symbolist line instead suggests that it is a mistake to take alien thought systems at their face value, to interpret them solely in terms of the content they carry on their literal surfaces. This school of anthropologists, which can be considered to originate with Durkheim, instead see the elements of traditional thought systems as metaphorical symbols which stand not for their literal referents but for, say, certain aspects of the social structure. Thus totemic creatures might be interpreted as really representing the different kinship groups in a society: beliefs involving totemic animals would then be construed as metaphorically embodied judgements about the relationships of these kinship groups to each other and to other elements of the social structure. The beliefs uncovered by this kind of 'decoding' turn out as a rule to be quite sensible opinions about the implicit subject matter. So the symbolist approach avoids invoking distorting influences to explain the apparent irrationality of traditional beliefs by reinterpreting those beliefs so as to make them implicitly rational.[3]

It would, of course, be a mistake to think that a correct approach to alien belief systems in general could be decided on *a priori* grounds alone. What interpretation is appropriate for any given system of thought must depend on the actual characteristics it displays, to be discovered by factual investigation, and cannot be decided solely by the philosopher in the proverbial armchair. Still, it is possible to make some progress by straight philosophical reflection. Indeed, advances in this area have to a large extent been hampered by persistent conceptual difficulties with such notions as 'symbolism', 'rationality' and so on. As we shall see, *a priori* considerations are certainly powerful enough to expose various deficiencies in the standard approaches to alien belief systems and to suggest alternative lines of analysis.

2. RADICAL INTERPRETATION

How is it possible to find out what an alien people think in the first place? This is a deceptively deep question and needs to be answered with care.

In Chapter 4 I argued that it is in principle quite possible to find out what beliefs and desires other people have. But at that stage I took for granted two quite crucial assumptions: firstly, that we can understand what people say, and, secondly, that we can judge what beliefs they will form when faced with given evidence. Without these two assumptions trying to find out someone's beliefs and desires would be a most uphill task, for all we would have to go on would be their brute non-verbal behaviour.

These two assumptions must now be re-examined. When we are trying to understand people from an alien culture, rather than members of our own, part of our problem is obviously finding out what their utterances mean in the first place. And similarly, we cannot simply assume that we know what beliefs someone will come to in given circumstances, if that someone does not necessarily share our framework of concepts and general assumptions about the world.

These two problems that we must now deal with are not independent, but it will be simplest to begin with the first, about the understanding of an alien language: this will lead us fairly quickly round to the other.

Let us suppose that we have some idea of which native expressions count as assertions: that is, which utterances they take to express claims about the facts of some matter. (I am not requiring that these claims have anything to do with the actual facts of any matter; the only weight the notion of *assertion* carries here is that which contrasts with *question*, *wish*, *command*, etc.) What we want to know is what the alien assertions mean.

Drawing on the discussion in Chapter 4, I shall take it for the moment that assertions have meanings by virtue of expressing beliefs. That is, for each assertion there is some kind of rule according to which a speaker is only entitled to utter that assertion if he has a certain belief. Given that the speaker expects to be taken to be conforming to the rule in question, he will utter the assertion with the intention of being taken to have that belief. And so, given that he is not trying to mislead his hearers, somebody making an assertion will have the belief the assertion expresses.

This suggests a way of decoding the meanings of the assertions in an alien language. We want to know which assertions express which beliefs. Let us look at the occasions on which particular individuals make standard utterances of a given assertion ('standard' here meaning that they expect to be taken to be conforming to the rule for using that expression, and are not trying to mislead their hearers). Then the meaning of that assertion will be the belief that is held in common by those individuals on those occasions.

But of course, this line of attack begs the question in a fundamental way. The basic principle suggested is to pair each assertion with the belief that is common to those that make that assertion. Yet how are we to know what beliefs particular aliens hold independently of under-standing their assertions? For all that has been said so far, we will be completely in the dark about this. Perhaps we are slightly better off than we would be trying to reconstruct their beliefs from their non-verbal behaviour alone. For at least we can suppose that all those making a certain assertion (standardly) will have some belief in common, even if we do not yet know what it is. But this is scarcely enough of a constraint to get us going on any detailed attribution of beliefs to the aliens.[4]

It is clear at this point that we need to bring in the other source of information invoked in Chapter 4, and attempt to identify the aliens' beliefs from our knowledge of what circumstances they have been in and what evidence they are consequently acquainted with. This independent source of knowledge about their beliefs might then give us enough to construct the requisite pairing of beliefs held with assertions made. Thus, to take a trite example, we might assume that when any alien individual has been outside on a rainy day he will judge *it is raining*. And then if we find some form of words asserted by just those individuals we could conclude that it must express that belief.

But this now brings us up against the second difficulty that was observed at the beginning of this section to arise in investigating an alien people: we cannot simply take it for granted, as perhaps we can with somebody from our own culture, that we know in general what beliefs they will form when faced with given evidence. For what beliefs people form in given circumstances depends, in a manner of speaking, on what concepts they have for comprehending the matter, and there is no reason to think this will remain invariant from culture to culture. What would entitle us, for instance, to assume that the natives in our example above will have a concept of *rain* as such at all? Perhaps they have one undifferentiated notion covering mist, fog, and light rain up to a certain strength, and another unified concept for heavier rain, hail, and snow. If this were so, there would be no one belief they would form in those circumstances where we would judge it is raining. (Talk of 'concepts' is of course only a manner of speaking, and should not be taken too seriously to refer to mental entities such as images, ideas and so forth. All I intend by 'concepts' are the components which make up beliefs. That beliefs must be articulated into such components follows from the fact that any person can grasp an unlimited number of different beliefs.)

There are plenty of examples showing that people from different cultures classify things in different ways. Favourite examples illustrating this are the forty or so kinds of snow and sand discriminated respectively by the Eskimos and the Bedouin. In making such discriminations these peoples clearly form beliefs which would escape the modern Westerner, say, in the same circumstances. There are also less trivial examples of such conceptual variation, where one society has concepts which not only lack simple equivalents in another society, but are somehow not expressible in the other's thought at all. Whorf has argued for instance that this is true of the Hopi concepts for space—time: his claim is that the concepts the Hopi use in this area are simply not equatable with anything we think.[5] And, whatever one might think of Whorf's argument, there are certainly many plausible examples of different peoples having fundamentally different concepts for ordering their social environment, even if not for their natural environment.

The possibility of conceptual relativism across cultures is often viewed with a certain amount of suspicion, not least because of the obstacle it seems to place in the way of interpreting the thought and language of any alien culture in the first place. But there is no real basis for this suspicion. For we can perfectly well succeed in understanding an alien culture even while allowing for the possibility of conceptual relativism.[6] But we do need to abandon the idea of starting from independently based knowledge of what the natives must believe on given occasions. If we cannot be sure of what concepts they work with this line can only come to a dead end. Somehow we have to use their linguistic practice itself to give us an initial indication of what is going on inside their heads.

How is this to be done? The way out is to attend directly to the way the alien people use their language in relation to evidence and arguments.

That is, rather than trying to guess straight off what beliefs they will come to in given situations, we should look directly at what they *say* in which situations, and try to chart correlations between their making given assertions and their being acquainted with certain data. Thus we might find out that Eskimos will describe the snow with a certain epithet once they have seen it to have a certain texture; or that the Hopi have a quantity word for relating events which they apply to two events depending on an indiscriminate amalgam of the spatial and temporal distance between them.

Then, once we have established that a certain assertion is characteristically used in relation to certain external data, we can conclude that the belief 'behind' the expression must be the one appropriate to that use. That is, we infer that the assertion in question expresses that belief whose content makes it understandable that they should use the assertion as and when they do.

So instead of assuming that we can tell what beliefs they will come to independently of examining the structure of their linguistic practice, we should use the structure of that practice in relation to the external world itself to show us what kind of beliefs they formulate. In our earlier manner of speaking, this will mean that we have grasped the content of the concepts they work with. And, *then*, of course, we will be able to judge what belief a particular alien would come to in given circumstances, even if he does not express that belief in an assertion. But these judgements will no longer be a means to the interpretation of the alien language: for they will only be possible *after* we have reached a general understanding of what their expressions mean and therewith an understanding of what concepts they work with.[7]

In the next section I shall say more about the implications that follow from the necessity of interpreting in this way. But one point worth making here is that there is nothing in this method of interpretation that requires the aliens to have the same concepts as are present in the interpreter's own culture. It might be felt that, unless they did, the translator would not be able to recognise what features of the world their expressions related to. But all that we really need require of the interpreter is that he be able to *acquire* the ability to recognise those features of reality the alien expressions pick out, in the process of trying to understand their language, not that he have it beforehand. Interpreting a language which might be underlain by concepts inconsonant with ours should be like learning a first language, rather than a matter of pairing its expressions with those in a language already understood. Since it is possible to learn a first language, it should be possible to learn an alien language with different concepts. Of course there is a perhaps insuperable problem in the way of *translating* such an alien language into ours. I shall have more to say about this below. But there is no particular reason to suppose that understanding a new language requires being able to represent it in a language one already speaks.

3. THE LIMITS OF IRRATIONALITY[8]

In this section I shall argue that the way we go about interpreting the assertions of an alien people forces us to accord them a certain measure of rationality in forming beliefs. In basic outline the reason is as follows. In order to identify the content of their beliefs we have to proceed via their use of language in response to external circumstances. And this means that there is no alternative to the supposition that their sentences have those meanings which make it reasonable for them to assert the sentences they do. To be more precise, what the argument of the last section shows is that, in epistemological effect, the beliefs expressed by the sentences they assert are just those beliefs which are justified by such circumstances as are shown in their general linguistic practice to warrant the assertion of those sentences.

To illustrate this point, consider a people who had what was identifiably a colour term 'grebe', which they applied indiscriminately to both blue and green things. Or again, that they had an epithet for humans, 'hevi', which they applied to just those men who were big and strong. One possibility would be to interpret 'grebe' as *blue* and 'hevi' as *clever*, and to suppose that the natives are somehow incapable of realising that green things are not blue and that big, strong men are not all clever. But clearly this interpretation is indefensible against the alternative construction that 'grebe' means *green or blue*, that 'hevi' means *big, strong man*, and that native judgements on these matters are basically sound. The point is that there is no alternative to the view that their assertions have those meanings which make the beliefs the natives express ones they have reasons to adopt. The diagnosis that a people are systematically irrational about some matter cannot be successfully defended against the criticism that in coming to this diagnosis we have misidentified the concepts behind their words. For we have no other hold on what concepts these are other than what they show in their use of language.

Having stated my initial claim thus baldly and simplistically, I shall now proceed to qualify it in various directions. Notwithstanding the cursory argument just rehearsed, many will undoubtedly and quite rightly wish to insist that it is quite possible and all too often actual for people to adopt beliefs which are unwarranted. What, for instance, about the possibility of somebody convincing himself of something in order to justify an otherwise disreputable action? Surely I do not want to rule this out *a priori*.

I think this kind of phenomenon can be accounted for without abandoning the general thrust of my claim that it must always be a mistake to diagnose the speakers of a language as systematically irrational in forming beliefs. We can see the issue as follows. To have an interpretation of a language is to have a method of deciding the content of the belief that would be expressed by any possible assertion in that language. Given such an interpretation we can read off, from what assertions are actually (and standardly) made, which of the possible beliefs their concepts allow them the natives actually adopt as true. Now we can see it as a test of our interpretation (and in effect it is the only test) that we somehow be able to *explain* their having those specific beliefs that our interpretation makes them out to have. If we find it quite mysterious how they could have come to the beliefs our interpretation attributes to them, then we can only take this to cast doubt on the interpretation in the first place. What is relevant in the present context is that showing that someone had what the conceptual content of a belief indicates as good grounds for it is not the only way of explaining why he has adopted that belief. Beliefs can also result from the need to justify our actions, from wishful thinking, from various mental disorders and so forth. But what is also relevant here is that cases of this kind are in a sense essentially deviant, by contrast with the case where beliefs are produced by reasons. This is because in explaining a belief which is produced by something other than acquaintance with justifying reasons we are presupposing a grasp of what the belief *is*, a grasp of the content of the assertion that is taken to manifest the belief. This can only come from a consideration of those cases where we do not have any special 'non-rational' explanation of why the people in question have adopted the beliefs their assertions express. And because of the argument outlined above, we have no alternative, in considering these unspecial cases, but to come up with the conclusion that the beliefs their words express are just those which are justified in the circumstances where they use those words. So adopting beliefs on rational grounds is the norm, from which other sources of belief are derivative cases. It is in the former cases that the identity of the belief is constituted and displayed; and that identity is presupposed in 'irrational' explanations of why people come to believe *it*.

Consider our 'hevi' example again. Suppose it were argued that after all this does mean *clever*, and that its deviant application is due to the psychological discomfort that the people in question feel if they ever admit to themselves that their lives are being run by big, strong, *stupid* men. This story might seem implausible, but it is not immediately obvious that it is incoherent. But a moment's reflection shows that it only makes sense if there are *some* contexts which show that when other things are equal 'hevi' is applied on the basis of displays of intellectual, not physical, ability. In the absence of *any* such indications of the 'real' meaning of 'hevi' we will be in no position to start offering psychological explanations of why it is *mis*applied.

Still, there will no doubt be many who feel my claim is far too strong. Surely, they will say, there is a multitude of obvious examples of people accepting ungrounded beliefs even on matters where they have no particular axe to grind. Do I really want to say that individuals cannot simply *err* in adopting beliefs, that there must *either* be good *or* non-rational explanatory reasons for any ideas about witches, sorcerers, gods and suchlike that might be received in traditional societies?

An observation might help here. It is not part of my claim that all ordinary beliefs must be true. (Henceforth in this chapter I shall use 'ordinary' to refer to beliefs lacking any out-of-the-way explanation.) All I am saying is that they are always based on good reasons. Good reasons can be short of conclusive to a greater or lesser degree. So it is perfectly possible that the facts are actually such as to make some ordinary beliefs false. But this by no means undermines the thesis I am arguing. Consider the case of a belief in some universal generalisation about a potential infinity of cases ('All fruit is edible'). Here it is actually inevitable, given the problem of induction, that grounds for this belief will fall short of establishing its truth. Even so, to ascribe to an alien people such a belief we need to hypothesise that a certain assertion expresses it. And this hypothesis will only be defensible if their linguistic practice shows them to accord greater credit to the supposed generalisation the stronger the body of positive instances they know of, and to discredit if they know of negative instances. For them to do otherwise, in the absence of any specific non-ordinary explanation, would merely serve to show that the expression in question did not have the hypothesised meaning.[9]

I am quite prepared to admit, then, that some of the 'ordinary' beliefs we attribute to an alien people can be false. Indeed, it might well be the case on occasion that we, as external observers, know of definite grounds for rejecting a belief which we attribute to an alien people. All I require is that those grounds be not known to them, for our attribution of *that* belief to them requires that *they* have good reason for adopting it. Still, even this is unlikely to palliate all scepticism about my main claim. What, it might be asked, about the Azande who are prone to decide people are witches after performing autopsies? Or the many peoples who will attribute illness and other misfortunes to the machinations of sorcerers or the ill-favour of ancestor spirits? It is not just the case that we know these beliefs to be false; surely such beliefs lack good grounds of any kind (even though there are not always 'ulterior motives' for their adoption).

I agree that more needs to be said about such examples as these. But still, a careful analysis of the issues they raise will show that there is a sense in which we must allow that they are rational, if we are to maintain our attribution of *those* beliefs to the people being considered.

4. THE THEORY-DEPENDENCE OF ALIEN CONCEPTS

When someone accepts a given proposition rationally it is not always on *direct* grounds. A proposition can often be accepted because it *follows* from *other* propositions already accepted. Thus, when the Azande decide a particular individual was a 'witch' (*ira mangu*) after cutting him up *post mortem* and examining his insides, it is because they hold that anybody with a certain detectable 'witchcraft substance' (*mangu*) in their abdomen is a witch, and they have detected the substance in this case.[10] In general, it will be possible to find similar rationales for many of the apparently groundless beliefs found in traditional societies. Thus, there is a sense in which such beliefs are indeed rational, and can be explained in the kind of way I am arguing is required if we are to justify our attributing them to our subjects.

But this only displaces the problem somewhat. Anybody who objects to my position is not going to be satisified by being told that most apparently irrational beliefs in traditional societies can quite soundly be inferred from other beliefs. For he will ask, what about those other beliefs? What about the idea that all those with 'witchcraft substance' in their stomachs are witches? Surely this belief lacks any grounds? And does this not mean that the beliefs which follow from them are also, absolutely speaking, irrational, in line with our original intuitions? All, of course, showing that in interpreting an alien language we cannot after all be constrained to make all their ordinary beliefs come out rational.

Is it all that clear, though, that it is irrational to hold that all those with witchcraft substance (*mangu*) in their stomachs are witches (*ira mangu*)? The arguments of Chapter 2 become relevant at this point. We discovered there that conceptual considerations become entangled with evidential ones as soon as we move away from particular judgements about specific situations to the abstract postulates which make up a theoretical framework. Scientific concepts are theory-dependent, in the sense that their content derives from the structure of general assumptions containing them as much as from anything. The same is true of the concepts in traditional belief systems. Part of what is required to grasp the notion of an *ira mangu* is a recognition of the assumption that *mangu* in the stomach shows a man to be an *ira mangu*.

What this means is that the question of the rationality of this assumption cannot be posed in any simple way. It is only after we have a definite hold on some concept that we can ask whether specific assumptions involving it are warranted by the appropriate evidence. The basic assumptions of a theoretical framework play a part in fixing the content of the concepts they involve, in specifying what will count as evidence for other more local beliefs involving those concepts. There is thus no obvious sense in which we can question the validity of those basic assumptions without simultaneously disrupting our grasp of the concepts involved.[11]

Still, it might be felt that there is something sleight of hand about this argument, even if it is not clear where our attention has been distracted. Surely I have to admit that in the end the Azande have definite empirical beliefs which lack the evidence which is quite straightforwardly required. For instance, what about their belief that anybody with witchcraft substance in their bellies will cause misfortune to his enemies?

But even here I would deny it is possible to demonstrate any simple irrationality on the Azande's part. Here again the 'theory-ladenness' of all descriptive concepts is relevant. For the Azande, *mangu* is that substance possessed by *ira mangu*, and the enemies of such beings are those on whom misfortunes get visited. If the apparent enemies of someone whose *post mortem* seemed to show *mangu* did not have any particular history of misfortune, perhaps that only shows it is not as easy to tell who is a witch's enemy as we thought, or perhaps that not everything that looks like *mangu* is really *mangu*. For the Azande, as for the natural scientist, it is always in principle possible to account for the appearance of unexpected empirical results by appealing to the more central, concept-constituting tenets of his theoretical system and questioning the reliability of observational procedures.

By now it should be clear that there is going to be no obvious way in which I have to admit that traditional belief systems are ordinarily irrational. Specific judgements within an alien belief system, such as that a particular person is a witch, can characteristically be supported, given the concepts involved, by reference to certain observations. And the basic postulates of the belief system themselves play a part in fixing the content of those concepts, in indicating which observations are so relevant, which means that the question of empirical evidence for or against those basic postulates does not arise in any straightforward way.

Perhaps it is worth emphasising at this point that I do *not* hold that there is nothing to choose between traditional thought systems and ours, that we cannot justify our natural intuitions that ours have a superior grip on reality. My claim thus far is only that if we are to interpret correctly what traditional thinkers say we will have to allow that their beliefs are ones the evidence supports, insofar as the question of evidence arises in any straightforward way. It is, it must be admitted, an implication of my argument that we cannot simply dismiss traditional beliefs as false in the way indicated at the end of the last section, by appealing to extra evidence we know of to that effect. For the point of this section has in a sense been to show that there are not in fact any evidential considerations with which such beliefs as the Zande view that certain people are witches are definitely inconsonant. Still, even if there is nothing in particular we can put our finger on to show that specific beliefs within traditional thought systems are unsatisfactory, there will still be room to argue that the systems of concepts out of which such beliefs are constructed are themselves a relatively inferior means of representing reality. I shall return to this in the last section.

There is a further set of observations worth making at this point. We have seen that grasping a belief involves knowing what will count as evidence for it, and that what this evidence is in turn depends on the overall structure of theoretical assumptions involving the concepts out of which those beliefs are formed, as much as on any direct associations with elements of observational experience. It follows that it will always be invalid to identify beliefs from one culture with those of another culture which differs on the relevant theoretical tenets; or, what comes to the same thing, to translate an expression from the first culture by an expression of the second.

This does *not* mean that we, as modern Westerners will never be able to succeed in *interpreting* an alien language and grasping the concepts behind it. To do this, all we have to do is identify the structure of theoretical assumptions and associations with observation which defines what count as good reasons for applying their expressions and concepts. To know what that structure is is to know what their expressions mean and their concepts are, even if there is nothing matching in our culture. But it *does* mean that to represent some proposition from a traditional belief system in say, modern English, is of necessity to *mis*represent the alien proposition. To simply say that the Azande hold that 'Anybody with an inflated gall bladder has powers of doing evil' is to omit the more general context which surrounds the Azande notions of *mangu* and *ira mangu* and which gives them the sense they have. It seems likely that it is precisely when people take such translations at face value and ignore the surrounding context that they come to the 'common sense' conclusion that the average Azande must be in the same deviant and puzzling state of mind as a modern Westerner would be who thought inflated gall bladders signified evil powers. This conclusion would be far less tempting if due regard were paid to the full content of the Zande notions in question.

Must then any anthropologist who writes a monograph in his own language be guilty of this error of divorcing alien notions from their intellectual context? Of course not. For what can be done, and is done in the classic studies of alien beliefs, is to describe the overall structure of the alien thought system by specifying which concepts are linked to which by the general postulates therein, and by giving some idea of how some of those concepts are applied observationally. Often the anthropologist will use the actual alien words (*ira mangu*) in doing this. In a sense he is *extending* his own language, by defining in it expressions which adequately represent the alien concepts and which were not previously present in his language. And of course, it is precisely works that do in this way adequately represent the content of alien thoughts that remove the misplaced impression that ordinary alien beliefs are puzzlingly irrational.

This point is sometimes obscured by the fact that we often already have a term in our language which approximates reasonably closely to some alien term and which, with *caveats*, can happily be pressed into service to represent it—for instance, 'witch' for *ira mangu*. This might seem to show that we can well have a term synonymous with an alien term, even when we do not accept the structure of postulates which I say is required for such synonymy. But this is to forget that *we* do not actually *use* the term 'witch' to describe reality—insofar as it has a use at all for us it is restricted to characterisation of the thoughts of other peoples in the historical or geographical distance. So in a sense 'witch' is already an extension of our language, introduced to aid the characterisation of alien thought. The reason we do not seriously use the term 'witch' ourselves to describe reality is that even if we can grasp and entertain the theoretical structure which gives it the meaning it has, we quite sensibly do not *accept* such a structure.

5. SYMBOLIC BELIEFS

Let us now turn to the idea that the assertions made by members of traditional societies to account for their religious and magical activities are not to be read literally. Perhaps this 'symbolist' approach can illuminate the difference between traditional and modern thought.

According to the symbolist, when a native explains his devotions at some shrine by saying that he is showing respect to the spirits of his ancestors, whose shrine it is, we should not take his assertion at face value, but rather understand him as referring to his kinship group and expressing its importance to his social being. His actions, correspondingly, should be read as not *really* aimed instrumentally at appeasing any spirits, but rather as a *symbolic* performance enacting the social significance of his kinship group.

Now there is certainly nothing difficult about the idea that an assertion should be understood metaphorically rather than literally. When somebody says in English, 'His blood was boiling', or, 'She is a bitch', we do not understand what he says in terms of the normal meanings of the words in his assertions. Boiling blood is a symbol for anger, and bitches are symbols of malevolence. And so we recognise that in this context the speaker's words do not, so to speak, stand for the symbols themselves, but for what they are symbols *of*. They mean something like, 'He was angry', and, 'She is malevolent'; and correspondingly it is these latter beliefs that are to be attributed to the speaker in question.

But there are difficulties involved in applying this model to the kind of utterances which are made in connection with traditional ritual practices. As English speakers we recognise that expressions like 'His blood was boiling' has *two* senses, one literal and one metaphorical. (Or, in cases where the metaphor is quite dead, we will merely say it is ambiguous between two literal sense.) And this shows itself in our allowing that, when applied to a given person, 'His blood was boiling' can simultaneously be both true and false—it can be understood as an accurate description, even though, of course, 'His blood was not *really* boiling'.

This standard property of common-or-garden metaphors is not in fact a characteristic feature of the traditional utterances under consideration; nor is it claimed to be one by those anthropologists who adopt the symbolist approach to alien belief systems. It is not part of the symbolist account of traditional thought to argue that the native always *knows* that his ritual practices and his justifications for them are to be understood metaphorically. In general, the native takes himself to hold, and be acting on, the belief that his words express in their literal meaning. He will not be prepared to admit, as we are with our metaphors, that there is one sense in which his words are true but another in which they are false.

Still, why should we insist that metaphors be recognised as such by the people using them? Could they not mistake the real significance of their own utterances, and hence the nature of the beliefs they really hold and are acting on? The dangers in entertaining this possibility can be brought out by recalling some points about interpreting an alien language. An interpretation of an alien language specifies what belief is expressed by each possible assertion in that language. The interpretation is tested by checking whether we can account for the people in question holding those beliefs which the interpretation implies that they actually accept. Insofar as we cannot account for those attributed beliefs the interpretation is suspect. But this ceases to be a test at all if we are allowed *carte blanche* to impute metaphorical meanings to certain of their assertions. For then, whenever we are faced with their seeming to adopt some inexplicable belief, we can simply deal with the problem by maintaining that in this context their words should be understood nonstandardly as a metaphor for some different (explicable) belief. And by such ploys we could defend any interpretation of their language against any evidence whatsoever.

To take a philosophically much-debated example, the Nuer describe human twins in terms which are usually rendered into English as, 'They are birds'. Faced with this rendering, it is obviously attractive to conclude that in this context the Nuer term for 'bird' does not have its usual literal meaning, but is merely a metaphor for the special significance that twins have in the Nuer scheme of things. But what shows that this is the right account, against the possibility that we have in the first place misunderstood the significance of the Nuer term we have equated with our 'bird'? In the absence of any special evidence about a metaphorical use of the Nuer term in describing twins, surely it is right to search for some different interpretation of their term, one which will make it explicable why they apply it to twins. Such an interpretation is given when we are shown how the notion their term expresses fits into a spirit cosmology which has as a consequence that both human twins and feathered bipeds partake of the same spiritual essence.[12] For this interpretation gives their term a unitary literal meaning which succeeds in allowing us to understand why they apply it to both categories of beings.

What I am suggesting, to put it crudely, is that a laissez-faire attitude to attributions of metaphor is in the end simply a licence for bad translations. Or, to be crude the other way round, that a proper attention to the precepts of translation outlined earlier will remove the motivation for attributing metaphorical meanings to expressions which the people who use them take to be literal. If we get the meaning of the Nuer term right, then we can understand why they use it as they do, without having to accuse them of implicit equivocation. (It might well be that 'bird' is the closest and most convenient equivalent in English for the Nuer term. But this rendering will be relatively harmless as long as we do remember that it is inaccurate and misleading without a grasp of the kind of theoretical context which gives the Nuer term the significance it actually has for them.)

To decide that some term is ambiguous or metaphorical we must have something more to go on than the fact that our presumed literal interpretation of the term makes it mysterious why it is used as it is. The kind of thing required has already been indicated—a recognition on the part of the users that in certain contexts the term can be construed in two ways. For then one construction can be used to validate the literal meaning, and the other to indicate the metaphorical reading. If the Nuer admitted, so to speak, that though it was appropriate to describe twins as 'birds' they were not *really* 'birds', in the sense that birds are 'birds', then of course the metaphorical interpretation could stand. However, as I said, it is no part of the symbolist approach under examination to claim that the Nuer, and traditional thinkers in general, make this kind of admission. In view of this, I find it difficult to see how this approach can in any way substantiate the attribution of symbolic contents to the general run of alien belief systems.[13]

There are of course a number of quite different ways in which traditional thought and practices can involve symbolism. One quite straightforward case is where there is a magical belief in the power of symbols to affect the things they are symbols of. Sticking pins into effigies is the classic example. There are a multitude of variations on this theme to be found in traditional societies. But it would be a mistake to take such actions and the beliefs informing them as coded metaphors for implicit concerns which stand behind their explicit contents. The native in such cases *will* explicitly recognise that his spells or rituals involve words and symbols for certain things, and he will literally believe that manipulating them will produce certain effects involving those things. That his belief happens to be about the manipulation of what is explicitly recognised as a symbol does not make the belief or the consequent action themselves symbols for something else. He is not thinking metaphorically by *using* symbols, but thinking literally *about* symbols.[14]

Sometimes what people seem to have in mind when they say that alien beliefs and practices are symbolic is that their existence somehow serves the interests of the society in question or certain groups in it.[15] How far such claims are true (and, if so, explanatory) in particular cases is of no special interest here.[16] For even if they are, the idea that any effect or cause of some phenomenon is 'symbolised' by it simply empties the notion of a symbol of any distinctive content.

A related idea is that alien beliefs in general symbolise the desire of traditional peoples to overcome their subservience to the uncontrollable forces of nature.[17] It is of course arguable that in general people do develop explanatory theories for just this reason—in an attempt to anticipate and control the workings of nature. But this would not make their theories *symbolise* this concern: their theories would simply be results of that concern. And in any case this idea will scarcely serve, as it is intended to, to distinguish traditional superstition from modern scientific thought. For science also alleviates our fear of natural forces. The fact that science works, in a way traditional thought does not, is not to the point here. For traditional man *thinks* his theories work—indeed it is essential to their reducing his fear of nature that he should do so. We have been given nothing to show that his beliefs have a qualitatively different kind of 'symbolic' content from that of modern scientific theory.

Even more vaguely, there is a tendency to label as 'symbolic' any associations, co-classifications or generalisations in alien thought which seem puzzling to the interpreter, *without* any further claim that the items involved are symbols *for* anything.[18] As this section will have made clear, I am sympathetic to the idea that the elements of alien beliefs are what they seem and not coded versions of something else. But, given this, it seems to me simply confusing to continue to call such beliefs 'symbolic' just because they associate things which to us seem unconnected. This terminology suggests that we have found some inherent qualitative feature which will help to explain why alien beliefs are so different from modern ones, when in fact all we have done is pose the problem.

6. ALTERNATIVE RATIONALITIES

What now of the idea that traditional belief systems involve quite different kinds of rationality from modern science? In a way my argument so far might seem to have lent support to this view. I have claimed that in general traditional beliefs are to be read literally, not metaphorically. And I have argued that we will only properly grasp their literal content when we see those beliefs as rational, as supported by the evidence which is appropriate to them.

Given then the wide range of differences between the many systems of traditional thought and between them and Western science, am I not saying that what is rational, what the evidence shows, varies from system to system? It certainly seems to be part of my claim that what is rational for one society need not be rational for another, and that what is rational for the scientist might be something else again.

But I do not think it is necessary to see this as a matter of different societies having different *types* of rationality. I would prefer to say that the differences in question stem from the possession of different *concepts*, not different rationalities as such.

A man who sees diseases as resulting from spirit possession will come to different judgements about a particular sick man from someone who attributes diseases to germs. But both thinkers will start with the evidence of their senses and then use standard logical processes to infer the conclusions that their different systems of postulates, their conceptual schemes, entitle them to. The difference in their conclusions need not indicate any difference in *forms* of reasoning, but only a difference in what concepts they bring to bear on the matter. If 'alternative rationalities' are supposed to imply different standards of what counts as a logical argument, we have no more reason to attribute different rationalities to this pair than, say, to a geologist and an agricultural scientist.

Still, do differences between thought systems *have* to be merely a matter of different concepts? I have indicated how a particular case might be read in this way. But why should we be entitled to completely dismiss out of hand the possibility that different peoples might have different logical standards?

However, once we examine it seriously we see that this is not a real possibility at all. In the first place, we can appeal once more to considerations about translation. Logic—our logic, that is—is primarily concerned with the inferences that we draw from a proposition in virtue of its structure with respect to such particles as *and*, *not*, *or*, *if* . . . *then*, *all*, *some*, etc.[19] Could an alien people have a different set of such inferences? Could they, say, sometimes refuse to make the move from some proposition *p* to the rejection of its negation *not-p*? I think not. Consider the situation from the translational point of view. We will have interpreted two of the sentences they actually assert, one presumably a simple transformation of the other, as respectively equivalent to '*p*' and '*not-p*', for some proposition *p*. But surely this would merely show that we have misinterpreted their meaning, that it cannot be right to translate the particle in question as our 'not' rather than, say, as 'luckily' or 'certainly'. As before, if our translation makes an alien people out to believe obvious absurdities it is the translation, not them, that gets discredited.

Of course, an alien people can accept *un*obvious logical contradictions. We do too, as is shown by our sometimes being able to *prove* to ourselves, from premises we accept, that other of our currently accepted beliefs must be mistaken. But this does not mean that there is some deviation in logical assumptions, on their part or ours, only that complex inferences are not always drawn. What defeats a translation is an attribution of inexplicable beliefs, or combinations thereof. There is nothing inexplicable about a people sometimes missing complex inferences.[20]

The translation argument will work with other logical inferences in the same way as it does with those involving 'not'. For instance, I had occasion to argue earlier that we cannot be right to represent an alien construction as a universal generalisation ('All As are Bs') unless the people in question recognise counter-examples as refuting it. We have, it is true, since seen that in order to save some generalisation a people might decide that what *seemed* like a counter-example could not really *be* one. But that is a different point—it does not show their insensitivity to logic but just the opposite.

Still, the translational argument only gets us half-way. We have shown that *if* we are to hold that certain alien words mean the same as our 'and', 'all', etc., then, by the nature of the case, those people must make the same logical inferences as us. But what shows that an alien people must have particles synonymous with our logical words? Could they not have a different logic, which simply failed to translate into ours? When talking about alien concepts in general I insisted that equating their concepts with ours required that they displayed the same use of those concepts as we did, but the general implication drawn was that their concepts differed from ours. Why should we not similarly conclude that, so to speak, the logical concepts of traditional thought are not commensurate with ours? But while it is not difficult to see how different peoples might apply quite different non-logical concepts to some area of reality, there are good reasons for doubting whether there could be similar divergences on basic logic. If a people can be said to have beliefs at all, it must be that they distinguish between things actually being as a belief represents them and things not being so. And as such they cannot but have the notion of negation, of things *not* being as a given belief represents them. Similarly, the notion of conjunction must emerge in the judgement that two beliefs *both* represent things as they are. Again, it seems that all thinking must involve identifying entities (people, plants, places) and characterising them in various ways (male, edible, near). And, insofar as this is so, it is hard to see how a thinking people could fail to make judgements about *all* or *some* of the entities sharing a given characterisation.

Before concluding this section it is necessary to enter a general *caveat*. There is still an abstract possibility that we might not find anything corresponding to basic logical expressions in the sounds made by an alien people. [21] If the argument of this section and in particular of the last paragraph is sound, this would simply show that those sounds could not express beliefs. In a way this is a kind of possibility that has been with us throughout this chapter. Interpreting an alien language is a matter of finding some systematic procedure for pairing possible alien beliefs with types of alien utterances. This can be regarded as part of a general project of explaining their actual utterances by reference to what they actually believe, and explaining those beliefs in turn in terms of their experiences, environment, innate capacities, etc. In undertaking this project we make the assumption that the people in question have a mutual understanding that certain sounds express certain beliefs, and that they use this understanding in making and interpreting assertions. The point to be recognised here is that there is nothing inviolate about this assumption—it is in principle possible that we might simply find ourselves quite unable to fit beliefs to their sounds in the requisite way. It is unlikely that we would accept defeat quickly, for we have an awful lot of room to manoeuvre in. We do not need to suppose that the aliens work with the same concepts as we do, but can look to the general structure of their linguistic practice itself to show what content their expressions have. Then, if certain expressions seem to be used inconsistently in certain contexts, we can try the hypothesis that those expressions are ambiguous or metaphorical in those contexts, and look for independent evidence to support that hypothesis. What is more, we can always revise our initial suppositions about which sounds count as *assertions*, and instead try to explain some of them as questions, commands, exhortations, ejaculations or whatever. And, apart from this, we can always try to account for a deviant use of an utterance which we *do* take to express a belief as a 'non-standard' case where the speaker is being insincere, or where he has failed to grasp the established meaning of that utterance. These various ploys mean we have a great deal of leeway. But each is capable of, and would require, independent corroboration by reference to our general view of how human actions, including linguistic actions, depend on the agent's mental states. And so, just as this general view is a corrigible theory, to be elaborated and revised when necessary, so is the more specific assumption that any community of *homo sapiens* will have agreed sounds for expressing their beliefs. There is nothing to rule out *a priori* the possibility that *none* of the sounds made by some community could be interpreted as consistently expressing determinate beliefs with contents fixed by accredited reasons, even after we had tried all the available ways of accounting for apparent incoherence.

So it is possible, if unlikely, that we should come to doubt that any of a people's sounds were assertions at all—either because we failed to find any logical apparatus in their language, or, more generally, because we were unable to grasp any regular evidential pattern in their use of language by which we might fit determinate contents to their expressions. What we should say in such a possible case I am not sure. But it would scarcely be something that lent support to the notion that alien beliefs emerge from 'alternative rationalities'. For the conclusion we would have been forced to is not that the alien sounds expressed beliefs that were somehow deviantly derived, but that those sounds could not be interpreted as expressing beliefs at all. Whatever the right explanation of those sounds, it would not, by hypothesis, be in terms of any determinate views of reality we attributed to the people making them, and so the question of the rationality, alternative or otherwise, of any such views would not arise.

7. ACCOUNTING FOR DIFFERENT BELIEF SYSTEMS

The 'common sense' view has it that traditional thought systems are simply confused superstitions, to be explained by the intrusion of distorting influences on the thought of their adherents. In effect I have already argued that this view cannot be right on any simple level (even if we can understand how 'bad' translations might tempt people to it). We can, it is true, allow that individuals in traditional societies sometimes will be led to beliefs by influences other than the appropriate evidence. One of the Azande, for instance, might deem someone to be a witch, not because he knows him to have an inflated gall bladder, nor because his enemies suffer misfortune, nor for any of the other accredited reasons, but simply because he dislikes him, and the belief that he is a witch is conveniently consistent with this attitude. But this cannot be the norm amongst the Azande, for it is only insofar as beliefs as to who is an *ira mangu* are ordinarily arrived at via the accredited reasons that there will be a determinate content to the notion of an *ira mangu*, against which we can see certain applications of the notion as resulting from distorting influences, as, say, expressions of ideology or the need for rationalisation.

It is not as if what was odd about what are called 'alien belief systems' was that they consisted of explicably aberrant applications of concepts which in other contexts the traditional thinkers applied in an un-distorted way quite acceptable to Western investigators. The idea of witchcraft and associated notions permeates the whole of Zande life, and it is the standard uses of these concepts, as much as others, which initially seem to present a puzzle. The need we feel for an explanation of traditional beliefs is not somehow dispelled if we restrict our attention to those cases where there are no ulterior explanations.

But now we seem to have stuck ourselves with a problem. Why then do people in traditional societies believe such outlandish things? If their beliefs are not metaphors, if they are not the products of alternative rationalities, if they cannot be deemed the product of distorting influences, what *is* the explanation?

I have argued that ordinary beliefs in traditional societies are accepted literally, as a result of normal processes of reasoning with the concepts current in those societies. If at all, we are going to get an explanation of the difference between traditional thought and our own by asking why it is that the concents they work with are so different from ours. I have taken it that concepts are constituted in essential part by the structure of basic postulates by which they are related to other concepts and to observational procedures. So we can approach our problem by considering why it is that traditional societies have the structures of postulates that they do.

In a way modern philosophy of science is concerned with the way in which such structures of postulates are constructed and developed. I have in mind here the writings of thinkers like Kuhn, Lakatos and Feyerabend, which I discussed towards the end of Chapter 2. What emerged from that discussion was that scientists will characteristically defend their core of central postulates from observed anomalies by adjusting the auxiliary hypotheses which surround that central core. They will continue to do this as long as is possible without abandoning altogether any attempt to account for what happens, and only on rare occasions will they be forced to rethink their basic assumptions and start anew.

This picture of science suggests an interesting question. Why should traditional thought not be seen as the product of just the kind of concept-elaborating process characteristic of modern scientific development? Given the understanding of modern science we have reached, this would account quite happily for the fact that alien belief systems are different from ours. The naive view has it that scientific truth is obvious—that anybody applying correct scientific methods to some area is guaranteed to arrive fairly quickly at the uniquely correct theory. In reality, however, the received scientific account of any one area is always developing—goodish frameworks of postulates are superseded by better ones, and in time those are succeeded by still better ones. And there is no fixed route along this path, with a given starting point and a predetermined sequence of subsequent stages. What concepts are scientifically appropriate for a certain subject matter is not something which automatically emerges from some pre-theoretical contact with that subject matter. The framework of concepts some intellectual community will initially bring to some subject matter will depend on any number of things—on which ideas are consonant with their social values, on what models are available to them from other areas, or the extent of their creative inspiration, etc. And the same will apply when basic revisions are required and a new set of concepts needs to be installed—exactly what revisions are to be put forward is not something dictated by scientific methodology alone, but again can depend on any number of methodologically accidental factors. All that the canons of scientific method require is that the framework accepted at any given time should continually be put to the empirical test, refined so as to be made consonant with what such tests show, and, when necessary and possible, replaced by *some* other system which promises a more comprehensive account of the area in question.

So there is nothing immediately incoherent about the idea that alien belief systems are products of just the same scientific methodology as our current theories. Their difference from us would then be no more puzzling than the fact that earlier Western scientists, like Galileo and Newton, held theories different from those we currently accept. Nor need the absence of anything in our Western intellectual history corresponding to certain kinds of traditional belief system be taken to show that the latter are somehow unscientific—it would simply reflect the fact that the exact form of what emerges when science calls for conceptual innovation always depends on the social context as much as on scientific method itself.

What is more, this suggestion has a kind of egalitarian attraction, in that it allows us room to defend our intuitive preferences for our own theories over traditional belief systems without having to impute any intellectual deficiencies to traditional thinkers. We could, as it were, see them as Newtons to our Einstein. To put the point another way, we can allow respectability to alien belief systems, even up to the point of allowing that they are developed in accord with every canon of scientific practice, without having to conclude that those systems represent reality as well as ours.

But having made this point—and it is worth making, given the all-too-common assumption that we cannot properly reject traditional thoughts unless we can find epistemological errors in traditional thinkers—we now need to ask whether traditional belief systems are indeed products of scientific method. And in fact there remains plenty of room to doubt whether traditional thinkers are good scientists. For all the slowness and indeterminacy of the development of scientific frameworks, science is still essentially a *critical* activity. Scientists recognise an obligation to account for anomalies in non-*ad hoc* ways, by producing explanations which are themselves further testable. It is because of this obligation that they on occasion come to recognise that even their most basic conceptual assumptions need to be replaced by others.

It is by no means clear that traditional thought is 'open' to development in this way, that there is a similar preparedness to entertain the possibility that the accepted view of reality might be wrong. Traditional thinkers do not seem concerned to make their system of postulates precise, to ferret out hidden inconsistencies in their assumptions, to see whether independent evidence can be found for the explanations they offer for unexpected events. When a magical spell fails to work, it is often attributed to its having been somehow incorrectly cast. There is nothing unscientific about that in itself. But what is unscientific is simply leaving it at that, rather than trying to specify exactly what omissions were responsible for the failure, and then checking to see whether rectifying those omissions does in general ensure the desired results or, at least, increases the probability thereof. And insofar as traditional thinkers are nonchalant in this way about the need to elaborate, refine, and check their ideas, they will never be forced into the situation where they have to reconsider whether their basic postulates are sound.

To some extent it might be felt that the 'closedness' of traditional thought should be attributed to the *content* of the explanations traditional thinkers give, to the *kind* of concepts in terms of which they view the world. Is there not something about theories involving the dispositions of gods and ancestral spirits, or the efficacy of supernatural powers and magical symbols, which makes them inherently incapable of being tested against the empirical evidence? But I think this is the wrong diagnosis. As we saw in Chapter 2, it is quite possible to test theories about unobservable entities, given that we have assumptions about how these entities relate to each other and to directly detectable phenomena. There is no intrinsic reason why the magical and religious systems of traditional thought should not satisfy this requirement. The gods and spirits of primitive religion, for instance, are not the whimsical characters of Greek myths, nor the ineffable entities of modern world religions, but by and large beings who are taken to react to and act upon the natural everyday world of human beings in well-defined and regular ways. Primitive thought is not inherently unsuited for giving the kind of explanations and predictions which relate different natural events to one another; and indeed it is characteristically applied in this way. If anything, the real difference between the traditional and the scientific thinker is that the former is characteristically content to suppose that there is *some* explanation within his framework for anomalous events, without ever carrying out the detailed and sophisticated checks which will eventually show him there is not. If he is to be criticised it is not so much for the content of his world view as his approach to it.

We should be careful before concluding that we have indeed here found something different about traditional thought. For one thing, the impression that alien belief systems are 'closed' to change might well be an artefact of the way anthropological research is done. Detailed studies of alien belief systems have mostly been carried out by anthropologists doing field work of limited duration. Even in those cases where people have returned after some time to the societies studied, or lived amongst them for relatively extended periods, we scarcely have the kind of time-scale in which we would expect significant intellectual developments to manifest themselves. Moreover, writers such as Kuhn have shown us that modern scientists themselves are not all that quick to recognise when an unexplained phenomenon indicates a deficiency in their theoretical system. They are quite happy to shelve problems for considerable periods of time, and will suppose that the failure to find a solution within the system will be overcome once adequate intellectual resources are directed to it.

Still, even given these *caveats*, the evidence does seem to indicate that traditional societies lack even that programmatic concern to find definite solutions to anomalies that is uncontroversially part of modern science and which ensures that, in the long run at least, received ideas are replaced by others.[22]

Perhaps there is something to the common sense view of alien belief systems after all. Even if within their thought systems traditional thinkers are no more subject to distorting influences than we rational moderns, it now seems that at the level of those thought systems themselves such influences might well play a predominant role. We saw above that social and ideological factors can play some part in the development of even properly scientific thought—what new frameworks are proposed will often depend on what is consonant with or suggested by the surrounding context. But in a scientific community the source of new frameworks need be of no lasting significance—such ideas will survive only insofar as they out-compete the alternatives. But in a traditional society, where there is no such competitive pressure, then it seems that ideas adopted because, say, they fit in with the values of the society, or the dominant sub-group therein, will simply survive by default.

But even on this level there is something misleading about the 'common sense' view. For it is scarcely accurate to say that there are unscientific *pressures* which *distort* traditional thought, by comparison with scientific thought. At the level of the introduction of new frameworks of thought the two are on a par—in both cases conceptual systems can initially be attractive for such reasons as their consonance with the social context. Thereafter scientific practice differs from traditional practice. But, if anything, it seems to be scientific practice that requires special explanation in terms of intruding pressures. Human history in general seems to show that the complacent acceptance of received ideas is the norm, that it is natural to men (including those modern men we find in streets rather than research institutions) not to question the basic premises of their thought. So we scarcely need to invoke any abnormal influences to account for the persistence of traditionally established ideas. The right question is not what prevents traditional thinkers from being sceptical, but what makes modern scientists so abnormally critical.

Should we conclude then that it is scientific thought that is an aberrant outcome of particular social values? Is it science that is ideological and traditional thought that is normal? To resolve this question we need to examine the notion of ideology, to consider the way people's values interact with their view of reality. This will be the subject of the concluding chapter. In this I shall be primarily concerned to decide how far, if at all, it is possible, or desirable, for the social sciences to reach 'value-free' conclusions. But along the way I shall have cause to return to the paradoxical idea that it is scientific rather than traditional theories that result from distorting social pressures.

7 Facts, Values and Ideology

1. 'FACTS' VERSUS 'VALUES'

It is difficult to give any brief specification of the problems raised by the relationship between 'facts' and 'values'. Perhaps the best way of introducing the topic is to consider the contrast between *beliefs* and *desires*, which has been assumed at various points earlier in the book.

These two kinds of mental states both consist of the subject having a certain attitude to a certain proposition. But the attitude is different in the two cases. Beliefs are judgements about what *is*, or has been, or will be. Desires are about what *ought* to be, or have been, the case. To have a desire is to hold that something is or would be somehow satisfactory. To hold a belief is to have a view about the facts of some matter. (At least, this is how *I* have been using the term 'belief'. In ordinary language the application of the term is rather wider.)

As we saw earlier, beliefs and desires interact in the genesis of action. Actions are oriented to the satisfaction of desires. To be zeugmatic, desires are what the action and the agent are *for*. His beliefs then indicate which actions seem best suited to satisfying his desires.

Beliefs raise questions of justification. A person can be deemed correct or incorrect in adopting a certain belief. The having of a certain desire does not similarly raise an immediate issue of justification. It makes sense to ask if the facts bear out someone's belief that Spain is a republic or that inflation is slowing down, but not whether they bear out his liking for power, wealth, or ice-cream.

Given the distinction between beliefs and desires we can define two kinds of utterances. *Assertions* are utterances which express beliefs. *Evaluations* express desires. Assertions raise questions of justification, corresponding to whether the beliefs they express are justified or not. Similar questions are not immediately raised by evaluations. There are of course questions about the linguistic competence and sincerity of someone making an evaluation. We can ask whether the speaker knows

159

what desires his utterance is taken to express, and, if he does, whether he really does have the desire he is expressing. But given competence and sincerity there does not remain any further question about the justification of the view expressed, as there does with assertions.

What about those central assumptions in a theoretical structure which play a part in giving meanings to the terms involved, such as the physicist's assumption that force equals mass times acceleration, or the Zande claim that an *ira mangu* can visit misfortune on his enemies? As we have seen, questions of justification for such judgements do not arise in any simple or straightforward way. Nevertheless I shall take it for now that these judgements are beliefs, expressed in assertions, and not evaluations. For on the face of it they certainly seem to be about what *is*, rather than about what *ought* to be. And even if questions of justification are not here as straightforward as they are with more specific beliefs, they are not entirely inappropriate. Later on in this chapter I shall return to judgements of this concept-constituting kind and discuss the special problems they raise in connection with the issues at hand.

The contrast between beliefs and assertions, on the one hand, and desires and evaluations, on the other, is crucial for the standard arguments about 'facts' and 'values'. But there are terminological difficulties here. In the first place, our initial dichotomy is not between 'facts' in the sense of *justified* beliefs, against all views which fail to be justified. Rather it distinguishes views which might be justified or not, from views for which the question does not arise. Justified beliefs are merely a sub-class of beliefs in general. And correspondingly views which fail to be justified include both desires, where justification is not at issue at all, and *un*justified beliefs. The terminology of '*facts*' versus 'values' suggests that unjustified beliefs should be assimilated to 'values'. This is perhaps attractive, insofar as one explanation for someone's accepting an unjustified belief can be that it somehow fits in with his evaluations, in a way to be examined later. But it is also confusing, for it obscures the important point that adopting an unjustified belief is not itself to make an evaluation, even if evaluations can explain why the belief is adopted. So I shall use the term 'values' to refer specifically to desires or the evaluations that express them, and should not be understood as including unjustified beliefs or assertions under this heading. Correspondingly, when I talk of 'factual' judgements I should in the first instance be taken to be referring generally to claims as to the facts, whether or not the actual facts justify those claims.

A further terminological difficulty is that the problem of 'values' is normally presented as especially concerned with difficulties associated with *moral* views. Whereas I have explicated 'values' in terms of desires in general. Since nearly everybody with views on the question will deny that all desires involve moral judgements, or that all moral judgements involve desires, or both, my terminology is rather unconventional. But it will be convenient to stick with it, for the problems we shall be concerned with will turn out to arise specifically, and generally, with the intrusion of desires, whether or not those desires have anything to do with moral judgements.

What exactly is the relation between desires and moral judgements? It depends on what view of morality is adopted.[1] *Subjectivists* about morality hold, roughly speaking, that moral judgements are simply expressions of certain kinds of desires. Amongst subjectivists there is some dispute about what exactly is required for an expression of a desire to count as a *moral* judgement. Some subjectivists hold that we make moral judgements when we express approval or disapproval in a way which exhorts others to concur. Others argue that moral attitudes are those which instantiate general principles which do not accord the speaker any special status. But on any subjectivist view, moral judgements are certainly evaluations in my sense, albeit a special case of such evaluations. Then there are *objectivist* theories of morality, according to which the essential feature of moral judgements is that they ascribe certain real properties to things, such as being conducive to human happiness, or ensuring that humans are treated equally in certain respects, or, perhaps, having a certain 'non-natural' attribute intuitable by means of a special moral sense. It is objectivists who will find my terminology of 'values' most contentious. For they will take moral judgements to be in principle subject to questions of evidential justification, and in this respect on the same logical level as any other beliefs as to the facts. All I can say is that it is not part of my intention in adopting this terminology to suggest that moral objectivism is mistaken—indeed I find it a rather more attractive view than subjectivism, insofar as the terms of the debate allow any serious solution. It is just that the specific 'fact–value' problems I shall be concerned with arise specifically when there is a possibility of people's *desires* somehow intruding on their *beliefs*. It would be tiresome in discussing these issues to have to keep on saying that insofar as moral values count as factual claims they are not implicated in the 'problem of values'. So when I take it from now on that 'values' are not objectively assessable against the facts, I should *not* be taken as denying moral objectivism but rather as assigning any factual components of moral judgements to the category of beliefs.

Having dealt with these preliminaries, let us turn to the question of 'value-freedom' in the social sciences. What we might call the 'establishment' programme for the social sciences is that they should emulate the natural sciences in consisting of assertion rather than evaluation, and moreover that those assertions that get accepted should be those the evidence bears out. The rationale for this programme is the idea that social choices, like any others, will best be made if based on justified beliefs rather than conjecture.

Many are currently sceptical about the 'establishment' programme. Whatever might be possible for the natural scientist, they doubt that it is possible for the social scientist to restrict himself to those factual assertions that the evidence supports. The specific nature of the social scientist's subject matter, they feel, makes it inevitable that evaluations will intrude on his thinking. I shall distinguish three specific problems that the sceptic might pose for a defender of the establishment view.

Firstly, is it possible to distinguish at all between assertion and evaluation in the social sciences? What I have said so far has presupposed that this can be done. But we shall see that there are problems in principle and practice in deciding what counts as assertion and what as evaluation.

Secondly, if it is possible to distinguish assertion from evaluation, can social scientists manage to stick solely to the former? Can their theories consist solely of assertion, or must they inevitably include or imply certain evaluations in their conclusions?

And thirdly, even if we concentrate on such parts of social scientific theories as consist of pure assertion, there remains the question of whether those assertions will be, or could be, made because of evidence which justifies them, or whether they will be accepted because of the theorist's evaluations instead.

The first two of these questions will be answered in the next section. The third will then occupy the rest of this chapter.

But before proceeding we may as well get out of the way one kind of relationship between beliefs and values which does not *in itself* give us any reason to answer any of these questions in the sceptical negative even if there are other reasons for doing so. The relationship in question is that our beliefs indicate to us the best way, if any, of achieving our ends. That is, given certain desires, our beliefs will lead us to value certain courses of action as means to the satisfaction of those desires. Firstly, this does not show we cannot tell the difference between beliefs and desires, between assertion and evaluation. To believe that X will lead to Y is one thing. To desire Y, and hence X, is another. Secondly, this does not show that the social scientist cannot stick to pure assertion and eschew evaluation. That the social scientist can tell us what will lead to what does not in itself show why he has to have any view about whether those results are desirable or undesirable. And, thirdly, the possibility of beliefs helping to show what ought to be done does not automatically mean that those beliefs are going to be adopted for any reason other than the existence of evidence for them. In the equation 'Ends + Beliefs $\rightarrow$ Means' the beliefs and the ends are, so to speak, independent variables, and the means the dependent variable. It would be a mistake to think that this process in itself shows that beliefs get adopted because they tally with a certain choice of means. In the above schema it is only *after* the belief, and the ends, have been arrived at that the appropriate means is indicated.

2. 'VALUE-LOADED' TERMS

It is now time to take another look at the distinction between assertions and evaluations. How are we supposed to tell whether a given utterance is one of the former or one of the latter?
Unreflectively we might suppose that this can be done simply in terms of vocabulary—that the utterance will carry a mark of its status on its surface. Thus one might demarcate evaluations as those utterances containing such auxiliary verbs as *ought* or *should*, or such epithets as *good, right, satisfactory, desirable*, or their contraries. And then factual assertions would be those utterances not containing any such expressions.

But this apparently simple syntactic procedure collapses as soon as we come to consider what are commonly known as 'value-loaded' terms, such as *democracy, fascist, terrorist, nigger*, and so forth. Statements made using such terms cannot straightforwardly be classified as either assertions or evaluations. For they are characteristically used to express both beliefs as to the facts and views as to whether those facts are satisfactory or not. Thus two people who differ on whether some group are 'terrorists' or 'freedom-fighters' might well agree on the factual properties of the group—that they use violent means in pursuing certain aims—and disagree only in their approval or disapproval.

Now it is undeniable that many of the terms and phrases used in the social sciences are 'value-loaded' in this way. This raises immediate doubts about the 'establishment' answer to our first two questions. For it makes it unclear how we can distinguish factual claims from evaluations in what a social scientist says. And, *a fortiori*, it suggests that it will be impossible for the social scientist to stick solely to assertions about the facts.

A popular establishment response is to urge that the social scientist ought to forswear the use of value-loaded terms altogether, to make sure that all his expressions are purely factual, free of any evaluative connotations.

This does not seem to me a workable suggestion. A term has evaluative meaning if it is mutual knowledge that someone applying the term will have an attitude of like or dislike to the thing described. But the attitude that people have to something is not going to change because some new terminology is decreed. A rose by any other name will smell as sweet, or sour. So a new 'neutral' replacement for an old evaluatively charged word will quickly accrue the old connotations. So long as most of the people using the new word retain the previous evaluative attitude to the thing described it will soon be generally assumed that someone using that word has that attitude. A classic example of this process is the succession of terms used to refer to Afro-Americans (sic): 'niggers', 'negroes', 'coloureds', 'blacks' . . . . As each word comes to gain general currency, largely as a result of people not wanting to express their negative attitudes, the old overtones quickly accrue, because it is realised that most people do have the negative attitudes they are striving to conceal.

In particular, it will standardly happen that people's shared *moral* feelings will give rise to value-loaded terms. It makes no difference whether we hold, with the subjectivist, that ultimately what it is for oppression, say, to be 'bad' is for us to disapprove of it; or whether we agree with the objectivist that it is bad in itself, in virtue of its nature and consequences, in principle quite independently of the fact that most of us happen to share negative feelings about it. For on either view we will have people sharing distaste for a situation with certain factual features, which, as above, will mean any factual term for that situation cannot but acquire negative evaluative connotations.

The use of value-loaded terms could be entirely avoided only in a linguistic community whose members did not have any common evaluations about the same factual matters. In particular, this would seem to require that the members did not agree in moral feelings on any issue. While there is perhaps something suspect in requiring that social scientists ought always to agree morally on what they are studying, a methodology which requires *a priori* that they should never have common moral feelings about anything they investigate is absurd. If this is the price of avoiding value-loaded terms it is surely too high.

These remarks show that most writing about human and social reality is inevitably going to express certain evaluations, thus indicating the sceptical answer to our second question. But I do not think that the inevitability of value-loaded terms need force us to be similarly sceptical about our first question, about the possibility of *distinguishing* factual claims from evaluation in what the social scientist says. The factual meaning of an utterance indicates what evidence justifies accepting it. The evaluative meaning of an utterance is the emotional attitude it is recognised as expressing. Why should the fact that claims about society will characteristically have both these kinds of meaning stop us directing separate attention to the factual content of what is said? When a certain society is described as *oppressive*, say, why should we not be able to count the question of whether it actually has those factual characteristics implied by this description as in principle separate from the issue of whether it is to be disapproved of? To hold we can do this—and I see no reason in what has been said so far for thinking we cannot—is not of course to say there is anything *wrong* with people, including social scientists, basing evaluative conclusions on their factual claims, nor with those evaluative conclusions being naturally and inevitably built into the very terms in which they express those claims. All I want to urge is that the question of whether those factual claims are borne out by the evidence is in principle separable from the further evaluative questions.

Even if we use, as we no doubt do, concepts like *terrorist* or *oppression* in our thinking, as well as in our talking and writing, the same points apply. Such concepts will give rise to attitudes which are neither beliefs nor desires, but somehow a mixture of both. But there is nothing to stop us discerning in such portmanteau attitudes a separate belief aspect (that the group has certain aims which it pursues in violent ways) and a desire aspect (of disapproval), and treat them each as such.

Is this all there is to the 'problem of value-loaded terms'? What I have said so far might seem rather too glib. And indeed there is an aspect of the matter I have glossed over so far. Consider again terms like 'democracy', 'fascist', 'oppression', etc. The trouble with these terms is not only that they force us to include evaluations in any social description. We will also characteristically find disagreements in the first place about what *factual content* these terms are supposed to have. People will *contest* the defining characteristics of 'democracy', each usually arguing for those defining criteria that make the political organisations they favour come out 'democratic'.[2] In a way the existence of such 'contested concepts' is a puzzling phenomenon. For the disputants are not just differing on which political organisations they approve of, but also on how a certain word is to be understood factually. Not that this is a disagreement on facts themselves—we are in a position to disagree about whether a statement is faithful to the facts only *after* we have agreed on its constituent expressions' factual meanings. The puzzle is to understand what point there is in disagreeing about definitions, rather than simply settling the matter by convention and moving on to more substantial matters.

What is actually going on in such cases is that the parties to such a dispute are each trying to commandeer the positive evaluation intrinsic to the term 'democracy' in such a way as to attach it to those organisations they independently happen to approve of. Thus those sympathetic to capitalism will seek to define 'democracy' so that it turns out to be, perhaps exclusively, true of capitalist organisations, while socialists will aim at a definition making socialist organisations 'democratic'.

This kind of process has a general significance which will be brought out in the section after next. The immediate issue to be considered is whether it undermines the strategy of considering separately the factual and evaluative components in statements involving value-loaded terms. For it might seem that in the case of concepts like 'democracy' the factual meaning is inseparable from the implied evaluation, with different thinkers moulding the meaning so as to make it cohere with their prior values.

However, the difficulty is still more apparent than real. If, on the one hand, there is a complete lack of definite factual content to a term like 'democracy', then the term has ceased to be a value-loaded term altogether—for there will be no factual component to load the values onto, and the term has become purely evaluative. So if we are looking for factual claims in what someone says we can ignore such statements altogether. On the other hand, if, as is more likely, two social thinkers have clear enough ideas about what each means factually by 'democracy', there are still no special problems. Even if they understand each other as meaning different things factually, there is no reason why they should not each appreciate the factual content of the other's statement, and separate that from the prior evaluative content that they both attach to the term 'democracy'.

Of course, it will not always be clear what factual content, if any, is being attached to some term; and people might even on occasion positively strive to conceal their deviant factual use of certain expressions, in order to get the evaluation that actually goes with the *standard* usage attached to the situation *their* usage is designed to apply to. But if this is the situation then proper attention to the use of terms will reveal it—and if we are interested in extracting the factual claims in what someone says it will pay us to devote such attention.

3. 'IDEOLOGY'

We can now turn to our third question—will the values that people adopt affect what beliefs they come to hold? (Here and henceforth 'belief', 'assertion', 'factual claim', etc. will refer not only to purely factual judgements, but also to the factual components of value-loaded portmanteau judgements. A corresponding usage will be adopted for 'desire', 'evaluation', 'value', etc.)

To claim that beliefs are *affected* by values is quite different from claiming that beliefs *are* values. Indeed the former claim presupposes that beliefs and values are distinguishable, in saying that *one* influences the *other*.

To many it is obvious that people in general and social scientists in particular cannot help favouring those judgements about the fact which 'fit in' with their values. But in spite of its general popularity this is a somewhat obscure claim. In the first place, what is meant by a factual judgement *fitting in* with certain values? Many of those who want to argue that their so fitting in characteristically influences the adoption of factual judgements will also recognise the existence of a 'logical gap' between facts and values. They will allow, and often insist, that information about the factual properties of some situation always leaves us perfectly free to come to our own conclusions on the desirability or undesirability of that situation. But if values are in this way equally compatible with any facts whatsoever, what sense is there to the idea that some beliefs will 'fit in' better than others with given values?

Nor is there anything in the discussion so far which will help to clarify how certain values might 'favour' certain beliefs. Beliefs can indicate the best means for the ends we value. But, as pointed out at the end of the first section, our having certain ends in itself leaves us neutral as beliefs about what means will in fact achieve them. Again, certain descriptions automatically carry certain evaluations with them. But this does not show why those descriptions should ever be applied in the absence of the relevant evidence. That people's antipathy to homosexuals is loaded on to their terms for referring to them does not in itself give us any reason for thinking that those terms will be applied to anybody other than those individuals who evidence homosexual characteristics.

Perhaps the idea is supposed to be that people are characteristically inclined to believe that what they value exists, or is achievable, even when the evidence does not bear out these beliefs. This certainly suggests some definite content to the idea that certain beliefs 'fit in' with certain values. But, unfortunately, it could with equal plausibility be argued that people are characteristically inclined to believe that what they value *not* exist and is *not* achievable, even when the evidence suggests that it is. Why should we not conclude that it is pessimistic beliefs about the fulfilment of our values, rather than optimistic ones, that really 'fit in' with those values?

If we are going to be serious about the idea that certain values *favour* certain beliefs we clearly need a firmer foundantion than some vague hypothesis about a characteristic human tendency to optimism, or a conflicting hypothesis about pessimism. However, if we do stop taking these matters entirely for granted it does become possible to develop such a foundation. Consider, for example, a factory owner who is not averse to the material benefits of his position, but who also, as a moral man, acknowledges that the material level of the general population ought to be ensured as far as possible; or, again, consider a man who is an avid cigarette smoker but who is also concerned to avoid lung cancer. For the first man there would be something definitely attractive in the idea that a political system allowing private ownership in fact produces and distributes more material goods than the alternative systems. And similarly there would be a natural tendency for the second to reject the theory that smoking leads to cancer.

These should be seen as examples of a general tendency towards what we can call *attitudinal consistency*.[3] People are generally disposed to 'aim' or move towards states in which there are no salient conflicts in their total set of beliefs and values. If the factory owner did not adopt the belief in question he would be left with an awkward choice between pursuing his own interest and pursuing what he acknowledges as the general welfare; and correspondingly the smoker would be in a dilemma as to whether to continue smoking or to try to decrease his chances of cancer. Human beings find conflicts between different evaluations bothersome, the more so the less clear it is which evaluation should dominate. And one obvious way of reducing such conflicts is to adopt those beliefs about how things in fact work which will make one's different desires weigh together rather than against each other in deciding the merits of possible actions and states of affairs.

Attitudinal inconsistency arises specifically when two or more potentially conflicting desires are involved. This is why neither the simple means –end schema nor the use of value-loaded terms gave us any real grip on the sense in which certain beliefs can *fit in* with certain values. Insofar as we were focusing solely on one value (the desired end, approval or disapproval for a certain kind of situation) we avoided the question of whether any beliefs involved brought that value into conflict with *other* values over some issue. [4]

In a sense we can say that beliefs adopted because of the need to reduce attitudinal inconsistency are *ideological*. The common notion of an 'ideological' belief would, I suppose, be of a belief which is promulgated in order to defend actions or policies which are in the interests of a certain group, by presenting those actions or policies as having results which are accepted as being in the general good. But few who take this to be an important phenomenon want to imply that the favoured group is consciously and conspiratorially pulling the wool over the masses' eyes—on the contrary, the members of that group are standardly taken to be as convinced of the truth of the ideological claims as anybody. The ideas developed in this section can explain how this might happen. To start with, those favoured by the acceptance of certain beliefs will *themselves* adopt those beliefs, in an attempt to achieve attitudinal consistency: to accept that the policies needed for the satisfaction of their sectional interests in fact had results which frustrated the general good would face them with an uncomfortable conflict. Then, of course, given power and influence, they will encourage the general dissemination of the beliefs in question, and resist as disturbing or threatening any 'dangerous' arguments marshalled against them.

In one respect *ideology*, as standardly understood, is rather narrower than the category of beliefs adopted because of attitudinal conflict. For 'ideology' does carry the specific suggestion of reconciling sectional interests with generally accepted *moral* values—it is precisely in such cases that the belief is suitable for *persuading* the general public to sectionally useful policies, that the belief claims a *justification* for those policies. While attitudinal conflict in general can operate in cases where only personal, non-moral desires are involved. The smoker who came to doubt the connection between smoking and lung cancer would be a case in point. Still, the term 'ideology' is a convenient one, and since nearly all the interesting and important cases of attitudinal conflict are those where it is moral justification that is sought, it should not be seriously misleading to adopt it for my purposes. My usage is also somewhat deviant in the other direction. As well as referring to the inculcation of *beliefs,* 'ideology' also standardly covers the kind of process by which a group will come to adopt and persuade others to certain *values* in terms of which their sectionally preferred policies can be justified. The emphasis on 'freedom' as a moral value in competitive capitalist societies might well be seen in this light, for instance. But I shall not be talking about this latter kind of process when I use the term 'ideology' henceforth. For my primary concern in this chapter is with whether factual judgements about society are conditioned by values rather than evidence; where the values themselves come from is of no direct relevance to this question.

4. WHAT IS WRONG WITH IDEOLOGY?

It is important to realise that nothing so far said implies that it is *inevitable* that people will adopt those beliefs which make their values consonant with each other. Or, to be more specific, even if I am right in claiming, as I want to, that there are some circumstances which lead to people adopting such beliefs, it does not follow that they will do so in all circumstances.

Let us accept that there is a real tendency to remove the discomfort engendered when a belief implies that two or more values are inconsonant. Even so, a rejection of the belief is not the only way for the conflict to be removed. An alternative would be for one of the values to be abandoned, perhaps aided by a marshalling of considerations suggesting its satisfaction was not such a good aim anyway. Thus our property owner might simply stop worrying about the general material level ('life is always going to be a lottery'; 'how drab it would be if everyone were equal'); or the smoker might come to lose his yen for cigarettes ('I never enjoyed them anyway'; 'smoking completely destroys your sense of taste'). We call this sour grapes. A rather less obvious case of reducing conflict by altering values, rather than by altering beliefs, is the definitional contesting of terms like 'democracy'. To admit that a society one favours is nevertheless evaluatively deficient in respect of not being democratic would produce attitudinal imbalance. But this imbalance can be avoided if one ceases to care about 'democracy' as originally defined and, so to speak, transfers one's positive attitude to something different—even if this new social attribute still goes under the label 'democratic'.

Whether it is values or beliefs which are altered to restore balance would seem to depend in part on the weight of the relevant evidence for the beliefs that the individual is acquainted with. The possibility of resisting some belief will be diminished the more the acknowledged evidence weighs on its side and the less opportunity there is to preferentially gather contrary evidence. At the extreme, there is little room to avoid the concrete beliefs presented to us by the evidence of our sense, however much those beliefs show our values to be inconsonant.

Exactly how and when imbalance changes people's attitudes is essentially an empirical matter; and indeed it is something very actively researched by contemporary social psychologists. There are a number of competing and overlapping 'attitude consistency' theories, involving different conceptualisations of the phenomena, and leading to different empirical claims.[5] This is not the place to go into any details. But the common sense points made in the last few paragraphs indicate that, whatever a complete account might show, it is at least not always automatic that imbalance will result in people's *beliefs* being affected by the values they hold.

Still, it might be felt that I have already allowed enough to discredit the possibility of a social science in which decisions on factual judgements are generally made in a value-free way. If, as I am suggesting, there are general empirical truths about when people's beliefs will be influenced by their values, then surely there *will* be cases in social scientific research where this does happen. The evidence for factual judgements about social matters is rarely clear, and there is often potential for intense conflict between deep-seated values. Surely, if there are *any* kinds of conditions which will ensure the ideological adoption of beliefs, it is in the social sciences as much as anywhere that they will operate. And insofar as this is so, would it not be futile to continue worrying about the problem and what to *do* about it?

But this argument slips into the fallacy of fatalism. There is no reason to suppose that the presence or absence of circumstances sufficing for ideology is something independent of our choices. In particular it may well be—indeed it would be extremely surprising if it were not—that one of the conditions which will prevent ideological decisions on beliefs is precisely a conscious commitment to deciding one's beliefs in a value-free way. True, there is little doubt that the official social sciences as they are actually practised at present contain plenty of instances of con-clusions arrived at ideologically. But this might well be empirically due merely to the absence of institutions and values which favour the tailoring of beliefs to the discoverable evidence rather than consonance with values. And, if so, we *can* do something about ideology—uphold and encourage such institutions and values.

At this point a rather different question arises. *Why* should we try to prevent ideology? There are people who deny that this is an aim worth pursuing, who suggest that it would somehow be bad faith for anybody who cares seriously about political issues to keep his theoretical conclusions separate from his values. Now perhaps there are rhetorical occasions where the importance of some programme justifies exaggerating its beneficial consequences to those who need to be persuaded. And of course there is nothing wrong with social scientists investigating how, if at all, certain values can be achieved, with their work being 'value-relevant' in Weber's sense. [6] But, for all that, I do not see how it can ever be worthwhile to be ideological in the precise sense under discussion here. In general actually *adopting* (as opposed to merely professing) beliefs which lack evidence can only be self-defeating. For one's actions best lead to the satisfaction of one's ends if they are based on accurate beliefs about what is in fact conducive to those ends. If we believe our ends are mutually compatible, when in fact they are not, we will misjudge the results of actions intended to pursue them. The man who kids himself about the smoking–cancer link is likely to produce results contrary to his own preferences. Even our property owner is best advised to find out how the general welfare actually fares in the system that favours his own. For only then will he really be in a position to decide if that system is the one he wants. (By hypothesis, he must at some level have a real concern about the general welfare—otherwise what pressure would there be in the first place for him to convince himself that the existing system fosters it?) This argument for adopting only those beliefs which are supported by good evidence is admittedly not entirely general. Not all possible beliefs are relevant to one's choice of actions—some relate to matters that are beyond one's power to affect. But this lacuna will be of little help to those who want to argue that there is merit in *a priori* commitment to *ideological* beliefs. For the beliefs they are standardly concerned with are specifically those relevant to political issues, those which suggest some definite answer to the question, 'What is to be *done*?' It is precisely this kind of context that gives force to the argument that adopting unwarranted beliefs is only going to obscure from oneself how best to achieve one's ends. There is room for dispute about how wicked it is to mislead others on political matters. But it is just stupid to mislead oneself.

As I said above, the theories that actually get adopted by practising social scientists are often nothing more than ideologies favouring powerful social groups. This can well be argued to warrant an initial scepticism about factual claims which legitimate the advantages of such groups. But it would be the antithesis of political seriousness to elevate any scepticism into the conclusion that those claims *must* be false. For this would be to adopt, in a negative way, just the kind of *a priori* commitment to ideologically attractive conclusions that I am criticising as inevitably self-defeating. Even those who disapprove of the advantages enjoyed by certain sections of society need to know whether or not the factual claims legitimating those advantages are actually discredited by the evidence—if certain aspects of general welfare do indeed depend on a certain group having certain privileges, then surely this is something that needs at least to be taken into consideration in deciding whether to resist those privileges.

This last point raises an issue of more general significance. A belief, even if adopted for ideological reasons, is a claim as to the facts, and as such needs to be assessed for correctness against the empirical evidence. We should not think that a belief's being ideological gives it a distinctive kind of content—that it somehow *converts* it into a value and so removes the necessity for its evidential assessment. For a belief to be ideological is for it to have been adopted as a result of a certain kind of process— namely, because it fits with the values of those adopting it. But it is still a belief for all that. And so there might still *be* evidence for it, if only we take the trouble to look. This point is sometimes obscured by a related consideration. For there is a sense in which exposing a belief as ideological discredits not only the person who has accepted it, but the belief itself. As a general rule people adopt those beliefs that the evidence impresses on them. So we standardly assume, when somebody manifests a certain belief, that there must be evidence in its favour. And consequently we will credit it ourselves. On the other hand, when we conclude that somebody has adopted a belief for ideological reasons our general predisposition to assume there must be evidence for the belief breaks down. For we then have an alternative explanation of his adopting it, which does not imply that there must exist evidence for it for him to be acquainted with. Thus the judgement that a belief is ideological removes a general *prima facie* reason for supposing there must be evidence for it. But this does not affect the general point that ideological beliefs call for evidential assessment as much as others. To remove a *prima facie* reason for accepting a belief is not to have a positive reason for rejecting it.

Let us now briefly recapitulate the arguments of this section. The existence of processes by which values affect beliefs does not imply that beliefs are always so affected. Even if these processes do at present operate in the social sciences, there are good reasons for thinking that we can avoid them if we try, and also good reasons for making the effort to do so. The sceptical response to our third question might be right about what the social sciences are, but it is wrong about what they can and should be.

5. IDEOLOGY AND THEORETICAL FRAMEWORKS

At the end of the last section I distinguished two ways in which we might explain someone being led to a belief. On the one hand we can show him to be acquainted with appropriate evidence or reasons for the belief. Here we not only explain his belief but also show that he is entitled to it. Alternatively we might show that he has adopted the belief because it fits in with his values. Although it remains in principle open that there might still be grounds for the belief, in itself this kind of explanation removes our standard reason for crediting his belief.[7]

Let us now shift our attention from those specific beliefs for which it is clearly laid down what counts as appropriate evidence to the basic postulates found at the centre of theoretical structures. In particular, let us consider whether the contrast just drawn applies also to explanations of why scientists accept such basic postulates. At first sight there certainly seem to be difficulties here. For, as we have seen in previous chapters, basic theoretical postulates in a sense play a part in constituting the concepts they involve, and this means that there is no question of straightforward evidence for or against such postulates. Given a clear notion of 'bureaucracy', say, there will be no difficulty in principle in deciding whether a particular organisation satisfies the requisite criteria or not. But things become messier when we come to consider such general questions as what are the prerequisites for the development of bureaucratic forms of organisation, what the effects of such organisations are, what conditions will lead to their modification or disappearance. These questions inevitably become entangled with, though by no means reducible to, the issue of what criteria are to be recognised as showing an organisation to be bureaucratic. And so, given a dispute about the effects of bureaucracies, say, there seems no real possibility of showing that it is one side's view rather than the other's that has emerged from acquaintance with the accredited evidence. For part, though not all, of what is at issue cannot help being which evidence is to be so accredited.

This suggests that on the level of basic postulates at least, ideology might be inevitable. If *legitimate* reasons for a belief are not clearly laid down, then surely the only possible way of accounting for someone's adopting it is in terms of its somehow fitting his values. Something like this view is adopted in Mannheim's influential writings on ideology. *Relative* to the dominant intellectual perspective of a given society, we can distinguish between correct and incorrect beliefs. But according to Mannheim there is no question of which such perspective is *absolutely* correct—underlying theoretical commitments are always and inevitably simply results of the influence of the surrounding social context.[8]

Still, is it really inevitable that science should collapse entirely into ideological relativism? Remember that, for all the indeterminacy of scientific theory choice, there remain, in the long run at least, scientific principles for choosing between alternative theoretical frameworks—a research programme which over time proves unable to account for anomalous phenomena without simply decreasing its explanatory content is thereby shown inferior to a competitor which copes with this task more satisfactorily. The time factor involved here, which reflects the impossibility of ever having conclusive evidence for choosing between programmes, allows that it can be scientifically appropriate to adopt embryonic programmes which have yet to overtake their competitors but which hold out some promise of doing so, or to stick with degenerating programmes which have fallen behind their rivals but which may yet catch up again. But, as we saw, this temporal dimension does not make science entirely arbitrary. Even if scientific method never shows immediately or definitely which of two competing theoretical frameworks is to be preferred, it does lay down guidelines as to when continued adherence to an unsuccessful view is unlikely to be fruitful.

So there *is* an alternative to the external social context always determining which theoretical frameworks get accepted. If such a framework repeatedly fails to produce any explanatory successes then it can eventually be rejected on those grounds, independently of how much the view of reality it presents is attractive to dominant social interests. Some of the observations made in the last section in connection with more straightforward epistemological decisions are applicable here. There is little doubt, for one thing, that in actual practice theoretical frameworks are not always given up when scientific standards finally call for them to be abandoned. Their attractions for powerful social groups will often encourage their persistence well past this point. But, again, to say that existing practice falls short of what the canons of scientific methdology require is not to say that ideological influences *must* obtrude on scientific requirements. It may well still be that sufficient institutional and normative encouragement for scientific standards could ensure that theoretical frameworks came to be chosen solely by reference to such standards rather than in accord with ideological interests.

Still, it would be foolish to think that it would be a simple matter to ensure value-free choices at the theoretical level under discussion. The delicacy of the scientific judgements involved obviously means that it will be all too easy for ideological pressures to exert a distorting influence on which frameworks are deemed acceptable. And of course the social sciences will be especially susceptible. It is not that theories in the natural sciences can never be favoured or disfavoured because of what they imply for the consonance of conflict between certain human values and interests. Debates about the physiological effects of cigarette smoking or of atmospheric radioactivity would be cases in point. But this kind of thing is scarcely the norm in the natural sciences—nobody has any ulterior motives for favouring one view rather than another about the behaviour of elementary particles or the structure of space.[9] In the social sciences, by contrast, ideological pressures will almost invariably be present. By the nature of their subject matter the claims made by theories in the social sciences cannot help but be about the empirical connections between various states of affairs that different groups will be interested in preserving or preventing.

There is a further reason for not being overly optimistic about the possibility of overcoming ideological influences on decisions about abstract theoretical frameworks. As I have had occasion to remark at various points earlier, the canons of scientific method have little to say about the *discovery* of such frameworks, about the *origins* of conceptual innovations. It is no scientific disqualification of a theoretical framework that it might originally have been proposed and elaborated because of its consonance with external social values. Provided it is thereafter evaluated relative to its competitors by reference to its actual explanatory progressiveness it is of no special methodological consequence that its proponents might have found it initially attractive for ideological reasons.

But what if all the frameworks which get a proper hearing in a certain intellectual community are uniformly those that support certain powerful social interests? For instance, it is arguable that the great majority of the proposals mooted in modern academic economics have embodied the underlying assumption that the optimal allocation of resources is best ensured by unrestricted competition amongst private owners of capital. Clearly the rigorous rejection of degenerate lines of research will do little to stop ideologically favoured views being accepted, if the dice are loaded by only those frameworks which are consonant with dominant social values getting on the agenda in the first place.

Perhaps the appropriate response to this difficulty is to require that scientists should make the effort to play fair—they should positively encourage the pursuit of programmes which have ideologically uncomfortable implications. But this does seem a somewhat idealistic suggestion. And in any case it is difficult to see how people could be *directed* to adopt views to which they are initially disinclined. We can see here the sense in Mannheim's idea that ideology can only be avoided in a community of 'free-floating' intellectuals who lack any particular social attachments, or in the view held by some Marxists that objective knowledge will only be possible in a classless society.[10] For the uniform bias we are worried about will arise precisely when a dominant class is able to exert preferential pressure in favour of views which present its sectional interests as being conducive to the general good. If there were no such class, or if the intelligentsia was free of their influence, then the possibility of *systematic* bias at least would be avoided. But the Marxist and Mannheimian suggestions can also be charged with excessive idealism. Even in societies lacking the standard economic divisions there will be groups whose interests do not coincide with those of the rest of the population, and whenever such groups are for any reason disproportionately influential or powerful they can be expected to exert pressure in favour of views which favour them. And as long as there are any such pressures there will always be the danger of the intelligentsia succumbing.

This discussion of abstract theoretical choices suggests that in the end there are real obstacles to an entirely value-free social science. But it should not be forgotten that, as before, the issue is essentially an empirical one: we are asking what conditions, if any, will as a matter of practical fact prevent ideological influences illegitimately distorting accepted views of social reality. And so, even a pessimistic answer does not affect the normative point that it would still be better for people to accept those views that most accurately represent reality rather than those which unnecessarily distort it. In particular, anybody who is serious about disputing the accepted orthodoxy on some matter will still have an obligation to vindicate his scepticism by producing an alternative which can in time actually be shown to be scientifically superior.

6. SCIENCE *AS* IDEOLOGY

Let us consider further the observation made towards the end of the last section, that scientific method has little to say about where new ideas should come from. Insofar as this is so, it follows that it is no discredit to a scientific theory if its emergence is *explained* by reference to the external social context. For example, it would be no criticism of Darwin's theory of evolution by natural selection to show that it was first entertained because of its analogy with the workings of high competitive capitalism; nor, for that matter, would it be a criticism of the theory that any capitalist economic system inevitably suffers periodic crises to demonstrate that it was initially prompted by a disaffection for such economic systems. This is not just the point that there might always still always *be* evidence for a belief even if those adopting it have done so for illegitimate reasons. At the level of abstract theoretical commitments it does not even discredit the *adoption* of some view to show that its development was due to social influences. Once more, the evidence is never quick or conclusive in showing whether some basic theoretical position is acceptable or not, and even when it does give some such indication it is merely a matter of showing that the position in question is preferable to its rivals, not that it is *the* right account of the relevant area. And so there is no question of a scientist only being justified in a basic theoretical commitment if it has been forced on him by his acquintance with the relevant subject matter.

Of course, there *is* something wrong if a scientist persists in his commitment to some position beyond the point where its explanatory failures do recommend its being abandoned. But still to infer from *any* demonstration that external social influences have played a part in the acceptance of a given theoretical position that its acceptance is unwarranted is to betray too unthinking an adherence to the simple model whereby a 'rational' explanation validates someone's belief and an 'irrational' explanation discredits it. Even if this model works for those more specific beliefs for which there are clear criteria of correctness and incorrectness, it breaks down when we come to the 'sociology' of more abstract theoretical knowledge.

A similar point can be made about the even more abstract matter of the adoption of the scientific method as such. At the end of the last chapter I raised the puzzle that it was the critical scepticism character- istic of science, rather than the intellectual complacency of traditional thinking, that seemed to call for explanation in terms of external social influences. And I wondered whether this showed that in the end it was science rather than traditional thought that presented a suspect view of reality. We can now dissolve this anxiety. It is not as if the principles of scientific method emerge easily and uncontroversially as soon as anybody forms the desire to understand reality as it is. So why should it discredit the scientific approach to show that its adoption results from certain social influences? Once more, the idea that an intellectual stance is unwarranted unless it has been impressed on an open mind by the relevant data is an illegitimate extrapolation from the case of those specific local beliefs which have well-defined criteria of justification.[11]

Still, perhaps there is a problem about the scientific method as such. Why should we indulge in the theoretical restlessness the scientific attitude calls for, why *should* we strive to push our theories to their logical limit and then test them by means of carefully controlled observations? The reason social influences do not discredit choices of research programmes is that the guidelines scientific method lays down for justifying such choices leave perfectly proper room for such social influences. But what is supposed to justify the choice of the scientific method itself? And how do we know that the social influences on *that* choice do not discredit it?

There is a school of thought that holds that the scientific method *is* in certain respects discredited by its association with the external influences that encourage it. This is *Critical Theory*, the contemporary inheritor of the Hegelian — Marxist tradition of the Frankfurt School of Sociology.[12] According to Critical Theory the defining characteristic of science is that it serves the 'technical interest'. Science aims specifically at 'nomological' knowledge, at the discovery of universal laws which specify invariable relationships amongst empirical phenomena. Critical Theorists argue that this aim is to be understood in terms of the suitability of such knowledge for facilitating the control and manipulation of the phenomena under study. To know of laws stating sufficient or necessary conditions for the occurrence of some event is to know how to produce, or prevent, those events—namely, by ensuring the presence of those sufficient conditions, or the absence of those necessary ones.

Critical Theorists infer from this that empirical science has no right to a 'cognitive monopoly' of reality. They argue that the picture of reality presented by empirical science is specifically one oriented to the technical interest of potential control. Other 'cognitive interests' (the aim of *communicating* with people, or of *emancipating* them) will call for different conceptions of reality.

This analysis leads the Critical Theorists to reject the application of the empirical scientific method to the social realm. Perhaps, they allow, a purely technical interest is appropriate to the natural world—we need to be able to control our natural environment.[13] But the ability to control *people* implies a system of social domination where the people who are the objects of the empirical 'science' of society are manipulated by those who administrate that system. Thus empirical science is condemned as 'ideological', at least in its application to the social realm, in the sense that it involves an implicit commitment to systems of political domination, and precludes any concern to understand people's real needs or to emancipate them from oppression. As we can see, this is not our earlier notion of illegitimate 'ideology', not a matter of people's values influencing them to beliefs to which they are not entitled by scientific standards. On the contrary, it is the acceptance of 'scientific' standards in the first place that is being condemned as itself concealing a commitment to illegitimate values.

Is this attack on an empirical science of society valid? There is little to dispute in the observation that a scientific understanding of some area gives us the potential to control and prevent certain occurrences. But we need to be careful about exactly what this implies for either the *explanation* of why people have adopted the scientific method, or for the *evaluation* of the legitimacy of their doing so.[14]

Consider first the question of whether science's 'technical' utility explains its actually having been adopted as a method. Here I think we need to give different answers for its application to the natural and the social realms. It is doubtful whether the technical interest as such had much to do with the adoption of the scientific approach to the study of the natural world. In the history of the natural sciences the large-scale support by industry and governments for research which they hope will be of technological or military use is a relatively recent phenomenon. And it is implausible to argue that individual natural scientists have often been motivated by any concern for the technical implications of their research. Exactly what did lead to the emergence of the natural scientific attitude and the development of scientific institutions in Europe during the seventeenth century is a complex and unanswered question. But it seems clear that the place to look for an explanation is in the fundamental transformations of religious and political attitudes occurring at the time, rather than in any desire for the technological applications science might yield.

When we turn to the application of the empirical scientific attitude to the social realm, however, there does seem to be a closer link between the technical interest and the historical adoption of the scientific approach. What I have in mind here is the phenomenon, first pointed to by Weber, that with the increasing complexity and bureaucracy of modern society there is an increasing need to anticipate and control social activities. The behaviour of such things as costs, demand, discontent, output, etc., are crucial to the running of complex enterprises. Without the ability to 'calculate' such relevant factors it would be impossible for the large-scale organisations characteristic of modern society to function at all. The historical timing of attempts to develop precise empirical theories in the social sciences certainly suggests that such attempts can be attributed to these 'technical' needs specific to modern industrial societies.

Let us now turn from the question of why people *have* adopted the scientific approach to the issue of whether they *should*. As I pointed out above, at this kind of level there is no direct link between the explanation of why someone has a certain intellectual stance and his entitlement to it. Indeed, this point is appreciated by those more careful proponents of Critical Theory who take pains to make clear that their characterisation of science as essentially 'technical' is not a claim about its historical emergence, but only about its inherent rationale.[15]

What then is the point of science? Recall that in Chapter 2 I argued that general principles for choosing between scientific research programmes could be understood and evaluated by reference to the implicit aim of developing comprehensive anomaly-free *versions* of such programmes. But I there said nothing about the justification for that aim itself. This is the question we must now face up to. *Why* should we want to discover systems of generalisations which relate as many different empirical phenomena as accurately as possible?

It is rather difficult to get a proper grip on this question. On the one hand there is the view of the Critical Theorists that this aim is inherently oriented to the technical interest, that different 'cognitive interests' would call for qualitatively different kinds of theories. To this we can counterpose the more 'realist' view that if we can find general patterns in a given subject matter it must be because there are general patterns there, and that insofar as this is so a nomological science needs no other justification than that it accurately represents a certain aspect of reality. From this point of view the fact that science can serve the technical interest is simply a fortunate by-product of reality's regular behaviour.

One problem in assessing the Critical Theorists' view lies in their conception of alternative forms of knowledge. For they characteristically take an extremely 'positivistic' view of science itself. In particular they assume that since science has to deal with observables it cannot comprehend the desires, frustrations and sufferings of human beings, nor the meanings of their actions. And so they hold that people will only be able to understand each other and see that they can and must transform their situation if they transcend the empirical scientific attitude and embrace some alternative approach to social reality.[16] From the point of view developed in this book these worries about science are quite misconceived. Once we have a proper grasp of what scientific method actually requires we no longer need to suppose that an understanding of human subjectivity is beyond its ambit, and we can dismiss the idea that a scientific view of society has of necessity to hide people's real experiences and potentialities. Of course a view of social reality without human subjectivity would be reprehensibly incomplete. But there is nothing in 'technical' science, properly understood, that condemns it to such incompleteness.

But perhaps we can give a rather different sense to the idea that the reality science presents is one specifically oriented to the technical interest. Consider a traditional African witchcraft theory like the Zande theory mentioned in the last chapter. As an attempt to develop a detailed set of generalisations which enable a wide range of events to be systematically explained such a theory should be deemed a failure. But, nevertheless, as we saw, it will not anywhere be in straightforward conflict with what is observed to occur. What is more, it could well be argued that such belief systems have advantages which compensate for their lack of explanatory precision. For instance, traditional man is largely free of the existential anxieties brought on by the cold and infinite world of modern physics. And his relatively comfortable world views have the additional, if paradoxical, advantage of *stability*: precisely because of their somewhat loose relation to the data they do not require perpetual modification and relearning. So there does seem to be some room to ask *why* we should take the pains we do to have theories that accurately specify general connections amongst a wide range of events. And, once we ask this question, it is difficult to avoid the answer that such theories serve the technical interest better. For it is precisely when we have definite and reliable knowledge about general connections amongst phenomena that we are able to control and anticipate the behaviour of our environment.

So even if the Critical Theorists are wrong to think that science cannot comprehend human subjectivity, perhaps there is after all something to the claim that science is in some way specifically tailored to the technical interest. The point at issue here is a deep and difficult one. It is hard to get rid of the notion that the reality the scientific method is aiming at is *the* reality. And there is perhaps something rather dubious about the merits of comfort and stability just attributed to the theories produced by the alternative approaches to reality found in traditional societies. Still, it is difficult to see what substantive disadvantages there are to such alternative approaches other than their ultimate failure to serve the technical interest. Fortunately it is unnecessary to resolve this issue here. For even if we do allow that science is inherently oriented to the technical interest, in the sense now under consideration, there is no reason whatsoever to conclude that there is something reprehensible about science, that its application to the social realm is inherently supportive of systems of political domination and oppression.

All choices, political or otherwise, need to be based on general assumptions about what means or policies will best achieve the intended range of ends. And so, as I have already had occasion to stress, anybody making such a choice will be best advised to ensure that the general assumptions on which he bases it are as reliable as possible. If there is indeed something distinctively 'technical' about empirical science, this merely serves to show that the knowledge it yields is just what is needed to inform our choices of action. Of course actions or policies can be aimed at bad ends as well as good ones. But what is wrong with, say, the political decisions made in oppressive social systems is that the *ends* aimed at are reprehensible, not that technical scientific knowledge is used to select the means. That science can help to achieve bad ends is no argument at all for thinking we need some alternative procedure for pursuing good ones.

Perhaps it needs to be recognised that there is a real if unfortunate historical tendency for scientific knowledge of society to be used for bad rather than good. Recall the point made earlier, that it is specifically complex industrial societies that call forth a technical social science. In such societies most social decisions will be made by the minority that control and administrate, and they will affect the majority that are controlled and administrated. And so it is all too likely that as a general rule the choices informed by technical social science will be directed towards the interests of that minority rather than to the needs of the general population.

But even if we allow that as a matter of historical fact a scientific understanding of how society works is in this way more likely to be used for bad than for general good, we have scarcely established any intrinsic link between the status of such technical scientific knowledge and its social effects. For nothing that has been said rules out the eventual possibility of a situation where such social science would be used for the good. And in such a situation the good would still better be served the more 'technical' was that science. Perhaps there is little reason to be over-optimistic about people's real needs ever getting properly onto the political agenda. But if they ever did get there it would be a pity not to know what policies could lead to their satisfaction.

Notes

NOTES TO INTRODUCTION

1. Comte himself included *both* a rigorous empiricism *and* the idea of a continuity between the natural and the social sciences in his 'positive philosophy'.
2. D. Papineau, 'Ideal Types and Empirical Theories', *British Journal for the Philosophy of Science*, Vol. 27 (1976).
3. See R. P. Dore, 'Function and Cause', *American Sociological Review*, Vol. 26 (1961); also L. Wright, 'Functions', *Philosophical Review*, Vol. LXXXII (1973); and L. Wright, *Teleological Explanations* (University of California Press, 1976).

NOTES TO CHAPTER 1

1. E. Durkheim, *The Rules of Sociological Method* (Free Press, 1964). See especially Chapters 1 and 2, and the Preface to the second edition.
2. Ibid., pp. 1–2.
3. Ibid., p. 110.
4. Maurice Mandelbaum, for instance is a 'Durkheimian' who holds that individual decisions can affect external social facts. See the last paragraph of his 'Societal Facts', *British Journal of Sociology*, Vol. 6 (1955), and Section IV of his 'Societal Laws', *British Journal for the Philosophy of Science*, Vol. 8 (1957).
5. This is not in fact a particularly accurate way of formulating the genotype–phenotype distinction. But it is satisfactory enough for the issues under discussion.
6. See P. Vorzimmer, *Charles Darwin: The Years of Controversy* (Temple, 1970).
7. Chapter 6 and 7 of J. D. Y. Peel's *Herbert Spencer: The Evolution of a Sociologist* (Heinemann, 1971) give an illustration of the way genetic assumptions influenced Victorian social thought.
8. 'The Continuity of the Germ-Plasm as the Foundation of a Theory of Heredity', in A. Weismann, *Essays upon Heredity and kindred Biological Problems*, ed. E. Poulton *et al.* (Clarendon, 1891).
9. That current genetic ideas had an influence on Durkheim's thinking is suggested by certain arguments in Chapter 5 of *Rules of Sociological Method*, especially those on pp. 107–9.

NOTES TO CHAPTER 2

1. By 'classical' empiricism I mean of course the empiricism of Locke, Berkeley and Hume.
2. A. J. Ayer, *Language, Truth and Logic*, 2nd edition (Gollancz, 1946) is still the most accessible introduction to logical positivism in English.
3. See Vol. I, Part III, of D. Hume, *A Treatise of Human Nature*, ed. L. A. Selby-Biggie (Oxford, 1888). For a discussion of Schlick's views see K. Popper, *The Logic of Scientific Discovery* (Hutchinson, 1959), pp. 36–7.
4. See Popper, op. cit.
5. See A. J. Ayer, *The Problem of Knowledge* (Penguin, 1956), pp. 73–4, for a succinct statement of this point.
6. The most systematic presentation of this model is in Chapter 5 of E. Nagel, *The Structure of Science* (Routledge and Kegan Paul, 1961).
7. For a more detailed discussion of the issues raised in the rest of this section see Nagel, op. cit., Chapter 6, and also C. Hempel, *Aspects of Scientific Explanation* (Free Press, 1965), Chapters 4, 5 and 8.
8. A different argument against translationalism is that 'correspondence rules' only *partially* define theoretical terms, in that they only specify an observational import for such terms for those special circumstances where the selected procedure of measurement or observation is actually applied, although we certainly take it that theoretical terms can be quite meaningfully applied outside those circumstances. I have not pursued this line of criticism—only because it is of little direct relevance to my overall theme. Cf. Hempel, op. cit., pp. 126, 129–30, 188–9.
9. P. Bridgman, *The Logic of Modern Physics* (Macmillan, 1927).
10. The pyramid metaphor is an elaboration of the more common but perhaps less illuminating 'network' metaphor of scientific theories. Cf. C. Hempel, *Philosophy of Natural Science* (Prentice-Hall, 1966), p. 94.
11. Hempel for instance (ibid., pp. 80–1) fails to identify the seriousness of the difficulty facing the realist here.
12. An alternative argument against realism about theoretical entities arises from the point made in note 8 above. If correspondence rules only specify a meaning for theoretical terms when certain conditions of observation are satisfied, then what warrant do we have in the first place for understanding such terms as signifying things which purportedly exist unobserved in the absence of such conditions? This raises a central issue in the philosophy of language—can sentences have meanings which relate them to states of affairs the presence of which on given occasions we might in principle be unable to decide? (See M. Dummett, 'Truth', *Proceedings of the Aristotelian Society*, Vol. 59 (1958–59), pp. 156–62). I have by-passed this issue because the problem I have raised about realism remains even if we allow that we *can* have sentences whose truth depends on states of affairs beyond our capacities to detect. For even if we do allow this we would still need to know, so to speak, *which* states of affairs sentences about theoretical entities relate to. Our central problem is not so much that the meanings of theoretical terms are underdetermined by 'partial' definitions, but rather that they are *over*determined by 'multiple' definitions.

13. The extensive modern literature on this topic begins with Quine's 'Two Dogmas of Empiricism', in W. v. O. Quine, *From a Logical Point of View* (Harvard University Press, 1953).

14. N. R. Hanson, *Patterns of Discovery* (Cambridge University Press, 1965), Chapter 1.

15. Paul Feyerabend discusses this 'pragmatic' definition of observational language in his 'Explanation, Reduction and Empiricism', in H. Feigl and G. Maxwell (eds.), *Minnesota Studies in the Philosophy of Science*, Vol. III (University of Minnesota, 1962).

16. A number of writers make much of the possibility that the theory-ladenness of perception might on occasion actually lead scientists with different theoretical preferences to perceive given situations differently. It seems to me a much more important (and less controversial) consequence of perception's theory-ladenness that when scientists *do* have perceptions which are theoretically unwanted, they have room to reject them. See Hanson, op. cit., Chapter 1; and T. S. Kuhn, *The Structure of Scientific Revolutions*, 2nd edition (University of Chicago, 1970), pp. 62–5.

17. Detailed argument for the thesis that *all* observational procedures are potentially revisable are given in M. Hesse, *The Structure of Scientific Inference* (Macmillan, 1974), Chapter 1, Section II.

18. P. Feyerabend, 'Consolations for the Specialist', in I. Lakatos and A. Musgrave (eds.), *Criticism and the Growth of Knowledge* (Cambridge University Press, 1970), p. 219.

19. Initially in 'How to be a Good Empiricist', in P. Nidditch (ed.), *The Philosophy of Science* (Oxford University Press, 1968), and other articles; more recently in *Against Method*, (NLB, 1975).

20. *Against Method*, p. 28.

21. *Against Method*, Chapters 6–11.

22. Kuhn, op. cit.

23. Ibid., Chapter IV.

24. Ibid., Chapter XII. It should be noted that in his more recent writings Kuhn has downgraded the importance of 'irrational' personal motivations in the process of paradigm change, and come to attach more weight to the influence of such 'rational' factors as the persisting presence of unsolved problems. See the 'Postscript' to the second edition of *The Structure of Scientific Revolutions*, and 'Reflections on My Critics' in Lakatos and Musgrave (eds.), op. cit.

25. 'Reflections on My Critics', p. 237.

26. The best introduction to Lakatos's ideas is his 'Falsification and the Methodology of Scientific Research Programmes', in Lakatos and Musgrave (eds.), op. cit.

27. The 'positive heuristic' of a research programme will contain suggestions for possible modifications or revisions. I have omitted mention of this as peripheral to my argument. Ibid., p. 135.

28. But see ibid., pp. 127–31.

29. Writers influenced by the French Marxist epistemologist Louis Althusser sometimes suggest that an observational concept will be unsatisfactory unless we can *fully* explain its use from within the relevant theory. This seems to me far too strong a requirement. See, for example, B. Hindess, *The*

Use of Official Statistics in Sociology (Macmillan, 1973), especially the Appendix.

30. For similar arguments see Quine's 'Epistemology Naturalised', in W. v. O. Quine, *Ontological Relativity and Other Essays* (University of Columbia, 1969).

31. Lakatos discusses this problem in his 'History of Science and its Rational Reconstructions', in C. Howson (ed.), *Method and Appraisal in the Physical Sciences* (Cambridge University Press, 1976). But his attempted solution is not convincing. (Cf. note 14 to Chapter 7 below.)

32. See Popper, op. cit., Chapter VI, for the idea of *degrees* of falsifiability.

33. Popper, op. cit., pp. 31–2.

34. Feyerabend, 'Consolations for the Specialist', in Lakatos and Musgrave (eds.), op. cit., pp. 215–18.

35. The view that the meanings of all scientific terms are always theory-dependent is not uncontroversial. In particular Hilary Putnam has recently attempted to use the 'causal theory of reference' to dispute this view and defend a more straightforward scientific realism. I discuss this attempt in my 'Meaning Variance the Theory of Reference', *Methodology and Science*, Vol. 10 (1977). In this article I also show in more detail that an account of objective scientific theory choices is quite compatible with the reality presented by scientific concepts always being specific to the theoretical context; that is, that such choices do not require any independent 'data-base' of theory-neutral judgements. Althusserians deny that the object of scientific knowledge 'within thought' can ever be identified with the 'real object'. This is, I think, correct. It does *not* follow that it is invalid to explicate the scientific acceptability of a theory as depending on its relationship to external reality. Cf. L. Althusser and E. Balibar *Reading Capital* (NLB, 1970), especially Part I.

36. In her 'Methodological Individualisms: Definition and Reduction', *Philosophy of Science*, Vol. 25 (1958), May Brodbeck similarly argues that although social concepts do not denote anything existing above the individual level they cannot always be defined in terms of it (pp. 2–7). But while she sees this a matter of (possibly fruitful) *vagueness*, I take it to be a standard instance of the way abstract scientific terms only need an indeterminate tie to their more observable indicators.

NOTES TO CHAPTER 3

1. See I. Hacking, *The Logic of Statistical Inference* (Cambridge University Press, 1965), especially Chapter VII, for a critique of the standard theory of statistical testing.

2. D. Hume, *A Treatise of Human Nature*, Vol. I, Part III, especially Section XV.

3. See for instance P. F. Lazarsfeld, 'Interpretation of Statistical Relations as a Research Operation', in P. F. Lazarsfeld and M. Rosenberg (eds.), *The Language of Social Research* (Free Press, 1955); H. M. Blalock, *Causal Inferences in Nonexperimental Research* (University of North Carolina

Press, 1964); and the various articles in H. M. Blalock (ed.), *Causal Models in the Social Sciences* (Aldine-Atherton, 1971).

4. This connection between causation and explanation is systematised in the well-known 'covering law model' of explanation. However, the architects of the covering law model intended causal explanation to be merely one special case of the nomological explanation of particular events. For instance, they took functional explanations to be non-causal instances of the model, namely ones where the explanans refers to a *later* event which is *necessary* for the explanandum. And they took statistical explanation to be another kind of non-causal explanation. (Cf. C. Hempel, *Aspects of Scientific Explanation*, Chapters 9, 10, 11.) The idea that 'functional explanations' are non-causal is discredited in the references given above in note 3 to the Introduction. And my criticisms of the thesis that causation is statistical in Section 8 of this chapter will also serve to undermine the (rather different) notion of a distinctively non-causal mode of statistical explanation. The point really demands more careful discussion, but it will be convenient to assume henceforth that all explanations of particular events are causal.

5. The account of causation given up to this point is now fairly standard. See, for example, J. L. Mackie, 'Causes and Conditions', *American Philosophical Quarterly*, Vol. 2 (1965).

6. A failure to appreciate that a requirement of minimal sufficiency can exclude irrelevancies can encourage the temptation to ask for causes to be necessary for their effects. For example, see M. Lessnoff, *The Structure of Social Science* (Allen and Unwin, 1974), pp. 22–3.

7. See J. L. Mackie, *The Cement of the Universe* (Oxford University Press, 1974), pp. 83–4, for a general demonstration of this point. The 'barometer' problem is fairly often mentioned in the literature, but the only neo-Humean account of causation which seems to come properly to grips with it is D. Sanford's 'The Direction of Causation and the Direction of Conditionship', *Journal of Philosophy*, Vol. LXXIII (1976). If I have grasped it adequately, Sandford's account is similar in spirit to the 'no-eclipsing' idea I develop in this section.

8. Apart from dealing with the problem of side-effects I think the 'no-eclipsing' requirement also holds some promise of helping with the temporal direction of causation. That is, I think it might be used to explicate the fact that later events are never causes of earlier ones. Unfortunately it would take us too far afield to pursue this here. But cf. note 18 to this chapter below.

9. In 'Spurious Correlation: A Causal Interpretation', *Journal of the American Statistical Association*, Vol. 49 (1954), H. A. Simon uses a rather less fundamental argument to show the need for such an ordering.

10. I am ignoring here the fact that F_1 will also be associated with any of its causal descendants which happen in turn to be causes of F_2. This is unimportant because it will be unnecessary to control for such 'intervening' factors as long as our interest is only in whether F_1 is *a* cause of F_2, as opposed to its being a *direct* cause. This point illustrates something I have largely glossed over, namely that the 'directness' of causes is normally taken relative to the detail of the analysis being conducted.

11. There is of course the danger of some kind of 'experiment effect'—that it is not going to an academic school as such but being-picked-out-in-a-survey-

and-sent-there that affects subsequent occupation. But this point is peripheral to the argument.

12. L. Kish, 'Some Statistical Problems in Research Design', *American Sociological Review*, Vol. XXIV (1959), is helpful on this point and on a number of related issues.

13. See the Appendix to Mackie, *The Cement of the Universe*, for a useful account of the logic of 'eliminative induction'.

14. See Kish, op. cit.

15. The analogy between the qualitative and quantitative case can be stretched further. The *correlation coefficient* between two causally related numerical quantities can be interpreted as a measure of the *importance* of the cause in explicit question by comparison with the unknown 'error' causes. ('How much of the variance in the dependent variable can be attributed to the independent variable?') In the same way we can take the extent to which a qualitative cause increases the probability of its effect (also a number in the interval $[-1, +1]$) as showing its significance relative to the other unknown causes. However, the *slope* of a regression relationship—the coefficient b which specifies how much Z will change on average for a given change in Y—has no direct analogue in the qualitative case. If quality A is a cause of quality B there is no further question about which 'values' of B A's presence produces.

16. 'Path analysis' is a currently popular technique for getting causal conclusions from partial regression analysis. This involves 'standardising' all variables by measuring them on scales which give them unit variances. This approach simplifies a number of numerical manipulations, but has other disadvantages. The 'path coefficients' lack an obvious intuitive meaning, since they are in general neither partial correlations nor unstandardised partial slopes. And insofar as it is generally more reliable to extrapolate (unstandardised) slopes from finite samples than to extrapolate variances or correlations, there are difficulties about generalising the results of path analysis. See the articles in Part II of Blalock (ed.), *Causal Models in the Social Sciences*.

17. W. Salmon (with R. Jeffrey and J. Greeno), *Statistical Explanation and Statistical Relevance* (University of Pittsburgh Press, 1971); also W. Salmon, 'Theoretical Explanation', in S. Körner (ed.), *Explanation* (Basil Blackwell, 1975).

18. Originally Salmon presented the 'screening-off rule' as independent of the homogeneity requirement. But see 'Postscript 1971', in *Statistical Explanation and Statistical Relevance*, p. 105. Salmon also observes that while an earlier event can screen off later events from each other, a later event does not seem able to do this to a pair of earlier ones (op. cit., pp. 72–6). While I disagree with what he makes of this observation, it is what I think can be used to show generally that the 'no-eclipsing' analysis of (deterministic) causation copes with the temporal direction of causal relationships. Cf. note 8 above.

19. Ibid., pp. 79–80.

20. See J. H. Fetzer, 'Statistical Probabilities: Single Case Propensities vs. Long-Run Frequencies', in W. Leinfellner and E. Köhler (eds.), *Developments in the Methodology of Social Science* (D. Reidel, 1974).

NOTES TO CHAPTER 4

1. It would be impossible to list here even a representative sample of either 'interpretativists' or 'materialists'. My 'materialism' of course includes behaviourism. 'Interpretativists' include amongst others Wittgensteinians, phenomenological sociologists, hermeneuticians and ethnomethodologists.
2. Cf. A. J. Ayer, 'Man as a Subject for Science', in P. Laslett and W. G. Runciman (eds.), *Philosophy, Politics and Society, Third Series* (Basil Blackwell, 1969). Ayer's line in this article is in rough agreement with the one I pursue in this chapter. For an importantly different version of the claim that reasons are causes, see D. Davidson, 'Actions, Reasons and Causes', *Journal of Philosophy*, Vol. LX (1963).
3. For the idea of subjective probability see the Introduction to and articles in H. E. Kyburg and H. E. Smokler (eds.), *Studies in Subjective Probability* (Wiley, 1964).
4. The 'minimax' and 'mixed' strategies of game theory are sometimes taken to be *alternatives* to desirability maximization as principles of rational choice. But from the point of view developed here they should be seen as equivalent to recommendations for estimating (and affecting) the moves of one's opponent, and so as *additions* to desirability maximization. See A. Heath, *Rational Choice and Social Exchange* (Cambridge University Press, 1976), Chapter 2, for a simple description of game theory.

   I have of necessity forgone a number of other observations which would have helped clarify the 'decision scheme theory'. Perhaps the most important is that it is *basic* actions that specify the rows of decision schemes and that therefore get explained by the theory. By a 'basic' action I mean an action individuated as one which (a) the agent *can* do (b) he does not think of as done *by* doing something else. (Condition (a) does not make the theory collapse, for we do have independent ways of knowing if people are able to do something on a given occasion other than by seeing if they do do it if they want to; for instance, we can reason from their past performance, training, physical make-up, etc.)
5. See O. Jones (ed.), *The Private Language Argument* (Macmillan, 1971).
6. See Chapter 3 of R. C. Jeffrey, *The Logic of Decision* (McGraw–Hill, 1965), for an exposition of these techniques, which are originally due to F. P. Ramsey.
7. Donald Davidson has suggested, in the course of arguing against reason – action generalisations, that no physically individuated entities would display the kind of rationality pattern we impose conceptually on human thought and behaviour. I see no reason for assuming this *a priori*. Indeed if (with Davidson) we adopt a monistic ontology, the undeniable if limited predictive utility of everyday action theory gives us a strong reason for *not* assuming it. D. Davidson, 'Psychology as Philosophy', in S. C. Brown (ed.), *Philosophy of Psychology* (Macmillan, 1974), p. 52.
8. P. Winch, *The Idea of a Social Science* (Routledge and Kegan Paul, 1958), especially Chapters II and III.
9. Ibid., p. 32.
10. I am for expository purposes drawing a slightly different distinction between 'internal' and 'external' aspects of rules from that originally drawn

by H. L. A. Hart in *The Concept of Law* (Clarendon, 1961), p. 55.

11. D. Lewis, *Convention* (Harvard University Press, 1969).

12. H. Garfinkel, *Studies in Ethnomethodology* (Prentice-Hall, 1967), pp. 68–70.

13. The 'ethnomethodological view' I describe in this section is a kind of composite which would no doubt be rejected in some respect by any actual member of the school. But see Garfinkel, op. cit. A useful collection is J. Douglas (ed.), *Understanding Everyday Life* (Routledge and Kegan Paul, 1971). The term 'ethnomethodology' was actually coined by Garfinkel. See H. Garfinkel, 'The Origins of the Term "Ethnomethodology"', in R. Turner (ed.), *Ethnomethodology* (Penguin, 1974).

14. See T. P. Wilson, 'Narrative and Interpretative Paradigms in Sociology', pp. 68–9 and R. Turner, 'Words, Utterances and Activities', p. 186, both in Douglas (ed.), op. cit.

15. See Garfinkel, *Studies in Ethnomethodology*, Chapter 1. The term 'indexical' is borrowed from analytic philosophy of language, where it describes terms like 'I' whose reference is a function of the context of utterance. But this is not in fact a good model for the ethnomethodological idea, since there *is* an absolutely invariant principle for reading 'I'—namely, that it always refers to the speaker. See Y. Bar-Hillel, 'Indexical Expressions', *Mind*, Vol. 63 (1954).

16. See Wilson, op. cit., pp. 71–9.

17. Cf. A. Blum, 'Theorising', in Douglas, op. cit.

18. Cf. J. Rawls, 'Two Concepts of Rules', *Philosophical Review*, Vol. LXIV (1955).

19. See A. Wootton, *Dilemmas of Discourse* (Allen and Unwin, 1975), Chapter 3, where this line of reasoning is particularly clear.

20. H. P. Grice, 'Meaning', *Philosophical Review*, Vol. LXVI (1957); and 'Utterer's Meaning, Sentence Meaning and Word Meaning', *Foundations of Language*, Vol. IV (1968). (My word-meaning' is neutral between Grice's 'sentence meaning' and his 'word meaning'; and like his notions it is not necessarily applicable only to spoken or written actions.)

21. A rather different case is 'non-verbal communication' like facial expressions and 'body language'. Here there does seem room for the actions in question to have a kind of established word-meaning, for the communications are not so much covert as simply below the level of explicit consciousness. I do not want to deny that here we might have a general but unconscious recognition that certain actions indicate certain attitudes. But it is not quite a full-blown 'language'. The lack of awareness deprives the regularity of normative force, and—a related point—we certainly do not unconsciously Grice-mean to produce an effect by our observers (unconsciously) grasping that that is our (unconscious) intention. (It might be objected that the intentions and understandings behind the everyday use of ordinary verbal language are usually not all that conscious either. But the important point is that we can become conscious of them easily enough if we attend to them.)

22. P. F. Strawson, 'Intention and Convention in Speech Acts', *Philosophical Review*, Vol. LXXIII (1964). Though Strawson is concerned with rather different points from those I am labouring this is a helpful article on the general connection between Grice-meaning and 'speech-act' theory.

23. Cf. A. Giddens, *New Rules of Sociological Method* (Hutchinson, 1976), Chapter 3.

NOTES TO CHAPTER 5

1. W. G. Runciman, *Social Science and Political Theory* (Cambridge University Press, 1963), pp. 127–32; M. Lessnoff, *The Structure of Social Science* (Allen and Unwin, 1974), pp. 97–9.
2. Both Runciman and Lessnoff are concerned to infer, from the necessity of such individual reductions, the further claim that social scientific explanation has to be interpretative and not causal. But we can consider their argument for the necessity of individual reductions independently of this further claim.
3. Of course in order to discover the individual explanation for some macro-law in the first place it would be necessary to investigate the actual histories of some actual individuals. But this is a different point—once the general individual explanation has been established there is no further necessity to apply it each time the macro-law is invoked to explain some particular social development.
4. L. J. Goldstein, in 'Two Theses of Methodological Individualism', *British Journal for the Philosophy of Science*, Vol. 9 (1958), is for instance led to deny that there is anything individual about typical individuals at all.
5. In the last section of her 'Methodological Individualisms: Definition and Reduction', *Philosophy of Science*, Vol. 25 (1958), May Brodbeck in effect suggests that it may turn out that certain macro-laws are resistant to such deeper understanding, in that the connections between the individual components of the social facts involved may be quite specific to the kind of social circumstance in question. This is a coherent possibility, but if it were realised it would invalidate my final 'anti-Durkheimian' argument in Section 8 of Chapter 2 above. (I have drawn freely on Brodbeck's important article in constructing the arguments of this chapter.)
6. J. W. N. Watkins is a good example. See his 'Ideal Types and Historical Explanation', *British Journal for the Philosophy of Science*, Vol. 3 (1952); and his 'Historical Explanation in the Social Sciences', *British Journal for the Philosophy of Science*, Vol. 8 (1957).
7. I doubt that anybody has unambiguously defended historical determinism as I have defined it. But even if my historical determinist is a straw man it will be illuminating to see exactly why he cannot stand up.
8. I do not wish to deny that economic factors are important determinants of social developments, nor even that they are in some sense the most important such determinants; it is just that they are not *always* the *only* ones.
9. This thesis is I think a more reasonable approximation to the position actually held by certain advocates of 'historical necessity'.
10. Cf. I. Berlin, 'Historical Inevitability', in his *Four Essays on Liberty* (Oxford University Press, 1969); see also the articles by Watkins referred to in note 6 above.
11. The literature on free will and determinism is of course extensive. As good an introduction as any to the standard arguments is Chapter 17 of J.

Hospers, *An Introduction to Philosophical Analysis*, 2nd edition (Rutledge and Kegan Paul, 1967).

12. The real problem with compatiblist freedom emerges on the moral level—it does not seem right to blame (or praise people for things that they were determined to do. But see C. L. Stevenson, 'Ethical Judgments and Avoidability', *Mind*, Vol. 47 (1938).

NOTES TO CHAPTER 6

1. J. Skorupski, *Symbol and Theory* (Cambridge University Press, 1976), pp. 25–9. The present chapter owes a considerable amount to Skorupski's book.
2. The clearest proponent of the alternative rationalities approach is P. Winch. See his 'Understanding a Primitive Society', *American Philosophical Quarterly*, Vol. 1 (1964); also *The Idea of a Social Science* (Routledge and Kegan Paul, 1958).
3. A number of rather different notions, to be mentioned in Section 5 of this chapter, are often conflated with the symbolist approach as I have characterised it. Leach and Beattie are probably closest amongst contemporary writers to my 'symbolist'. E. Leach, *Political Systems of Highland Burma* (Bell, 1954). J. Beattie, *Other Cultures* (Cohen and West, 1964).
4. A further difficulty is that the discrimination of *standard* assertions in itself presupposes the attribution to the speaker of quite complex aims and expectations concerning his audience. Here I think we simply have to start with a rough-and-ready guess as to when assertions are being made standardly and refine this recursively as our interpretation progresses. Cf. the argument in the penultimate paragraph of Section 6 of this chapter.
5. B. L. Whorf, *Language, Thought and Reality* (Wiley, 1956).
6. If, as some advocate, we deal with the problem of radical translation by simply presupposing conceptual invariance, then we are going to find, in cases where there actually *is* such variation, that there is no satisfactory way of interpreting the aliens, that *any* translation leaves some of them with some quite inexplicable beliefs. And then we will have to summon up the 'principle of charity' to select as the least bad translation the one that makes the aliens as sane as possible. Insofar as my approach in this chapter accords with charitable principles it at least explains *why* (and *when*) they should be upheld. See, however, D. Davidson, 'Radical Interpretation', *Dialectica*, Vol. 27 (1973).
7. It might seem unclear at this point why we should bring in beliefs to analyse the meanings of assertions at all. Why not just see the meanings of assertions as deriving straight from principles which govern their legitimate use in direct relation to the external world? The answer is the standard realist one—even if people's mental capacities are almost exclusively displayed in, and derived from, conformity to such 'external principles', they are still needed to *explain* such conformity.
8. Cf. M. Hollis, 'The Limits of Irrationality', *Archives Européenes de Sociologie*, Vol. VII (1967); also his 'Reason and Ritual', *Philosophy*, Vol.

XLIII (1967). My argument from radical interpretation is in rough accord with Hollis's, but I differ on a number of points, in particular on the necessity of a translational 'bridgehead' and on the epistemological status of the basic presuppositions of our theory of interpretation.

9. This paragraph illustrates that my argument from interpretation by no means requires that the meaning of an assertion be *equated* with the grounds on which it is ordinarily adopted. For even if we allow that assertions can have contents which transcend the grounds on which they are accepted, we can still only get at those contents via what the translatees' linguistic practice shows to be such grounds. This is quite enough for my argument. Cf. note 12 to Chapter 1.

10. E. Evans-Pritchard, *Witchcraft, Oracles and Magic among the Azande* (Clarendon, 1937), Part I.

11. As Quine has taught us, there is no clear point at which theoretical postulates stop making empirical claims and start constituting concepts. The arguments of this section and the previous two help to make it clear why this lack of an analytic–synthetic distinction undermines the possibility of identity criteria for beliefs across cultures. Cf. W. v. O. Quine, *Word and Object* (MIT, 1960), Chapter 2. (Not that Quine would want to put the point in terms of the interdeterminacy of identity criteria for *beliefs*.) I have avoided this problem because none of the arguments in this chapter (or in Chapters 2 and 7) which invoke 'beliefs' and 'concepts' actually require that they have clear trans-cultural identity criteria.

12. E. Evans-Pritchard, *Nuer Religion* (Clarendon, 1956). There are further complications to the Nuer cosmology, but not ones which warrant Evans-Pritchard's inclination to talk of 'symbolism'. Cf. Skorupski, op. cit., Chapter 13.

13. Perhaps there remains room for the idea that there is a real grasp of symbolism below the level of consciousness. But it is hard to see how this can get a grip, given that the people in question characteristically behave just as they would do without any such grasp. Cf. Skorupski, op. cit., pp. 37–41.

14. Cf. Skorupski, op. cit., Part II, where the logic of the magical and ceremonial manipulation of symbols is discussed in detail.

15. Ibid., pp. 23–4.

16. The questions which arise here are to do with the legitimacy of 'functional explanations'.

17. Beattie is prone to slip into this position. Beattie, op. cit.

18. See D. Sperber, *Rethinking Symbolism* (Cambridge University Press, 1975). Sperber argues that such structuralist analyses of myth and ritual as Lévi-Strauss's are best read as *not* being attempts to decipher hidden codes. This seems to me right. But, whatever the merits of Sperber's alternative account of alien thought systems as a kind of cognitive mechanism for assimilating literal but irrational beliefs, it then seems odd to continue talking of 'symbolism'.

19. It is a difficult and much discussed question in philosophical logic whether the difference between logical and non-logical structure is anything more than a matter of the degree of generality of the inferences sustained. If it is not, then the argument of this section can be taken as showing that all human thinking must share at least the *most basic* forms of reasoning

(namely, 'propositional' and 'predicate logic'). See, for instance, W. v. O. Quine, 'Mr Strawson on Logical Theory', in his *Ways of Paradox and Other Essays* (Random House, 1966), especially Part II.

20. Perhaps we can even attribute *obviously* contradictory beliefs to a people, in those cases where we can explain their accepting them as due to their faith in the supposed word of a superhumanly intelligent being. Thus, possibly, the Catholic belief in the doctrine of the Eucharist. Cf. J. Skorupski, 'Science and Traditional Religious Thought', *Philosophy of the Social Sciences*, Vol. III (1973).

21. That they might deal with basic logic by using rather different linguistic devices from ours is a much more concrete possibility; but this would be of no more serious import than the fact familiar to all elementary logic students that *our* everyday 'if . . . then' is rather different from the material implication of the propositional calculus.

22. The position I end up with here can be seen as a up-dated version of the nineteenth-century 'intellectualism' of Sir James Frazer and E. B. Tylor. For a far more thorough contemporary defence of intellectualism see R. Horton, 'African Thought and Western Science', *Africa*, Vol. XXXVII (1967), reprinted in B. Wilson (ed.), *Rationality* (Basil Blackwell, 1970). My final conclusions obviously owe much to Horton's article.

NOTES TO CHAPTER 7

1. G. J. Warnock, *Contemporary Moral Philosophy* (Macmillan, 1967), is a lucid survey of twentieth-century Anglo-Saxon theories about the status of moral judgements.

2. The notion of 'essentially contested concepts' is due to W. B. Gallie. In his article of that name Gallie is concerned to argue that rational considerations of a kind can be relevant to the way that the factual contents of such concepts develop over time. My concern is the rather different one of showing that the contestedness of a concept need not prevent objective decisions on such factual claims as it is used to make at any given time. W. B. Gallie, 'Essentially Contested Concepts', *Aristotelian Society Supplementary Volume*, XXX (1956).

3. Cf. M. Brewster Smith, 'Attitude Change', in D. L. Sills (ed.), *International Encyclopedia of the Social Sciences*, Vol. 1 (Collier–Macmillan, 1968), pp. 458–67.

4. Amongst writers on the possibility of 'value-freedom' it is Gunnar Myrdal who has seen most clearly that it is specifically *conflicts* between values that provide the threat. G. Myrdal, *Value in Social Theory* (Routledge and Kegan Paul, 1958), and *Objectivity in Social Research* (Duckworth, 1970).

5. See Brewster Smith, op. cit., for an introductory survey of such theories. Unfortunately the tendency of 'consistency theorists' to work with a portmanteau notion of an *attitude* which does not distinguish between belief and desire aspects has prevented them from focusing clearly on the question of when people's *beliefs* will be affected. (Cf. Brewster Smith, op. cit., p. 467.)

6. M. Weber, *The Methodology of the Social Sciences* (Free Press, 1949), p. 21.

7. It is often supposed that, although people are caused to have irrational beliefs, the explanation of rational beliefs conforms to a different non-causal pattern. But I see no reason for denying that acquaintance with good grounds can *cause* people to adopt a belief. We need to distinguish between someone's *adopting* a belief and the *belief* itself, considered in the abstract. The latter, not being an event, is of course not susceptible of explanation, causal or otherwise, but only of evaluation. But this does not mean that the *adoption* of a belief cannot be causally explained. Nor should we be confused by the point that some such causal explanations have the side-effect of implying that the belief which is adopted should be evaluated positively as 'rational' in the abstract.

8. K. Mannheim, *Ideology and Utopia* (Routledge and Kegan Paul, 1960).

9. Kuhn suggests that individual natural scientists are often motivated by personal ambition, or by pride in their past achievements. This is sometimes taken to show that even natural science is irredeemably ideological. But this view obscures an important distinction. Unlike the ideological 'motives' I have been discussing, Kuhnian motives have no direct connection with the *content* of the desired theory, with what it *says*, and so give us no reason to suppose that certain *kinds* of theories will be favoured in certain contexts. Kuhn might show that individual scientists are biased, but not that science as a whole is. Indeed Kuhnian motives seem just what is required for the mixture of tenacity and proliferation characteristic of a healthy scientific community.

10. Mannheim, op. cit. The idea that the abolition of classes is necessary for the end of ideology is largely specific to 'Hegelian' Marxists. And of course their reasons for this view are rather more metaphysical than the one I suggest in its favour.

11. Imre Lakatos and Louis Althusser have in different ways suggested that the notion of *scientific* practice can be pinned down by reference to the 'external' criterion of a practice *not* subject to ideological influences. But, unless 'ideological' collapses circularly into 'not ensuring science', this idea seems at bottom to derive from nothing more than the naive supposition that a natural approach to reality will somehow guarantee success. I. Lakatos, 'History of Science and its Rational Reconstructions', in C. Howson (ed.), *Method and Appraisal in the Physical Sciences* (Cambridge University Press, 1976). L. Althusser and E. Balibar, *Reading Capital* (NLB, 1970).

12. The most prominent member of this school is Jürgen Habermas. In particular, see his *Knowledge and Human Interests* (Heinemann, 1972). For an introduction to the whole Frankfurt tradition see P. Conerton (ed.), *Critical Sociology* (Penguin, 1976).

13. Earlier members of the Frankfurt School, such as Adorno, Horkheimer and Marcuse, reject 'technical rationality' even in its application to the natural realm. More recent members of the tradition are less extreme in this respect. T. Adorno and M. Horkheimer, *Dialectic of Enlightenment* (Allen Lane, 1973). H. Marcuse, *One-Dimensional Man* (Routledge and Kegan Paul, 1964).

14. The arguments in the rest of this chapter were originally presented as a reply to a paper by Michael Lessnoff at the Royal Institute of Philosophy Conference at the University of East Anglia in April, 1977. They have

benefited from the discussion with Lessnoff. The proceedings of the conference will be published in the forthcoming S. C. Brown (ed.), *Philosophical Disputes in the Social Sciences.*
15. See, for instance, K.-O. Apel, 'Types of Social Science in the Light of Human Cognitive Interests', in Brown (ed.), op. cit.
16. See H. Pilot, 'Habermas' Philosophy of History', in Connerton (ed.), op. cit., for a thorough discussion of Habermas's more sophisticated arguments against empirical science's competence to deal with intentions.

Index